T0005832

"A powerful and important book that charts the rich and dynamic history of Black women in the United States. It shows how these courageous women challenged racial and gender oppression and boldly asserted their authority and visions of freedom even in the face of resistance. This book is required reading for anyone interested in social justice."

—KEISHA N. BLAIN, author of *Set the World on Fire: Black Nationalist Women and the Global Struggle for Freedom*

"This book is a gift to anyone interested in a more complete—a more truthful—story about the United States. By starting the history about Black women on this land with us as free people and as people agitating for our freedom, by prioritizing all Black women's voices and coming up to the present day, Dr. Berry and Dr. Gross illuminate greater possibilities for our collective freedom dreams and struggles for collective liberation."

—CHARLENE A. CARRUTHERS, author of *Unapologetic: A Black, Queer, and Feminist Mandate for Radical Movements*

"Remarkably comprehensive and accessible, introductory and sophisticated, two groundbreaking historians have come together to produce a groundbreaking new history of Black women in the United States. To know the story of the United States is to know this indispensable story."

—IBRAM X. KENDI, author of *Stamped from the Beginning* and *How to Be an Antiracist*

"At a time when some women's voices seem to be more amplified than ever, the Black woman's voice is still being muted and distorted from the highest level of government, and the autonomy over our bodies is being stripped away, more and more every day.

"Daina Ramey Berry and Kali Nicole Gross have gifted us with a book of heroines whose voices are here to tell us we aren't the first, and though it may sometimes seem an unwinnable struggle just to exist as Black women in an ever more oppressive space of aggressively suffocating and weaponized whiteness and daily misogyny, we have come through much worse, and we can and do effect change every day.

"What a wonderful breath of fresh air to start our journey on American soil *before* slavery, with women who came by their own choice, to move through the strength of those who didn't just survive but persevered through the most unthinkable horrors of bondage, Reconstruction, the deep disappointments that came with the Great Migration, and the struggles (even internally) of the civil rights era. And how inspiring to end (or persist) with our very own living legends, like Serena Williams, Bree Newsome Bass, Angela Whitehead, and Patricia Okoumou.

"Black women have always been at the front line of change, and *A Black Women's History of the United States* shows us in no uncertain terms that our DNA will have us here sculpting and writing the next chapters. Tell your sisters, mothers, and daughters to get this book for someone they love, because we owe it to ourselves, our daughters, our sons, and our future to know the history that isn't being taught in our schools. And it starts with us."

—ANIKA NONI ROSE, actor, producer, and singer

"*A Black Women's History of the United States* is an extraordinary contribution to our collective understanding of the most profound injustices and equalities, as well as the most committed struggles to realize true justice and equality, that have shaped this nation since its birth. Through the courageous and complex voices of black women, and with deft attention to the lives that black women have led from the earliest moments of conquest and colonialism to the dawn of the twenty-first century, historians Daina Ramey Berry and Kali Gross have utterly upended traditional accounts of the American past in ways most desperately needed in our American present."

—HEATHER ANN THOMPSON, historian and Pulitzer
Prize–winning author of *Blood in the Water:
The Attica Prison Uprising of 1971 and Its Legacy*

A BLACK WOMEN'S HISTORY
OF THE UNITED STATES

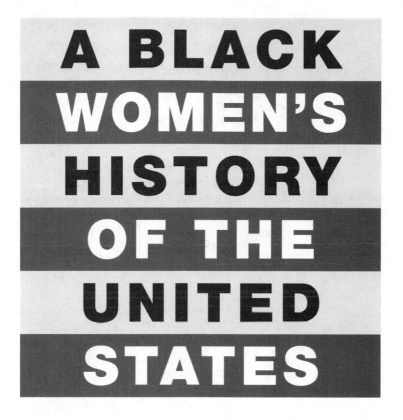

A BLACK WOMEN'S HISTORY OF THE UNITED STATES

ReVisioning American History

Daina Ramey Berry and Kali Nicole Gross

Beacon Press, Boston

BEACON PRESS
Boston, Massachusetts
www.beacon.org

Beacon Press books
are published under the auspices of
the Unitarian Universalist Association of Congregations.

24 23 22 21   8 7 6   (hc.)
24 23   8 7 6 5 4 3   (pbk.)

This book is printed on acid-free paper that meets the uncoated paper
ANSI/NISO specifications for permanence as revised in 1992.

Text design and composition by Kim Arney

Library of Congress Cataloging-in-Publication Data

Names: Berry, Daina Ramey, author. | Gross, Kali N., author.
Title: A black women's history of the United States / Daina Ramey Berry
and Kali Nicole Gross.
Description: Boston : Beacon Press, [2020] | Series: Revisioning American
history | Includes bibliographical references and index.
Identifiers: LCCN 2019026852 (print) | LCCN 2019026853 (ebook) |
ISBN 9780807033555 (hc.) | ISBN 9780807001998 (pbk.) |
ISBN 9780807033562 (ebook)
Subjects: LCSH: African American women—History.
Classification: LCC E185.86 .B475 2020 (print) | LCC E185.86 (ebook) |
DDC 305.48/896073—dc23
LC record available at https://lccn.loc.gov/2019026852
LC ebook record available at https://lccn.loc.gov/2019026853

Melvin R. Ramey, PhD
September 13, 1938–June 26, 2017

Mrs. June Maria Gross
March 2, 1941–December 3, 2017

Londa Ann Lovell
March 25, 1967–January 9, 2019

CONTENTS

AUTHORS' NOTE

ON A COOL SEPTEMBER EVENING IN 1832, Black and white women descended on Franklin Hall in Boston to hear a speech delivered by Maria Stewart. It was a special evening because Maria, who was Black, was the first American woman of any race to give public remarks, and this was only her second speech. "There are no chains so galling as the chains of ignorance—no fetters so binding as those that bind the soul, and exclude it from the vast field of useful and scientific knowledge," Maria proclaimed to her captivated audience. "Why Sit Ye Here and Die?" she asked in the title of her remarks, which challenged women to stand up and address racial and gender bias.[1] Speaking on behalf of African American women's rights, Maria urged her white counterparts to think about the condition of Blacks—in particular, women.

Maria's challenge drives this book and informs our thinking about creating a more inclusive history. Her mission guided our writing of this history of the United States in which Black women and their contributions are on full display. Here we lift the chains and explore the knowledge and influence of women like Maria who had something to say about their place in history. We also could not help but contemplate our own locations along that continuum.

Although we did not come of age during segregation, we spent much of our early childhoods witnessing African American women across the country speaking truth to power by declaring, "Black is Beautiful," and wearing their natural hair in Afros. We grew up on opposite sides of the country: one on the East Coast, the other on the West. And we were reared in different kinds of families: one born into a two-parent household where both parents held degrees in higher education, the other raised in a female-headed household where the sole caregiver and provider attended college but was unable to finish. One has ancestral roots in the American South; one has descendants who emigrated from the British West Indies in the early and mid-twentieth century.

We both attended college and eventually went on to pursue doctorates in history, yet despite our differences, the academy put the same obstacles in our paths, and as Black women historians, we confronted them continuously. Even with the major advances in the field of African American women's history by the 1990s, we still faced a biased system that did not believe in our potential as scholars or in the validity of our chosen area of study: Black women. It did not matter that one of us focused on enslavement and the other on crime and violence. That Black women in America had a history at all was itself contested, as was our capacity as Black women thinkers. Fortunately, we had Black women historians as advisers and role models, and we were the beneficiaries of incredible new books on African American women's history—works that energized and challenged us, and left us wanting to know more. But that was then.

Long before we learned about Beacon Press's ReVisioning American History series, we discussed the need for a new, dynamic history survey about Black women in the United States. At the time, we were at the same institution and had several conversations about creating a book such as this one. The past few decades have witnessed a thrilling burst of evocative works on African American women, in every conceivable area: from Black women fugitives on the run, to Black women's bodies being auctioned, bought, and sold in every stage of their life (and death), to political organizing in beauty shops, to fashion-forward sisters with Black Power ideals, to Black queer activists, to Black women enmeshed in the criminal justice system. With so much new scholarship, as well as pioneering works by historians such as Paula Giddings, Evelyn Brooks Higginbotham, Darlene Clark Hine, Sharon Harley, Jacqueline Jones, Rosalyn Terborg-Penn, and Deborah Gray White, the task of composing a concise, accessible, yet fresh and rigorous book about Black women's history was truly daunting. We knew that we needed to strike a balance between writing an overview of Black women's history and incorporating newer work on those stories, voices, and histories of Black women whose lives have nonetheless remained somehow shrouded.[2]

We want this book to be a new kind of survey on Black women's history, one that is purposely not comprehensive or attempting to be *the* definitive history of Black women in the United States. Instead, we see the book as a vivid introduction to Black women's history that aims to paint a richly textured portrait of Black womanhood in a manner that celebrates Black women's diversity and inspires readers to seek out more. We also want this book to be read by students, book-club members, aunts, uncles, grandads, artists, policymakers, activists, and by people in recovery and by people in politics, and everybody in between, so we do our best to avoid jargon and language that tends to exclude rather than educate.

This approach, together with our journey as coauthors, has challenged us to routinely discuss who and what to include, and who and what to leave out, and why. As much as possible, we chose to include the words of Black women themselves. We did so not only to have Black women's voices play a central role in the book but also because we fundamentally believe that what these voices tell us is crucial for understanding history and for using that history to help us navigate the challenges of today.

It is surely evident that this work is not simply an academic undertaking. We believe it is our responsibility to tell Black women's histories, to continue to resist the forces that attempt to marginalize Black womanhood, and to help inspire and support Black women wherever they are. Our work highlights key themes that dominate Black women's experiences in the United States, and the histories that result, exist ultimately as a testament to the beauty, richness, rhythm, tragedy, heartbreak, rage, and enduring love that abounds in the spirit of Black women in communities all across the nation. As we tell their stories and unleash their histories, Black women soar across the pages that follow with loose fetters and liberated spirits, just as Maria desired.

A NOTE ON USAGE: we use "Black" and "African American" largely interchangeably, though there are points when we clarify whether a Black woman has Caribbean, South American or Central American, or African origins. When it is historically relevant or appears in quoted material, we use the terminology of the period, whether it is a racial epithet or a historical term such as "Negro" or "Colored."

The term "slaveholders" is deliberately used to represent African Americans who held other African Americans in bondage. This word choice is different from "enslavers," which we use throughout to represent non-Blacks (i.e., whites and Native Americans) who enslaved African Americans. The term "enslaver" refers to someone who forces people into the system of slavery. The term "slaveholder" refers to someone who holds another person in slavery without the full power of a system to support the practice.

NANNIE'S LEGACY AND THE HISTORIES OF BLACK WOMEN

We must have a glorified womanhood that can look any man in the face—white, red, yellow, brown, or black—and tell of the nobility of character within black womanhood.

—NANNIE HELEN BURROUGHS

TO WRITE A HISTORY about the United States from the perspective of Black women is to chart a course where the incredible, the fantastic, and the triumphant meet, mix, and mingle, often simultaneously, with hardship, and terror. Although it largely defies uniformity, African American women's history is marked by the ways that we have marched forward, against all odds, to effect sustained change, individually, locally, and nationally. It is true that we embody the motto coined by Nannie Helen Burroughs for the school she headed in 1909: "We specialize in the wholly impossible." The motto, together with Nannie's own history, stands as evidence that a Black woman could, and did, push past daunting obstacles to live a life decidedly less ordinary.[1]

Migrating in the late nineteenth century, Jennie Burroughs, Nannie's formerly enslaved mother, moved Nannie and her sister from Orange County, Virginia, to Washington, DC, hoping to find better employment and educational opportunities. It was a moment when white supremacists re-cemented their power in the South and whites in the North withdrew support for Black civil rights. Reading the signs and riding the tumult, Jennie managed to make a new life for herself and her children, largely alone. Her husband, John Burroughs, was an itinerant preacher and was absent from the home for long periods. Nannie grew up watching her mother struggle to provide for the family. This instilled in Nannie a reverence for her mother's strength, a respect for the Black working class, and a profound commitment to helping Black women cultivate the skills necessary to gain a greater social, political, and economic foothold.[2]

"We must have a glorified womanhood that can look any man in the face—white, red, yellow, brown, or black—and tell of the nobility of character within black womanhood," Nannie proudly declared in a December 1933 address. Those ideals reflected her education and professional pursuits. Born in 1879, Nannie, who studied in Washington, DC, and later in Kentucky, would go on to become the president of the National Trade and Professional School for Women and Girls in the nation's capital. Throughout her stewardship of the institution, the school went from standing on a rough clay hill to an eight-building compound resting on several acres of land estimated to be worth $225,000. Ideologically, Nannie refused to be limited by the extremes of her day. Though many referred to her as "Mrs. Booker T. Washington," because of her emphasis on work and self-reliance, she embraced both industrial and classical education, and expressed early Black Nationalist and feminist ideologies. She encouraged race pride by celebrating dark skin, and she remained a champion of Black women's voting and labor rights. Three years after her death, in 1961, the educational institution she served for decades was renamed the Nannie Burroughs School.[3] Nannie's life and the fact that so many know so little about her touch upon the complicated threads that are interwoven into African American women's history.

Black women occupy a complex, paradoxical relationship to America. We are at once marginalized and ostracized, yet our very being has been exploited to help create and maintain white supremacy. When warring Africans and European traders kidnapped and sold thousands of West Africans into slavery, captive Black women and children together accounted for the majority of "those transported to the Americas during the entirety of the transatlantic slave trade."[4] African women were valuable knowledge producers and laborers, especially because many of them knew how to till the land. They possessed a skill set essential for helping European colonists not just survive in North America but thrive.

As enslavement became systemized into law, Black women's off-spring would become a vital asset for enslavers. But while America grew fat off Black women's bodies and coerced labor, Black woman-hood was depicted as dishonest, unchaste, and deviant. Black women were situated as the perfect foils against which notions of purportedly superior white male and female identities were drawn. In other words, not only have Black women been critical to the founding of this coun-try, but our very image has been a crucial component in the creation of dominant notions of white masculinity and femininity. Yet in examin-ing the experiences of Black women in the United States, it is equally important to understand Black womanhood in its own right, for all its beauty, intelligence, dynamism, and commitment to equality. The leg-acies of women such as Nannie Helen Burroughs deserve nothing less.

Moreover, there exists a profound urgency to remind the country of Black women's historical contributions, plight, and resistance, and to affirm Black womanhood against the tide of misogynoir. "Misogynoir" is a term used to describe gendered, anti-Black violence ranging from police beatings and murders of unarmed Black women (and often the deafening silence surrounding them, which birthed #SayHerName) to the racist targeting of leading Black female scholars, attorneys, jour-nalists, and political figures. This violence is in addition to the ongoing disparities in Black women's access to education, healthcare, employ-ment, and housing.[5] And all of this takes place while young Black girls struggle to "survive R. Kelly" and the internal and external structures that allow the sexual assault of Black women and Black girls to con-tinue, largely with impunity. Black women activists, like filmmaker dream hampton, amplified the women's voices and allowed them to tell their truths, which compelled the justice system to—in an all too rare instance—act on their behalf.

Such activism exists on a long historical continuum, as Black women are powerful change agents who have indelibly shaped the Black com-munity and the entire nation. Black women have used their formidable ability to collectively organize both to battle systemic oppression and to create unique sisterhood spaces all their own. This book honors and educates about this history, at the same that it serves the needs of Black women and girls in the twenty-first century. It combs through Black women's history to meaningfully showcase Black women's lives, attend to all our fraught complexities, and celebrating our incredible achievements and vibrancy. But most importantly, African American women drive the stories.

To that end, it is crucial that all kinds of Black women are represented: everyday and unsung sisters, as well as a few more well-known figures, but also we include those women who might otherwise be excluded from traditional histories. This book cannot cover them all, nor is it meant to. Rather, its objective is to feature select women who have significantly shaped our history and that of the country. We also endeavored to write in ways that are accessible to a wide readership.

Each chapter starts with a vignette of a specific Black woman whose historical experience embodies and reflects the spirit of her era. We feature a variety of women, including the enslaved, the free, educators, politicians, artists, queer folks, disabled people, and activists, as well as those who lived outside the law. Though there are many points where the book's organization is aligned with traditional historical periodization, we have endeavored to use a timeline most significant to Black women's lived experiences. This practice inevitably touches on broad events such as exploration and contact, enslavement, the antebellum era, the Civil War and Reconstruction, the Great Migration, the post–World War II period, as well as the civil rights and Black Power movements. The objective is to present the stories we want to tell while still allowing readers to understand them within a larger historical context. Sometimes the histories we tell are incredibly sad and difficult to get through; in other instances the women's hard-won victories will leave readers cheering aloud.

This book resists putting forth a history that imagines Black women as the same, but it also acknowledges a near-universal experience with respect to how the world views us. We refuse to regard Black women's history as purely oppositional or existing solely in combat with gendered, racist oppression—yet, we cannot deny the effects of its negative imprint. Despite our vast differences in class, education, skin color, religion, ethnicity, sexual orientation, and gender identities, the world—when it acknowledges us at all—often does so through a lens of disposability. Viewed that way, Black women's bodies are not the bodies that matter. They do not garner protection or respect, unless they are used and consumed for the benefit of those in the mainstream. Traditional Black female characteristics such as dark skin and fuller lips, hips, and buttocks tend to be regarded as unattractive until appropriated by white women. Black women's hair, fashion styles, and unique flavor are routinely policed and regulated by employers and even the federal government—recall the army initially banning braids and dreadlocks. Yet on white women, the same looks are wildly celebrated as cutting-edge beauty trends. But this book is not about cultural appropriation or the eclipsing of Black femininity. This is a history about Black women, for Black women and their allies, written by Black women—though it also seeks to educate and inspire all who read it.

We identify seven central themes in Black women's history that cut across time and space. Travel, motion, movement, and migration fundamentally underscore this history, as Black women's travails have not only remade whole societies and continents but also profoundly influenced cultural, political, and legal practices. Moreover, mobility also represented African American women's own desires to seek out new opportunities and new worlds, domestically and internationally; women such as Jennie Burroughs serve as an important example.

Violence in Black women's history, too, is extensive and multifaceted. We understand violence as physical, but we also acknowledge representational forms of violence such as the use of racist images and caricatures. We also examine the violence of exclusion as it refers to how Black women have been denied social and political participation and protection. The violence of poverty also cannot be overstated.

Activism and resistance are deeply embedded in African American women's histories. Black women have defended against rapist enslavers, transported children north in search of a better way of life, celebrated themselves with raucous partying, and organized as washerwomen and clubwomen. This legacy of struggle is also visible in Black women's political activism, whether working toward abolition or the right to vote, protesting police violence, declaring "Black Power," or running for public office. Resistance is steeped in Black women's embrace of their natural selves, as they often engage it passionately and courageously.

Few things have played a larger role in shaping Black women's destinies in this country than labor and entrepreneurship. Enslavement forced kidnapped African women into fields and houses, to toil alongside men. Discrimination and poverty would keep many there long after Emancipation, yet society stigmatized Black women for occupying these roles. Working outside the home effectively excluded them from being treated according to any commonly held notions of respectable womanhood. But African American women challenged universal symbols of femininity and virtue that privileged whiteness. Many powerfully called attention to the ways that white women could afford to remain at home and be ladies precisely because rigged economic circumstances demanded that Black women cook, clean, sow, and sew, never mind washing the clothes and nursing white children.

During the War of 1812, when the United States secured for the second time its separation from the British crown, thirteen-year-old Grace Wisher, an African American indentured servant from Maryland, helped sew an American flag. Grace worked alongside Mary Pickersgill, to whom she was bound as her servant, and Pickersgill's daughter Caroline and one of her nieces. This group of women "helped design the flag" that would later "inspire Francis Scott Key to write the national anthem."[6] Stitch by stitch, thread and needle in hand, Grace worked with red, white, and blue cloth to create a national treasure, one of America's greatest symbols, the American flag. Black girls and women like Grace have literally stitched themselves into our nation's history in places of prominence and behind the scenes.

Yet, no matter the time period, no matter if they were enslaved or indentured, Black women found ways to become entrepreneurs. They raised their own crops to sell during enslavement or hawked cooked goods like pepper pot stew, as they did near Philadelphia's Congo Square in the Colonial Era. After Emancipation, Black women entrepreneurs opened beauty shops that catered to African American women's unique skin and haircare needs. Black women could get their hair *fried, dyed, and laid to the side* in the parlors, but they could also laugh loud and trade scandalous gossip, all while cultivating grassroots activism.[7]

These laudable entrepreneurial efforts were essential for economic survival, especially since so many Black women faced stiff challenges in the workplace. From abolition through the 1950s, large numbers of Black women were confined either to agricultural work or domestic service. Few could secure factory work, and domestic service imperiled Black women by leaving them vulnerable to sexual assault in white homes and to accusations of theft that could swiftly find Black women on the wrong side of white justice.

Criminalization and incarceration also factored significantly into Black women's lives. Whether it was being convicted for crimes against property or for vice crimes, or for running numbers or for fortune-telling, Black women's experiences in the legal system highlight their clashes with state power. Their records also offer a glimpse of their own ambitions and motivations for living outside the law—laws they often understood as inherently biased and unequally applied. Even so, some Black women rolled johns while others swindled benefit societies, and still others pretended to be servants to gain access to wealthy white homes. Whereas the early history found them largely confined for larceny, the late twentieth century would find many Black women netted in the War on Drugs. This history and their responses to the carceral state are also central themes in the book.

Black women artists, performers, writers, singers, and dancers have without question played powerful roles in defining and enriching our culture, often defying oppression in the process. Black women artists have been instrumental in expressing the truth of Black women's inner lives, mapping our struggles outside and inside the Black community but also unearthing our humor and creativity. From the Colonial-Era poet Phillis Wheatley to the modern literary giant Toni Morrison, Black women writers have given voice to our humanity and generated writing that has reshaped America's literary canon. Black expressive culture also gives a rare sounding to sexual pleasure and does so beyond the narrow confines of promiscuity, victimization, and heterosexuality.

Black women's sexual practices and erotic desires are fundamental to explorations of African American womanhood and history. In some instances, Black women cultivated unique practices to navigate sexuality; their histories encompass deploying respectability and enacting what historian Darlene Clark Hine describes as a "culture of dissemblance"—the practice of purposefully concealing their sexuality to escape unwanted, potentially violent sexual advances. Yet other Black women boldly sought out illicit pleasures and occupied a range of sexualities.

We pay homage to and draw on an abundant historiography about Black women, in addition to scouring archives for precious primary source material. Whenever possible, we also make use of the growing repositories of historical and archival records online, and we often quote documentary interviews and cite video footage featuring Black women. Our hope is that this approach will more easily assist any readers who want to find out more about many of the figures and subjects in the book. Even with these efforts, there are times the historical record fails to adequately document Black women's experiences. Sometimes there are hardly any records at all. As historians we often find ourselves in the difficult position of relying on archival records not penned by Black women but instead chronicled by those who played central roles in obscuring and silencing their legacies. To balance this, we read against one-sided accounts and rely upon sources such as slave rosters and narratives, fugitive advertisements, census data, newspapers, and court records, together with Black women's own writings—speeches, reports, campaigns, organizational minutes, novels, poems, songs, and rap performances. Black women's voices animate this book, as few can more effectively describe the complexities of their lives than Black women themselves. From academic and journalistic prose to bold, jarring verses, Black women's voices defy simple characterizations.

All told, Black women's history in the United States is broad, beautiful, exciting, haunting, and crucial to understanding the nation. It is a testament to the intellectual richness and vitality of Black women. This history also holds the country accountable for its still unmet promise to make democracy serve all, equally.

CHAPTER ONE

ISABEL'S EXPEDITION AND FREEDOM BEFORE 1619

I demand justice.

—ISABEL DE OLVERA

IN EARLY JANUARY 1600, Isabel de Olvera, a woman of African descent, petitioned the mayor of Querétaro, Mexico for protection of her rights before joining Juan de Oñate's expedition to New Spain, which consisted of several regions in North and South America, including present-day New Mexico, Arizona, and Florida. As she was about to embark on the journey with Spanish explorers, Olvera believed she would be vulnerable to violence or captivity. "I am going on the expedition," she stated in her deposition, "and have reason to fear that I may be annoyed by some individual since I am a mulatto."[1]

Born the daughter of Hernando, an African man, and Magdalena, an Indian woman, she had always been free. Yet Olvera knew that those she encountered would deem her property, and she wanted the protection of "an affidavit" that she proudly noted would confirm she was "free and not bound by marriage or slavery." Her intent was to carry "a properly certified and signed copy" of this document to show anyone who might question her status. Her appeal ended with a final declaration: "I demand justice."

Women of African descent arrived in what became the United States as early as the sixteenth century. Their histories on this land are difficult to document because the archive hardly recognizes their presence. When they do appear, many are nameless figures, mentioned in passing, with little identifying information given about their experiences. We begin this study before the formation of the country as we know it today, at a time when rare women of African descent, like Isabel de Olvera, demanded justice. Ironically, even in this period, from 1400 to 1619, Black women were fighting for their rights, for their sense of belonging.

———————

THE EARLY HISTORICAL NARRATIVES of North America were not uniquely centered on Black women until now; instead, it was about discovery, colonization, and conquest. This history emphasized the "discovery" of land—a geography of multiple meanings depending on who occupied it. In the late eighteenth century, the territory that became the United States was home to indigenous populations for thousands of years before being occupied by the Spanish, Dutch, French, and British.

Why do we begin then, with Isabel de Olvera? Because her story reveals hidden or otherwise unacknowledged aspects of the history of this country. American history did not start when Europeans arrived in Pensacola in 1528, Roanoke in 1585, or Jamestown in 1607. It began in 5000 to 3000 BCE, during the Paleo-Indian era, when indigenous people settled here and lived in harmony with the land.

The first Black women who stepped foot on what we now consider American soil were not enslaved. In fact, some, like Olvera, were free, and they traveled as part of expeditions to explore land that had been inhabited by native populations for generations. These women did not arrive emaciated and distraught from being packed like sardines in the belly of slave ships. Instead, women of African descent arrived before the first ships disembarked their loads of human cargo in the American colonies. They came with Spanish and Portuguese explorers, and many could be classified as indentured servants, missionaries, interpreters, or simply leaders.

Black women arrived during a period of European conquest, colonization, and chaos—marked by warfare, trade, travel, and cultural clash. Much of this chaos began when Spanish and Portuguese explorers, authorized by Castilian law and the Treaty of Tordesillas (by papal law), came in search of new lands and trade routes to other parts of the world. They came to territories inhabited by native populations. They came searching for new continents and resources such as gold, iron, and food. Sometimes explorers were greeted with trust and admiration and were showered with gifts. Other times they were treated with trepidation, fear, and violence. Some were idolized as people with religious or supernatural powers. In these situations and circumstances, where European movement and mastery often proceeded hand-in-hand, Black women were present as well. And they witnessed the often sordid scenes. We learn about them through reports authored by explorers such as Vasco Núñez de Balboa, Hernán Cortés, Francisco Vázquez de Coronado, Lucas Vázquez de Ayllón, Hernando de Soto, and Juan de Oñate. Accounts of explorers' journeys sometimes mention women, and those that left silences in the historical record force us to construct Black women's lives through traces, conjectures, and sometimes speculation.

Before Olvera traveled to New Mexico, another Black woman made her way into present-day Kansas around 1594. Although we do not know her name, we know that she accompanied the Francisco Leyva de Bonilla expedition and almost lost her life after being severely burned in an attack near Wichita.[2] The woman was a member of Bonilla's small party and was traveling with them into the Kitikiti'sh Indian territory when Bonilla, a Portuguese captain serving Spain, was killed. The unnamed woman, described as "mulatto" (of African and Indian descent), and a young Spanish boy named Alonso Sanchez nearly died as well.[3] It is believed that the Oñate expedition to New Mexico four years later, which included several women, was partly a mission to find these two survivors.[4] Given the chaos of territorial warfare, it is no surprise that the expedition never found them and that the two women of African descent never made contact. Olvera probably interacted with only a handful of women like herself.

Black women are sprinkled throughout the history of the United States before 1619 in fragmentary documents. An occasional passage or reference does tell us, however, that they were in the territory doing all they could to survive, just like their male counterparts. In the Southwest, Black women arrived with large and small parties as early as the sixteenth century, well before the British colonists landed at Jamestown. They were among the first nonindigenous explorers of the region. We can uncover the women's history through Spanish archival records and a host of secondary sources. The travel records of explorers like Oñate and Bonilla suggest that there may be more documents and references to Black women in the American Southwest than the wider public acknowledges. In fact, hundreds of other women of African descent traveled in and occupied this land. Some of these women were the offspring of African explorers, and references to them reveal their vulnerabilities to the physical hardships of their journeys which included the constant threat of rape and other forms of violence.

In 1513, for example, Vasco Núñez de Balboa crossed the Isthmus of Panama and "discovered" the "south Sea," or Pacific Ocean. Accompanying him were approximately thirty Africans, including a man named Nuflo de Olano, whom scholars believe was enslaved. We do not have evidence of whether or not women participated in this expedition, but if Olano intermixed with native populations, his offspring, like Olvera and the unnamed woman who traveled with Bonilla, would be considered mulatto. Likewise, a little more than a decade later, in 1526, Lucas Vázquez de Ayllón founded the colony of San Miguel de Gualdape near the Pee Dee River in present-day Georgetown, South Carolina. Like Balboa, Ayllón brought approximately one hundred Africans with him to help set up the colony. These were the first African captives who arrived in the South as a group, and they rebelled shortly after their arrival. We know women were among them because documents suggest that there was a discrepancy in the payment of an unnamed woman. Conflict with local indigenous Americans proved fruitful for the African captives, who fled the colony and resided with Indians in the interiors.[5]

It is possible that there were other women of African descent among these early settlers, making them some of the first Black women in America, arriving *before* the women in Oñate's expedition. But how do we identify them in archives that hardly acknowledge their presence or through history books that omit them from their pages? *Who were the first women of African descent to step foot on American soil?* These women were the offspring of African male explorers and indigenous, Spanish, or Mexican women. Many of the women in this early period show up in the travel accounts and ship registers as nameless people, identified only by ethnic markers and gendered pronouns.

Starting with the story of Spanish conquest/invasion represents a shift in the story of Black women in America. The history of exploration and discovery produces traces of Black women in regions beyond the grand narrative, which often begins with the British. For example, in 1535, Hernán Cortés of Spain went on an expedition to present-day California, bringing with him three hundred enslaved people of African descent. Although Cortés traveled by horseback across Mexico from the port of Vera Cruz, he sent three ships, the *San Lazaro*, the *San Tomas*, and the *Santa Agueda*, carrying enslaved Africans to help settle the "new land" in the west.[6] Only two of the ships made it to Old Santa Cruz, which is located near La Paz, Mexico, on the east side of Baja, California. We do not know the genders of those on board, nor do we know much about what happened when the passengers and crew reached land, but it is quite likely that women were included in this group. People of African descent stepped foot on the Baja, California, coastline nearly 250 years before European settlement. They traveled with Spanish explorers, whom we learn were not initially trying to colonize the region but instead were searching for additional trade routes.

In times of "discovery," violence erupted as people from different parts of the world clashed with one another in their search for riches and quest for establishing territories. The first women to walk these territories were not immune from such conflicts, as evidenced by the mulatto woman in Wichita who was nearly burned to death. Some of these physical encounters may have involved force and could likely be classified as rape; others may have been consensual. Given that some women used the expedition to sever their marital bonds suggests that they were risk takers at a time when they had few, if any, rights. It appears that the majority of the people on expeditions were men and that the conditions were challenging, giving way to stress and violence. Parties traveled into unfamiliar territory that had been previously occupied for centuries. They brought supplies to outfit the expedition as well as tradable goods. As with any bartering relationships, negotiations sometimes ended in conflict and even war.

Members of the Oñate expedition, which originated in 1596, gladly gave up their worldly possessions to join the newly approved groups of additional explorers. In fact, "the news of the expedition was publicly proclaimed throughout the streets and plazas . . . and notices given of the privileges which would be granted those soldiers and colonists who enlisted in this enterprise."[7] Perhaps Olvera became excited about this opportunity and sought permission to join the group. The expedition crew brought with them supplies, including weapons:

leather shields, swords, daggers, helmets, buckskin jackets, and corselets with breastplates worn by men and women. The party traveled with 65 mules and 1,157 horses with heavy saddles (including war horses, riding horses, ponies, and mares). Oñate's companions also carried muskets and pistols, as well as a variety of "blade weapons," such as swords, machetes, fencing foils, and daggers. They needed these items both for protection and for trade.

The goal of Oñate's first expedition was to travel from Mexico City to a small base near present-day El Paso, Texas, where they attempted to set up residence. From there, the explorers ventured deeper into the west, northwest, and central plains on mini-expeditions to learn about life in these regions. During their travels they faced dehydration, hunger, fatigue, disease, and death. This was the environment Olvera would be entering when she asked to join the expedition at the beginning of 1600. She had to wait eight months for a rigorous legal process that scrutinized her status and ultimately cleared her to participate.

In order to travel, Olvera had to prove that she was free and unmarried. She called on three witnesses who testified under oath to confirm her identity. This was not always easy for women of African descent. Their credibility was constantly questioned, and courts did not always accept the women's testimony unless they had people to vouch for them. Olvera's witnesses were an enslaved man named Santa Maria, a free Black man named Mateo Laines, and a Mestizo (people "of mixed race" with Spanish and Native American ancestry) woman named Anna Verdugo. All three confirmed that Olvera was indeed the daughter of Hernando and Magdalena and that she was telling the truth about her identity. Ironically, from the earliest moments in American history, Black women like Olvera had to prove themselves free and clear of any forms of ownership (slavery and matrimony). Women's mobility and marital status needed legal confirmation, and even their status as free individuals required authentication. In this case it was necessary for Olvera to be investigated before joining the ongoing expedition. Olvera had never been enslaved, nor was she married, and in her words, she considered herself a "legitimate" daughter. The questioning of "unattached" women of color in the Spanish colonies of the late sixteenth and early seventeenth centuries was quite common. All three of Olvera's witnesses appeared before the mayor of Querétaro, a city in north central Mexico, and took oaths in a "legal manner by God and a cross" knowing that the consequences of false testimony meant excommunication from the Catholic Church.[8]

Olvera received permission to join the expedition on August 29, 1600, several months after making her request. We do not have evidence of what Olvera did during her long wait, but we know a great deal about the members of the expedition and some of the hardships they faced leading up to 1600, when Olvera joined them.

One year into the expedition, in November, 1597, after traveling for eleven days, the group took a rest to repair their carts. They also "buried a child, a son of Herrera." A few days later they buried a "servant who had been killed by a colt."[9] It appears the travelers tended to loss quickly and moved on. Every few months the Spanish government sent a representative to check on the members of the party. Officials took depositions and inventories of the travelers' property, examined their health, and replenished supplies. For nearly two years, Spanish rulers routinely halted Oñate's expedition and interviewed each male member of the party. In the group of nearly 400 men, 130 brought their families, including their wives, children, and servants.[10] The males ranged in age from fifteen to sixty years old, and there were no age-specific references to the women and children, only comments about marital status and occasionally ethnicity and names. There were about thirty women in the expedition, of whom eighteen were married. Of the total, eleven appeared as indigenous.[11]

So, what was life like for a Black woman such as Olvera, traveling as part of a major expedition? She knew she was taking a great risk entering volatile territory, but other women were present and actively engaged as interpreters, explorers, and servants, so she was not alone. In fact, Olvera traveled with a family as their servant, and they were supposed to care for her; we have no idea if they did so. Also joining her was a mulatto "girl of tender age," named Ysabel, and a number of Indian women, including Juana, Anna, Francisca, Catalina, Augustina, Maria, Francisca, and Beatriz, whom we only know by their first names in ancient records. Mestizo women, such as Magdalena and Ana, accompanied them as well. Some of these women used the expedition to leave their husbands, while others traveled with their spouses and children.[12] Some women gave birth during the long journey.

Many of the married women went as nurses, seamstresses, and body servants (who served as a personal attendant). We can speculate about their experiences through inventories (complete records of property including goods, food, weapons, and clothing) that appear in travel literature such as historical ballads, in which husbands choose to mention the women and acknowledge their presence.

Some men in listing their goods deliberately told officials they would not disclose their wives' possessions, to avoid theft. Instead they noted only that their wives and children accompanied them and had clothing and personal items of their own. Given the demographics of the women involved, it is clear that when Olvera joined the party two years later, she was surrounded by both married and unmarried women and by a handful of people of African descent. Oñate's personal servant was Black, and a man named Francisco de Sosa Peñalosa brought "four female slaves and one male slave."[13]

Some men sought to protect the identities of their wives because of horror stories that circulated about men on earlier expeditions. They did so by saying little about them in the depositions and by not disclosing their personal items; some even chose not to share their names. Esteban the Moor, one of the first African explorers in America, is said to have mistreated women. We don't know if this is true. However, we know that women accompanied him during the 1539 Coronado expedition through present-day New Mexico, Arizona, and California. At least one was an enslaved Indian woman, a prisoner of war. Esteban traveled with women who often served as interpreters, but legend suggests that they worshipped him and his comrades perhaps for their bravery. On a few occasions women gave birth on this journey, but we do not know who impregnated them. "Many times, it occurred that some of the women who accompanied us gave birth," one traveler shared, and as soon as "the children were born the mothers would bring them to us that we should touch and bless them."[14] Some accounts suggest that Esteban was abusive; others recognized him as being the main communicator with indigenous people. "The negro [Esteban] was in constant conversation," and Esteban, it was said by expedition members, "informed himself about the ways we wished to take, of the towns there were, and the matters we desired to know."[15] Other accounts viewed him as a great explorer who was not given credit for his bravery or for traveling to New Mexico.[16] Knowing about people like Esteban might have encouraged men like Hernández to withhold information about his wife and her possessions on the Oñate expedition nearly sixty years later. Not all sixteenth-century women received such "protections."

In 1577, while traveling the Pacific Ocean in his quest to circumnavigate the globe, Sir Francis Drake captured an enslaved woman named Maria off the coast of Guatemala. Described as a "proper negro wench," Maria was raped or gang-raped and was impregnated by either the captain or one of his crew. Her experience is one of the most chilling stories in the history of women in the New World. Yet we have no written narrative of her experience, just scattered references to her existence.

Drake decided to leave Maria and two Black men on a deserted island called "Crab Island" on the Maluku archipelago of Indonesia. Was Drake the father of the unborn child? This we do not know. However, we know that the woman was pregnant and rather than arriving in London with a baby of African and European ancestry, he and his crew disposed of Maria and the two men, and then continued their journey. What happened to the woman and her two counterparts? Did she give birth? Did the infant survive? History leaves us with no answers.[17]

Maria's brief mention confirms that Black women were being sexually exploited on ships in the sixteenth century prior to arriving on land. Ship captains such as Drake authorized, participated in, or turned their backs on such exploitation. They saw Black women's bodies as disposable, and as historian Jennifer L. Morgan argues, Drake's decision to leave Maria and her two counterparts on an island gave the "white crewmembers" a "hereditary freedom that would not be sullied by the birth of a dark-skinned baby."[18] The value of her life was not worth compromising the reputation of the captain and his crew. Such actions occurred on the eve of one of the most exploitative periods in Black women's history: the transatlantic slave trade era.

How might Maria have told her story? This we can only speculate. Given that she was described as "gotten with child," we can assume that her pregnancy was visible and that she may have been in her second trimester. Women at this stage in their pregnancies often feel a renewed sense of energy, which would have helped Maria survive being stranded on a deserted island. At the same time, women at that stage can also experience dizziness, leg cramps, and urinary tract infections. We do not know if Maria went through any of these changes or how long she survived on the island. We do not know who helped her give birth.

Maria may have welcomed the opportunity to depart from Drake's ship, where she experienced exploitation, most likely from the captain and several members of the crew. Yet, we do not know anything about her interactions with the two men with whom she was sent ashore. They were given "rice, seeds, and fire to populate the place."[19] Being on land might have given her physical relief as well. The instability of the sea could not have been pleasant during the early weeks of her pregnancy. But what was her life like on Crab Island?

We know that many of these islands in this archipelago are home to a warm climate, with average daily temperatures ranging from 73 to 85 degrees Fahrenheit. Most of this group of islands were mountainous, with active volcanoes, which could make them a challenge to navigate. European occupation in the late sixteenth century led to the discovery of spices such as cloves and nutmeg, and the region became known as the Spice Islands. But what about Maria, her unborn child, and the men who were discarded on an island said to be populated by crabs and bats? Would they be safe at night? Did they have a chance of survival? We will never know the answers to these questions or anything else about Maria, except that she was a woman of African descent who was impregnated while on a ship with one of the world's most renowned explorers, Sir Francis Drake, and abandoned soon after.

Unlike Maria, Isabel de Olvera and her experience in the late sixteenth-century era of exploration and navigation are better known to us because of her testimony and the Oñate expedition's travel and inspection records.

Upon being granted permission to join the expedition, Isabel traveled approximately 1,380 miles across Mexico and New Spain through mountainous regions, across rivers, and into desert valleys. She probably went from Querétaro, Mexico, to Santa Fe, New Spain in three important stages: (1) Querétaro to Santa Barbara, Mexico (approximately 640 miles), which took three to four months; (2) Santa Barbara to El Paso (approximately 435 miles), across mostly desert terrain, a journey of about three months; and (3) El Paso to Santa Fe (approximately 305 miles), which took about four months. Oñate had traversed this land on earlier travels, so he developed ways to save time by cutting through the Chihuahuan Desert on the last two legs of the journey. However, doing so put his comrades, perhaps including Isabel, at great risk.

On the crew's first trip to New Spain, before Isabel joined them, they were without water for three days. How did they maintain morale and cope under such extreme conditions? We know about these travel conditions through Gaspar Pérez de Villagrá, who wrote the first published history of any American commonwealth in 1610 and who accompanied Oñate and paved the way for others, like Isabel, who came to New Mexico after him. Villagrá talked about the "great distances" they "marched" along a "long ridge of mountains" to find safe passages. When they reached the banks of a river they named "Sacramento" in honor of "the Blessed Sacrament," they built a large chapel and used it as a place to rest and pray. "The women and children came barefoot to pray at the holy shrine," he wrote. One wonders if Isabel had the opportunity to pray at this place on her journey. If so, what would her prayers be? Did she know about the violence that had occurred at this site years earlier, when soldiers whipped the women and children "unmercifully until the camp ran crimson with their blood"?[20] She had to know the risks involved in exploration because she had petitioned for protection prior to her journey.

We can speculate that Isabel spent nearly a year traveling by foot to reach New Mexico. Her migration would have taken her from sea level to altitudes greater than three thousand feet. She would have walked through vast desert lands in the Chihuahuan Desert and crossed the Rio Conchos, Rio Grande, and probably the Rio Santa Cruz before entering northern New Spain, which includes parts of present-day Arizona and New Mexico. If Olvera was fortunate, she could cross rivers via the bridges Oñate's explorers built. If not, she would have to have exercised great caution and skill to avoid being swept down river. We know from accounts of Villagrá's experience crossing the Rio Conchas, for example, that "teamsters brought the wagons down the steep banks" where they had to "skillfully" maneuver them into rushing waters. The swift current must have been treacherous for anyone crossing since, as he recalled, "the rushing waves caught the wagons and tossed them about like ships in a heavy sea" while the horses and other animals used "every muscle" to reach the other side of the river.[21] How did Olvera manage? Did she know how to swim? Was the bridge that Oñate's men constructed a few years before still standing? Did Olvera have assistance traversing the steep riverbanks on both sides? Even if she was successful, there were still two or three other river crossings to make on the journey.

One wonders if Olvera traveled along mountain ranges or along the river to keep close to adequate sources of water. Months of travel had to be taxing on her body, particularly her feet. The harsh conditions likely diminished the travelers' morale, though Oñate was known for giving pep talks and encouraging words to his comrades when they set up camp. "Be not discouraged," he would tell them, recognizing that "sufferings and misfortunes seem to be our daily lot." With faith in God, "ill-luck cannot endure forever," he said. Reminding them of courageous men and "other heroes," he proclaimed that the "present trials and tribulations" occurred "for the express purpose of preparing" them "for the glorious future which awaits."[22] Did the leaders Olvera traveled with give words of encouragement to the women as well? We know that years earlier women took up arms and protected their homes against an attack from the Acoma people. Perhaps this legendary story inspired Olvera and the women she traveled with in 1600. Warfare was common in their period and groups at peace could quickly turn on each other. One always had to be on guard.

If Olvera made it to Santa Fe, she would have encountered a place where Spaniards, Mexicans, indigenous peoples, and Afromestizos set up society. Oñate held the governorship until 1607, when he was ousted for not obeying Spanish law. Thus, within a few years of her arrival, Olvera would have experienced the instability of early colonial life. Although we do not know all the details of her life, thanks to the testimony we are fortunate enough to have, we know that she may have gone on this expedition for several reasons, including traveling with a family to offer relief to those who were already in New Mexico. One thing is certain: Olvera knew that before she left, she had to protect her rights.

In trying to situate Black women in the early history of America, it is important to imagine the spaces and fill in the gaps as best as we can, especially when we know that Black women were present. Considering their thoughts and actions represents one way to correct their erasure when their voices have been silenced and their bodies disposed of. Given that Olvera chose to take a yearlong journey to present-day New Mexico speaks volumes to our understanding of the options and possibilities for Black women prior to British settlement and arrival of the British. From sixteenth-century accounts of Olvera's exploration and Maria's exploitation, we know that some Black women exercised their rights while others relinquished them. Some experienced sexual assault on ships while others sought legal protection, even if it did not guarantee they would be spared from assault. Their experiences would become more universal as time continued, and as a result, thousands of Black women arrived captive in the bellies of slave ships. This journey would soon mark their commonalities.

Starting with the seventeenth century, we learn of more women of African descent who were forcibly moved to the New World. These women had different experiences on this land than Olvera. They were unwilling victims of genocide in *the* largest forced migration in history: the transatlantic slave trade. Historians confirm that 1444 marked the first year a slave ship left the African coast to a Portuguese market, although this ship of 250 Africans did not come to the Americas; it went to Lisbon, one of the primary slave-trading centers at that time.[23] The ship arrived with grief-stricken men, women, and children. It is impossible to imagine the experience of this journey or the horror of being taken into captivity.

Consider for a moment the particular trauma of forced captivity for women. African girls and women might have been tending to children or engaged in other responsibilities in villages with family and friends when suddenly someone put a sackcloth on their heads and chains on their hands and feet. They were violently taken and forced to walk to places they did not know existed. When they arrived, some of them saw bodies of water that seemed to have no end. Even more frightening was the sight of their captors. This may have been the first time they saw people with white skin. Who were they? Ghosts? Cannibals? Evil spirits? Were their captors European or African? How did women make sense of and process what was happening? In the midst of this confusion, they were forced to walk in "slave coffles," chained by the neck and ankles to other captives, many of whom did not speak the same language despite the commonality of their skin tone. Those being transported may not have been from the same community. African people came from thousands of different ethnicities and spoke a variety of languages. Barefoot and sometimes naked, they were put into holding facilities with cold concrete floors and walls that did not have windows—a suffocating ventilation system. Bodily fluids such as vomit, blood, urine, and feces caked the floor and the walls, and the stench was overwhelming. The pole in the middle of the room that everyone avoided was where hands were tied to keep them still during floggings and branding, events that marked the commodification of bodies prior to being sent to the New World on ships. The shrieking sounds of distraught mothers, daughters, aunties, grandmothers, and infants moaning, crying, and screaming, were ear piercing and haunting. This was not a place anyone chose to visit nor cared to remember. It was a place they all wanted to forget.

Standing on the shores of the West African coastline, waiting to be put on a boat, African women were robbed of their liberty and identity. They left as individuals who were part of ethnic communities such as the Arada, Ashanti, Bakongo, Coromante, Ewe, Fante, Fon, Fulani, Hausa, Ibo, Tiv, and Yoruba. However, outsiders would soon impose general monikers on them: "Negras," "Wenches," or "Negars." Captains, traders, crew, and eventually enslavers (people who owned human property) saw them as African captives, and commonly made notation of the region from where they came: Angola, Benin, Calabar, Congo, Gambia, Gold Coast, Guinea, and Senegambia, overlooking the variety of cultural or language groups they represented. But these women resisted, especially when being shoved onto a small boat. There was something about the water and the large ship anchored in the distance that seemed even more daunting than the experience in the cold cement room. Having been in that holding facility for weeks, subjected to horrors difficult to describe, African women brought to the Americas faced trauma well before they were loaded onto ships and traversed the Atlantic.

When a captured and traded woman's feet first touched the water in the wooden base of the small boat that would take her to a ship that would make the journey across the ocean, she probably had no idea that she would never return to her homeland. The chances of her survival across the Atlantic were even more unlikely; nearly one third died in watery coffins that represented the belly of slavers. The rough waters brought a level of motion sickness that she probably experienced for the first time. Too many new experiences clouded her mind and depressed her spirit. What is this? Where are they taking me? Why am I subjected to this madness? Before she could fully consider these questions, she arrived at the ship, was forced up the plank and stuffed into the wooden dungeon/coffin/hold, a space she would occupy for the next several weeks. The latch closed and darkness and grief overtook her.

MOST OF THE WOMEN who came to the New World traversed the Atlantic in slave ships. However, women like Olvera and countless unnamed travelers arrived before the slave trade emerged in this country. From the dawn of the seventeenth century, Black women would change the shape of America through petitions, actions, and defying legislation that coveted their bodies and commodified their wombs. For the next several hundred years, however, the travel and exploration that was granted to Olvera, was denied to generations of Black women who followed her.

CHAPTER TWO

ANGELA'S EXODUS OUT OF AFRICA, 1619—1760

"He brought not any thing but 20. And odd Negroes, w[hich] the Governo[r] and Cape Merchant bought for victuall[s]."

—JOHN ROLFE

SOMEWHERE NEAR THE SHORES of Luanda, Angola, in 1619, between the Lukula and Kwanza Rivers, a group of Africans, including Angela, boarded the *São João Bautista*, a Portuguese ship en route to Vera Cruz, New Spain. Their forced entrance followed a journey of one hundred to two hundred miles, on foot, from their villages. Captain Manuel Mendes da Cunha received permission to carry upwards of these 350 African captives through a contract known as *asiento*, a right the Spanish Crown granted individuals, including ship captains, to enslave and deliver African people to the New World. It is likely that Angela experienced years of warfare and served as a prisoner of war before being traded into slavery and boarding the ship.

She came from a region rich with conflict between several groups, including the Kimbundu and Imbangala. Clashes and disunity occurred daily as droughts in the Sahara Desert region forced entire communities of North Africans to migrate south. This migration pattern caused conflicts that resulted in people being held as prisoners of war. To illustrate how pronounced this was, at one point, the value in human commodities outweighed the trade value of products such as gold, metals, and grains. In other words, the trade in human beings became the primary mode of negotiation and exchange among Africans and Europeans. Angela may have been captured due to warfare and then traded as a human commodity. As a result, she had no choice but to board the ship.

Life at sea was treacherous even for talented navigators like the Portuguese. Wooden ships tossed back and forth across the rough Atlantic waters. Saltwater seeped through cracks of the hold and violently splashed on the upper deck. The back-and-forth, up-and-down motion brought the realities of sea sickness to life. Nausea, dizziness, headaches, and cold sweats led to violent vomiting episodes, dehydration, and misery. Life on the ship touched all the senses. The stench of bodily fluids mixed with saltwater was enough to make anyone ill, while the ear-piercing sound of the waves crashing into the ship made the roar of thunder sound like whispers. Darkness suffocated vision while flashes of light were blinding. Friction from naked skin on the wooden planks gave way to splinters, skin chafing, and incurable infections. The sour taste of vomit remained in throats and dehydration led to dry mouth, split lips, and suppressed appetites. This was how Angela and hundreds of others lived on the *São João Bautista* for weeks.

African women populated ships in Atlantic waters in the fifteenth and sixteenth centuries and disembarked in Spanish American port cities well before British colonists claimed Jamestown, Virginia, in 1607. Over the course of a year, from June 1619 to June 1620, "six slavers arrived at Vera Cruz" directly from Angola with 1,161 African men, women, and children.[1] This marks the first period that enslaved people, and women in particular, arrived in large numbers on slavers. During the first few decades of the seventeenth century, women of African descent continued to voluntarily and involuntarily make their way to American soil. These women often arrived via a horrific crossing of the Atlantic as very few petitioned to settle in New World communities, unlike Isabel de Olvera, who came on foot. Instead they came as indentured servants and enslaved laborers entering ports such as Cartagena and Vera Cruz, not far from where Olvera began her journey.

The time most associated with Africans settling in America is August 1619, when John Rolfe "brought not any thing but 20. And odd Negroes, w[hich] the Governo[r] and Cape Merchant bought for victuall[s]." The "odd Negroes" included Angela and several other women, who arrived at Point Comfort, on the James River in Virginia. Their story is not always told. However, in order to learn about Black women's arrival, it is important to understand their experiences on the Atlantic Ocean. Although some started their journey on the *São João Bautista* heading for Vera Cruz, other captive Africans were captured at sea and placed on the *White Lion* and *Treasurer*, English ships sailing under the Dutch flag and bound for the Americas. When the ships arrived, a few days apart, in Virginia, the twenty Africans from the *White Lion* experienced their first official sale and were traded for provisions. Days later, it is believed that the captain of the *Treasurer* sold seven to nine Africans, then quickly left for the island of Bermuda, another English colony.[2]

THE HORRORS OF THE SLAVE SHIP represent one of the greatest atrocities in world history. The experience for women was especially treacherous and complicated by physical and sexual exploitation from the crew. Stripped naked and packed like sardines, female captives crossed the Atlantic in sex-segregated holds underneath the deck. It was a dark place with little ventilation. Some came to the ships after suffering in holding facilities (forts or barracoons) along the West African coastline for months. While there they were continuously inspected, as ship captains stopped at ports to fill their holds with select "human cargo." The merchants and traders who visited sexually abused some of the women.

At sea, the abuse continued, along with illnesses and diseases. The women frequently suffered from fevers, dysentery, and smallpox, and their poor diets caused starvation and extreme malnutrition. Equally troubling was the psychological trauma and stress captives faced. Their lives as they knew them had changed dramatically. They were torn from families and communities and forced into a living nightmare.

Records from eighteenth-century ship captains provide insight into life at sea. John Newton, for example, mentions several women in his journal. None are referred to by name; instead each of the captives received a number. This depersonalization robbed the women of their identities and ignored their personhood. African people became numerical figures recorded in account books, registers, and diaries without any consideration of their ancestry. Their given names did not matter to their enslavers, who were only interested in the number of bodies they took to New World plantation communities for sale. Making sense of this dispossession tormented African captives struggling to survive. Unfortunately, many lost their lives during the journey.

On June 13, 1754, Newton "buried a woman slave (No 47)" who had "not been properly alive since she first came on board." Perhaps she became ill from the treacherous journey to the coastline or at the fortification along the coast waiting to be shuffled onto a slaver. If she took ill before being forced onto the ship, the conditions on board certainly did not help. Poor ventilation, inadequate food, and unsanitary conditions led the bellies of slavers to serve as incubators for disease and, as a result, many died.

A burial on the Atlantic meant being thrown overboard. This is hardly the image one imagines when thinking about being "laid to rest." Being discarded in this way shows a complete disrespect for life. Tens of thousands, perhaps millions, of African people were unceremoniously tossed into watery graves. There, in the rough waters of the Atlantic, the bones of African people—known only by their assigned number, if even that—still remain on the ocean floor.

Newton buried another person, on June 24, 1754, "a girl (No 92)." One wonders if she came to the ship alone or with family. How did she die? Did she receive any medical care? How long had she survived on the ship? We know nothing else about "No 92" and only a bit more about a grown woman, "No 83." Crew member William Cooney "seduced" her "down into the room and lay with her brute-like in view of the whole quarter deck."

Imagine the humiliation she experienced to have others witness her sexual abuse. The violent nature of this is unsettling as Newton recorded that this woman, No 83, "was big with child."[3] Not only was she raped, but she was already pregnant and apparently far enough along in her pregnancy to receive the descriptor "big with child." But what else do we know about "No 83"? What was her experience like during the Middle Passage? How far along in her pregnancy was she? Did she receive any kind of medical care? Who was the father? Did she and her baby survive the trauma of being captured and raped? We do not have answers to these questions, but women like No 83 sear into our consciousness.

Her brief entrance into history is expressed by the language used to describe her. In addition to recognizing her pregnancy, Newton claimed that she was "seduced," as if she was lured into the quarter deck and tempted to participate. The act of seduction implies that she was enticed or drawn in by Cooney, but she never had a choice in the matter. Why would a captive pregnant woman want to have sex with a crew member in a place where others could watch? The voyeuristic gaze of the captain and crew added to her exploitation and humiliation. Even Newton was not pleased with Cooney's behavior and punished him for it. One can imagine that the act itself was punishment enough for the woman.

There is little surviving evidence or documentation to detail the experience of capture, life at sea, or the Middle Passage for the majority of the women who endured it. However, there is information about one woman, Ma Presence, a Mandingo captured near the Niger River in the nineteenth century, that provides some insight into the transformation from freedom to enslavement. Childhood for Ma Presence generated pleasant memories. "She lived in a village of huts surrounded by a high strong fence" to protect her community from wild animals and slave catchers. Her people were warriors, and she had vivid memories of "the gallant appearance" of them with their "trophies and spoil." She also vividly remembered the day she was captured. While Ma Presence and other children were bathing in a river close to the village, they heard the sounds of gunfire and screams, and then saw "flames rising from the huts." Just as she and her companions ran up the riverbank to find out what happened, Ma Presence was grabbed "by the arm, and dragged . . . away to the bush." At this point, she was forced into a "slave caravan" and walked to "the great Black Sea," where, upon first glance, "she covered her mouth with her hand and was lost in astonishment and fear."[4] Ma Presence did not recount much about the trek to the sea, and she did not share her experiences during the Middle Passage with those who knew her, even though she was known as a great storyteller. Perhaps the trauma was too painful. We know that she "was sold to a planter in Jamaica," before being sold and transferred to Bluefields, Nicaragua.

Black women like Ma Presence did not succumb easily to their captivity. Many fought back in the form of revolts and mutinies at sea. They used their knowledge of the ship's layout and crew behavior to inform other captives of the location of supplies and weapons, and about the living conditions and daily habits of the crew.

In the summer of 1730, a shipload of ninety-one African captives leaving Guinea for Rhode Island on the sloop *Little George* revolted and took control of the ship for nearly ten days. There were approximately sixty-one women and children among this group of captives and they participated in the rebellion that started one morning, a few hours before daybreak, at 4 a.m., when the ship was a hundred miles away from shore. The men were able to get out of their irons (perhaps with help from the women and children) and killed three watchmen: a doctor, a sailor, and the cooper. The other crew members grabbed their guns and stayed in their cabins trying to shoot at the rebels from their rooms. "At a loss at what to do," they used gunpowder to set ablaze a makeshift bomb made out of a bottle and attempted to throw it at the African captives. However, before they could do so, an African man hit the bottle with an ax and it exploded, killing the sailor who held it. Four to five more days of fighting ensued, and the African captives fully took over the *Little George*. As the ship neared land, a group of adults went ashore while the young children were placed on small boats and towed to safety.

One wonders how the women and children participated in the struggle aboard the *Little George*. Did any of them directly battle the crew? Or were they busy keeping watch and helping navigate the ship? Regardless of their activities, it is significant that women and children took part in a mutiny on a ship where they were the majority of those captive, even if the accounts that exist focus on the thirty-five men in this tumultuous battle on the water.

What happened to these women when they left the *Little George* in the middle of the night near Frenchman's Bay, Maine? We know they negotiated with the native people who discovered them, but we do not know if they all made it to freedom. Their incredible escape story of taking over a sloop for nearly ten days, making it to land, and disembarking safely in Maine, however, illustrates the resilience of African captives seeking freedom in a foreign land.[5]

Other women and men who rebelled on ships ended their lives on the open waters of the Atlantic. It is hard to know the various belief systems they carried with them, but the desire for liberty and freedom had to be key factors in their actions. According to historian Gwendolyn Midlo Hall, "Resistance aboard the slave-trade ships to Louisiana is well documented," and there were several uprisings at sea.[6] *Le Courrier de Bourbon* sailed for Senegal in the spring of 1723 with sixty males, forty females, and "four or five nursing babies." The journey was filled with rebellion and sickness. Some jumped overboard when they had the opportunity, others tried to fight the crew, and some were sick with smallpox. When the ship landed in the French Caribbean, the crew sold "a black man and a black woman with her nursing baby in exchange for food."

After the ship returned to sea, officers learned that the captives were planning an insurrection and two captive women who served as interpreters knew the plan. They tried to bribe the women into disclosing the details of the attack, but the women refused to share anything. In response the crew tied the two women to "a cannon to be lashed," and they "still said nothing." Several others took beatings as the crew tried to get the women to reveal the ringleaders. Finally, one of the women succumbed, sharing the plot with the crew. In order to make an example of the captive who was leading the insurrection, a forty-five-year-old man from Gorée, the crew tied him to the mast and shot him to death. *Le Courrier de Bourbon* arrived at the mouth of the Mississippi River with eighty-seven Black people in the winter of 1723, despite a voyage rich with rebellion, conspiracies, disease, and death.[7]

Not all disruptions on the water ended in death. Most ship uprisings were halted, and African captives were sold in New World communities. They were taken to places like Spanish Florida, Dutch New York, French Louisiana, and the British Colony of Virginia.

Women of African descent arrived in Spanish Florida in the early sixteenth century and lived in St. Augustine, in present-day Florida, in the 1570s and 1580s. Many came by way of Cuba after "the Crown ordered Havana to send royal slaves" to the region, including "twenty-three African men and seven African women."[8] They were forcibly removed to this region, yet they were instrumental in establishing a community, clearing land, and planting subsistence crops. By the turn of the century, in 1606, there were one hundred enslaved people in Florida, many belonging to the Crown.[9] Their presence confirms Black women's early arrival and importance in the history of this region. Although we do not know their names or much else about them, we do know they settled in this region around the same time Isabel de Olvera traveled to Santa Fe, New Spain.

Governed by Castilian law, this Spanish colony followed Las Siete Partidas, which was issued by King Alfonso X in 1265. This early legislation recognized that "all creatures of the world naturally love and desire liberty" and it addressed women in Law 4. Enslaved women could become free "when her lord puts her into prostitution to make money from her." This legislation was a crucial, and tragic, acknowledgment of how enslavers exploited enslaved women and even in "alleged" freedom claimed tyrannical control over their bodies, indeed, their vaginas. Law 4 was one of seven that addressed the few ways that Black women could become free, although working as a prostitute to make money for an enslaver is not by any standard a road to freedom. In addition to this stipulation about women, the seven laws addressed the ways in which society and its leadership should be governed.[10] This legislation was especially important as migration brought more people to the New World.

Free and enslaved Black women lived in regions that became the United States. They traveled as free and captive people and were essential to their communities. Some arrived on slave ships, some traveled openly in expeditions, and others were royal slaves sent from the Caribbean islands. When these early settlers arrived, they encountered indigenous peoples who had a variety of responses to their presence, including capture and warfare at one extreme and marriage and assimilation at another.

As the Deep South took shape in St. Augustine and the Southwest developed in Santa Fe, settlers also traveled north. In 1621 the Dutch West India Company received permission from the government of Holland to settle in New Netherland (present-day New York, New Jersey, Pennsylvania, Maryland, and Connecticut). By 1624 it had established communities from Manhattan to Albany using the Hudson River as the main thoroughfare. Most were settled in New Amsterdam, at the southern tip of Manhattan. Like their Florida counterparts, large numbers of enslaved people arrived in the North a few years after the Dutch West India Company initially imported eleven enslaved men. However, it is significant to note that "the Company, not individuals, owned these slaves, who provided labor for the building and upkeep of the colony's infrastructure."[11] The first known women of African descent arrived in 1627 in a group of three. By 1630 there were approximately three hundred white settlers and sixty enslaved people. Of the latter population, the Dutch West India Company owned half, while the others were in private hands. By the middle of the seventeenth century, the enslaved represented 25 percent of the community.[12]

Enslaved people helped construct Fort Amsterdam (1635) and "built roads, cut timber and firewood, cleared land, and burned limestone and oyster shells." Farming became an important industry, and the company hired overseers to manage the enslaved. Despite the presence of enslaved men and women, initial importations arrived "haphazardly" until the 1650s, when one of the largest shipments of enslaved Africans arrived in New Amsterdam on the *Witte Paert*. This ship docked in 1655 with three hundred Africans, and "residents knew of its arrival because of the stench that arose from the holds." Five years later, in 1660, "New Amsterdam was the most important slave port in North America."[13]

Black women and their male counterparts in this region were instrumental in establishing the infrastructure to create a permanent settlement in New York. As they cleared the land, timber and fur became two primary industries, and New Amsterdam became the hub for trading activities.

As colonial society took shape, African Americans began challenging their role and pushing for greater freedoms. For example, as early as 1635, enslaved "black workers petitioned for wages," representing one of the first organized labor actions in American history.[14] They also recognized inconsistencies in their legal status and immediately began filing petitions for freedom. In addition, they approached the Dutch Reformed Church, the major church of the region, to perform baptism and marriage ceremonies to solidify their unions and potentially provide another avenue to freedom. At that time Christians could not enslave other Christians, though this legislation soon changed. But by 1655, the church stopped baptizing enslaved people.

A decade later, however, approximately 75 out of some 375 Black people in New Amsterdam were free. Some gained their freedom because Dutch leaders used Black people as a cushion between white settlers and Native Americans, granting African Americans land ownership in a "buffer zone." By 1664 women like Dorothy Angola, Mayken, and Elary all lived in freedom. Some Black people lived on farmsteads that "spread over 130 acres," representing one of the first communities of "legally emancipated . . . people of African descent in North America."[15] There have always been free Black people in America, even during the early history of African arrivals.

Angela, however, was not among those lucky ones. Her Atlantic torment took her to Jamaica where she witnessed the sale of twenty-four children who had endured the journey with her. How did they make sense of this dispossession? After being torn from their homeland and forced to suffer through a traumatic voyage across the Atlantic, the separation from the children was sure to be agonizing for some. One can imagine adult women and men living this nightmare and trying to console the children as they screamed and cried for someone familiar, particularly as they disembarked in Jamaica. Perhaps they tried to make sense of the displacement and offer words of encouragement to help the children survive. But their separation from one another left little space for comfort. These women and children went from being free people to captives torn apart from their loved ones and sold into slavery.

When they landed at Point Comfort, near Jamestown, Virginia, Angela soon learned that legislation governed their lives, and within the first forty years of settlement, statutes focused specifically on their reproductive and productive labor capacity. As early as 1643, the Virginia Assembly allowed for African women to be taxed for their labor, while white women were not. Such legislation marked Black women's bodies as property, and they were expected to work in the fields, a distinction from white women.

Some women of African descent defied their status. Like their New York counterparts, they filed freedom petitions. On July 21, 1656, for example, Elizabeth Keye, the daughter of a deceased white man, Thomas Keye, and an enslaved Black woman, filed a petition for her liberty and that of her infant son. Elizabeth had fallen in love with a white indentured servant, William Grinstead, whom she later married. She won the suit and was one of the first women of African descent to receive her freedom. After her marriage to William, Elizabeth had a second son. Her case raised questions about the status of enslaved people that would be resolved at a later point in history.[16] Despite some successful efforts at suing for freedom, the Virginia Assembly enacted a law in 1662 that defined slavery by the status of the mother, reflected in the Latin phrase *partus sequitur ventrem*. Keye would not have won her case if this law had passed prior to her petition. The law stated that if one's mother was enslaved, then the children followed the condition of the mother and were also enslaved.[17] Colonial Maryland passed similar legislation in 1663, and the other colonies followed suit. By the turn of the eighteenth century, slavery was defined and carried out through Black women's bodies.

While the British occupied Virginia, the Dutch, New York, and the Spanish, Florida, the French controlled the territory of Louisiana all the way up to the Dakotas. The Code Noir (1685) governed the lives of the enslaved and established other regulations for French colonies. Created in Versailles under the leadership of Louis XIV, this sixty-article set of codes regulated life, death, religion, and the treatment of the enslaved in French societies. It allowed provisions for enslaved people in terms of their housing, clothing, treatment, respite on the Sabbath, marriages, and burials. It also allowed them to be baptized and educated into the Catholic faith and made provisions for seeking freedom.[18] When Africans arrived in Louisiana in the early eighteenth century, the French government issued a revised Code Noir (1724) that included stipulations against racial mixing in Article VI, forbidding "white subjects, of both sexes[,]" from marrying "the blacks." In addition, this new code provided some protection to disabled enslaved people. Article XXI said, "Slaves who are disabled from working, either by old age, disease, or otherwise, be the disease incurable or not, shall be fed and provided for by their masters." If their enslavers did not comply, the enslaved person was to be taken to the nearest hospital, which would collect payment for services rendered by placing a "lien on the plantations of the master."[19] Even in the early years of American history, enslaved people were treated as both people and property, to the extent that their care would result in property liens if enslavers did not comply with sound treatment.

Black women labored in homes and in the tobacco, rice, sugar, indigo, and wheat fields throughout the colonial regions. Labor governed their lives and shaped their early experiences in America. On farms and plantations, women followed the agricultural labor calendar based on the crops they produced. They conducted seasonal labor that began with plowing, planting, or flooding the rice fields, followed by a cultivation phase during which raw goods were prepared for the market. In urban areas they worked as laundresses, market

women, or body servants to their enslavers. Those who worked in
the homes of their enslavers prepared and cooked meals, cleaned the
house, entertained the planter children, and served as hostesses for
large events. Some of them washed and ironed their enslaver's clothes;
others helped dress them each day. They usually lived in quarters also
occupied by their enslavers and were watched with greater scrutiny
than their field laborer counterparts. Even if their living conditions
were similar to their enslavers', they still wanted freedom, and some
took it by running away.

After changing hands among three different enslavers, Phillis, also
referred to as Phillida, decided it was time to emancipate herself from
enslavement in New York. In June 1754, she left, taking with her
several items of clothing and her knowledge of the English language,
which she used to write a "false pass." At nineteen and described as a
"Mulatto *colour*," Phillis probably did not want to transfer to Robert
Campbell's property, as he would be her third enslaver, and so she
escaped. In the prime age of fertility, it is probable that Phillis, like
so many enslaved women in their childbearing years, was concerned
about being sexually abused. Campbell placed an advertisement and
a "forty shillings" reward for anyone who returned her to him. He
worried that she would lie and tell people she was free and looking for
a new master, and that she "may possibly endeavour to get on board
some vessel" to "better facilitate her escape." Campbell warned "all
Captains, Boatmen, and others" from taking Phillis with them on
ships. We don't know what happened to Phillis and whether she made
it to freedom, but the fact that she and many other Black women fled
slavery tells us a good deal about how they actively worked against
the system that oppressed them.[20]

Unlike their counterparts who filed lawsuits, Phillis and others
like her—including Nan, Elce, Sarah, and Jenny—chose a different
route to liberty. Instead of fighting the courts, they left the homes of
their enslavers, taking important items with them on their journeys
to freedom. Nan, a thirty-two-year-old house servant from Philadelphia, ran off with "a new Bonnett Lined with red Silk." Her enslaver,
William Chancellor, placed advertisements in the newspaper for two
weeks and offered a reward.[21] Jenny took many more personal items,
including beautifully colored dresses, coats, and other fine clothing
such as a "purple colour'd Peticoat, and a drab coloar'd Wastcoat, a

blue and white striped Cotton and Linnen Peticoat and a yellowish
Dest Gown roobed with red, a Hoop-Peticoat & a Bag of sundry
Linnens." It is likely that Jenny could use these clothes as she tried
to blend into free society, and it is also plausible that she had an at-
tachment to them as a seamstress or laundress. Her enslaver, Martin
Jervis of Philadelphia, owned a shop that sold all kinds of goods. He
described Jenny as a "lusty young Negro Woman . . . about Twenty
one Years of age," and someone who "speaks good English." She was
said to be a "yellowish Black" with "large lips," but one thing that
made her even more distinguishable was the fact that she "lost part
of three Fingers off her right Hand." Enslaved people were subject
to many injuries, and some were differently abled, like Jenny. It was
believed that Jenny escaped but stayed in the vicinity, which explains
why the advertisement ran for an entire year in the same newspaper.[22]
It appears that Nan remained at large, but other women were not
as fortunate.

One unnamed woman escaped her enslaver's wrath by running
away, but she was found dead soon after. Apparently, she managed to
remain out of sight for several days. Her enslaver, Captain Thomas
Wickham, placed an advertisement in a local paper for her safe return. However, he quickly learned that they found her "dead in a
meadow . . . frozen to death."[23] The local judge appointed a committee
to conduct an investigation, suggesting that the value placed upon this
woman was great enough for her enslaver to seek answers to her cause
of death. Had she committed suicide or did she die due to exposure to
the inclement weather? Was she murdered? It is impossible to know
this woman's full story. She enters the historical record only because
she was someone's property and her death caused him a financial loss.

Sometimes enslaved women deliberately chose to cause harm and
stress to their enslavers, and they paid a heavy price for doing so.
In the summer of 1731 one Connecticut woman "kill'd her Masters
[sic] Daughter, by cutting her Throat in her Sleep." Although we do
not know why she killed the girl, there are several plausible expla-
nations. The murdered girl could have recently been gifted the enslaved woman and would be her future enslaver. Perhaps the enslaved
woman sought revenge on her enslavers and knew that murdering
their daughter would cause great pain. Maybe the enslaved woman
had been gifted to her enslaver's daughter and tragically separated

from her own family. Maybe the girl exacted some kind of punishment on the enslaved woman, or the enslaved woman's own child had been snatched away from her, or the wretchedness of slavery had simply exacted its emotional toll? While the circumstances that gave rise to the Black woman's action will forever remain unknown, we do know she paid the ultimate price of her own life. She was hanged for murder on Thursday, September 16, 1731, in New Haven.[24]

Other Black women spared their children the yoke of slavery by committing acts of infanticide. An enslaved woman from Barnstable, Massachusetts, went to prison in December 1732, "on suspicion of murdering her Infant Child." Because another enslaved person allegedly "assisted in privately burying the said infant," local authorities had reason to believe that the enslaved woman was guilty. The infant had been buried for about two weeks before being discovered.[25] Acts of infanticide or the murdering of one's children was a form of resistance that some enslaved women chose to spare their children lives in slavery and to destroy the property of their enslavers. Since many offspring were products of rape, Black women might also have committed infanticide because they could not separate the children from their trauma. Other Black women chose to damage themselves. One woman in Salem, Massachusetts, wanted to return to her home country in Africa, but because she could not do so, she tried to take her own life. She did so by digging a hole in the ground, filling it with a bottle of rum and two "Biskets." Taking a knife, she "cut her Belly so much that her Guts came out," hoping that she would die right there in the ground. Although she was soon discovered and "her Wound was swe'd up," she died "a day or two afterwards."[26] With her suicide attempt completed, she probably found her final resting place away from a life of enslavement in America.

Some enslaved people created spaces for themselves beyond the confines of their enslavers' homes, farms, and plantations. Runaways who remained at large were referred to as *cimarron* in Spanish communities, "maroons" in English. These individuals were escapees who lived in the woods, caves, swamplands, and forests, places deemed uninhabitable, yet spaces where the enslaved found freedom. The communities they established in those places ranged from small groups formed for "less than a year to powerful states encompassing thousands of members and surviving for generations or even centuries."[27]

Many appear in the records as runaways, but they created permanent homes beyond the control of their enslavers.

Maroons in the early colonial period show up in legislation as runaways. In 1672, for example, Virginia colonists established "An Act for the Apprehension and Suppression of Runawayes, Negroes, and Slaves," because there were too many escaped people involved in "mischeifes," and the government worried that Indians and other enslaved people would join them. The raiding of plantations and small farms represented one of the greatest concerns about maroon activity.[28] Enslavers viewed maroons as outlaws who stole food, ammunition, and encouraged other enslaved people to join them. They amended and created new legislation to counteract maroon activity in 1680, 1691, 1701, 1705, and throughout the eighteenth century indicating that the "problem" of maroons continued as settlement and slavery expanded. South Carolina had a high concentration of maroon activity because the majority of their enslaved population in the seventeenth and early eighteenth centuries were of African descent, and there was widespread belief that African-born people were more likely to rebel and become maroons. This colony passed its first "Act to Prevent Runaways" in November 1683 and then a more extensive set of laws in February 1691, modeled after laws in Barbados.[29] One of the state's concerns was that "free-born African slaves were more likely to become maroons than native creole slaves were," because Africans brought "a determination to regain the freedom that had been taken from them."[30]

Although much of the literature on maroons focuses on men, we know that enslaved women joined these communities and, in some regions, served leadership roles like that of Nanny the Maroon of Jamaica. South Carolina colonists added legal stipulations to punish women runaways for maroon activity. If they ran away multiple times, they could receive the death penalty, a whipping, branding, or have their ears cut off.[31] Men also had specific punishments reserved for their role in maroon activities, including castration. The fact that the laws designated gender-specific punishments suggests that a sizeable number of men and women lived in maroon communities. Given that we have several records of Black women runaways, it is not surprising that they escaped and lived in isolated communities. Their role in maroon societies confirms that Black women fought for their freedom throughout every period of American history and that they were willing to receive scars and mutilation or worse if caught.

———————————

BLACK WOMEN LIVED in many parts of early America, from Louisiana to Florida and as far north as New England. They came here free, enslaved, and indentured for a contracted period of time. Those who arrived as captives responded to life in the American colonies by filing freedom suits, running away, pretending to be free, and taking their own lives and the lives of their children. During these early years they used whatever tools they had at their disposal to carve a space for themselves to be free or to survive captivity. Some chose to rebel on ships during the Middle Passage while others ran away when they reached the farms, plantations, and homes of their enslavers. They would continue to break the bonds of captivity, during the Revolutionary Era.

CHAPTER THREE

BELINDA'S PETITION FOR INDEPENDENCE, 1760–1820

*Flora said she "intended to kill him [her enslaver],
and was ready to be hung tomorrow for doing so."*

—FLORA[1]

AT TWELVE YEARS OLD, while praying in a "sacred grove" with her parents near the Volta River in Ghana, a girl who later had the name Belinda Sutton was about to experience a catastrophic event. Lodged safely between her mother and father, who held each of her hands as they worshipped together, she "enjoyed the fragrance of her native groves," the familiar sights of her village, and the security of being with her family. She needed this assurance because at night and sometimes during the day, she was plagued by dreams of terrible men "whose faces were like the moon, and whose Bows and Arrows were like the thunder and the lightning of the Clouds." Unfortunately, her nightmares became a reality that day when "an armed band of white men, driving many of her Countrymen in Chains, ran into the hallowed" space and tore Belinda away from her parents, from her homeland, and from her prayers. Severed from all that was familiar, Belinda now entered a place filled with "scenes . . . her imagination had never conceived." She was put in "a floating World," where she witnessed "the sporting Monsters of the deep" sea and the torture of life on a slave ship.[2]

Belinda was not alone. There were approximately three hundred other captives on the ship. The melancholy, grief, and confusion had to be overwhelming. Some hollered and cried, many put their heads down and surrendered, while others fought back in whatever way they could. Belinda would fight, too, but she did not have the capacity at that young age in the middle of the Atlantic Ocean. Her fight came fifty years and two children later, toward the end of her life, when she filed a petition for her freedom.

Belinda began, as Elizabeth Keye had, by filing a petition with the Massachusetts General Court in 1783. Her enslaver, John Royall, had fled the United States during the American Revolution and died in England. Belinda knew his will stipulated that she could have her freedom and a pension of thirty pounds upon his death, so when she learned of his passing, she pursued what she knew was rightfully hers. Belinda claimed her freedom and the pension promised to her so she could support herself and her two children.

While Black women were keenly aware of their rights during all periods of American history, the Revolutionary Era marked the forming of a new nation and was a particularly important time for women like Belinda to exercise their rights. While the whites in the country around them boasted about life, liberty, and the pursuit of happiness, Black women used the courts, and their feet, words, and actions, to liberate themselves from the yoke of slavery. In the process, they took refuge in swamplands, Europe, the Caribbean, and Canada.

———————

BLACK WOMEN CONTINUED to petition for their freedom into the middle of the eighteenth century, seeking protections and freedom to live as citizens in the American colonies. Just like women in the early Colonial Era, Black women of this period understood that liberty was innate, and they tested the boundaries of slavery and indentured servitude. In 1763 Jane Banks of Goochland County, Virginia, filed a suit for her freedom. She was an indentured servant of Judith Leak and believed she should be free given the status of her mother, Mary Brooks, who was a free mulatto woman. Unfortunately, Banks lost her case and remained in Leak's custody.[3] Clearly, Banks had a legitimate reason to claim free status, and even though her case was heard in court, it did not end in her favor. Other Black women, such as Elizabeth Freeman, also known as "Mum Bett" or "Mumbet," had more success.

Freeman was born in New York in 1744 and sold to the Ashley family in Sheffield, Massachusetts. She, like so many others, had a difficult life in slavery that included physical and psychological abuse. She was "married" in the kind of union enslaved people were able to have and became the mother of a daughter named Betsy. The American Revolution fueled Freeman's quest for freedom as she heard parts of the Massachusetts Constitution read aloud in the Ashley home. Of this she remarked, "I heard that paper read yesterday that says, 'all men are born equal, and that every man had a right to freedom.' I am not a dumb critter; won't the law give me my freedom?" She asked this question of attorney Theodore Sedgwick when she sought assistance with the case. Sedgwick represented Freeman in court, where he filed a freedom suit citing the new state constitution (1780) as evidence. Even though Freeman was illiterate, her desire and understanding of the law was remarkable. She had Sedgwick file the suit on behalf of herself and a co-plaintiff, an enslaved man named Brom (*Brom and Bett v. Ashley*). The case represented an attack on the legality of slavery, and it garnered financial support from other enslaved people in the area. Even though African Americans had few possessions and little money, they pooled their resources to fund litigation in freedom suits. Freeman and Brom won their case, making it the first successful freedom suit in Massachusetts history.[4]

Black women took advantage of the instability caused by war with Britain, as evidenced by the decade leading up to the Declaration of Independence when they wrote passes (documentation that established their liberty to travel) and tried to manipulate the law by liberating themselves and their offspring. From 1766 to 1769, enslaved women from Virginia, such as Agnes, Lucy, Tabb, Winny, and Amy, either wrote false passes or pretended to be free by their manner of dress. Standing tall, around five feet nine inches, Agnes may have used a "false pass" to pretend she was a free person able to leave the colony. However, she apparently had distinctive features that might have enabled someone to easily detect her. Agnes, who escaped in April 1766, was described in a newspaper as "a Virginia born Mulatto [who] speaks good English." Described as "lusty" with "small breasts" and a "small scar over one of her eyes," Agnes also responded to the name Agie. She left with "a striped red, white and yellow calimanco gown, a short white linen sack, petticoat of the same, a pair of stays with fringed blue riband, and a large pair of silver buckles." Her enslaver, Paul Heiter, offered two rewards for her capture—one in the colony of Virginia and a slightly higher fee if captured outside the region.[5] Given the clothing she took, it is clear that Agnes wanted quality material items that would allow her to blend into free society. Bright-colored clothing made of mixed materials, such as wool and satin, glazed and brocaded in floral, striped, or checked patterns, was not the typical dress of an enslaved woman. Likewise, colored ribbons and silver buckles aided in masking her enslaved status.

Black women of all ages pretended to be free during the Revolutionary Era. Tabb, a twenty-six-year-old "well made Mulatto" forged a pass in order to travel as a free woman. Her story is unique because she was "with child." Perhaps she fled to give birth in freedom or to be with family. The historical record does not reveal this information. However, we know a little more about thirty-five-year-old Lucy from Hampton, Virginia, who traveled about twenty-five miles to Norfolk in order to "pass for a free wench" in the fall of 1768. She was a skilled seamstress and ironer with two distinct "moles on one side of her nose," burns on three fingers from a childhood injury, "and a large scar on one of her elbows." Her enslaver, Booth Armistead, agreed to pay the customary fees for her capture within or beyond the colony.[6]

Some women traveled with male counterparts and masked their identities by changing their names. In one case, a couple emancipated themselves by allegedly murdering their enslaver. In the summer of 1769, Winny fled Stafford, Virginia, with Phill after he or both of them murdered John Knox. Both in their early thirties, they "went off together and have been several times taken up." They were captured on at least three occasions, but because they were "cunning and artful," they managed to repeatedly escape. Just like Tabb, Lucy, and Agnes, Winny and Phill passed as free people. They "forged indentures, with certificates . . . of their freedom," and they changed their names. Phill passed as "Daniel Watts," while Winny posed as a free woman named "Mimy Howard."

As with their counterparts who passed as freed people, clothing represented an important marker for Winny and Phill's new status. However, these two had "such variety of cloaths that their dress cannot be described" in the advertisement seeking their whereabouts. The reward for their capture exceeded that of others probably due to the alleged murder.[7]

Another couple, Amy and "a Mulatto man," went off together "near Petersburg, [Virginia,]" to live as a free married couple. Amy "carried with her a male child about two years old," and she wore clothing "which makes her appear more like a free woman." Like Winny, Amy used an alias, "Betty Browne," the name of a woman on a "stolen" indenture who was bound out to a Thomas Jones in 1744. Her enslaver believed that she settled in Norfolk and was now living as a free woman due to the language in the indenture.[8]

As the tension grew between the American colonies and Great Britain in the late 1760s and 1770s, enslaved women in Virginia continued to petition and pass as free people. In this decade, however, more women escaped with men and children, often described as their husbands and offspring. Some even created monikers to mark their status such as "Free Fanny."[9] Ben and Alice eloped and passed as free people; they were believed to be in Williamsburg. Alice was "about five feet eight inches high" and "of a yellow complexion" with "remarkable large eyes," while her partner, Ben, was a six-feet-tall, dark-skinned "fellow" with knock knees. Their enslaver, Edward Cary, assured those who encountered the couple that they had never been "ill used," but they were "outlawed" in King and Queen County and probably trying to board a boat. Of Ben, Cary noted that he "will not be taken easily (for many reasons), as he formally made several overseers fear him." Like most enslavers who advertised in the *Virginia Gazette*, Cary promised a reward for capture, with the additional stipulation that if the couple was found or brought in dead, he expected a "proper certificate of death."[10] As the war ensued, enslaved men and women had a new purpose for their petitions and desired freedom.

As Black women populated the thirteen colonies, they continued to test the limits of their freedom through petitions and feigning free status. From 1775 to 1783, however, they joined American colonists and fought for freedom from Great Britain. Other women fled to the British for their freedom. During the War for Independence, Black women understood the rhetoric of liberty and did all they could to guarantee their own. They were actively present at the formation of the United States of America and willing to support whichever side guaranteed their freedom. Historian Benjamin Quarles noted that their "loyalty was not to a place nor to a people, but to a principle," the principle of liberty. Thus, on November 7, 1775, when British

General Lord Dunmore issued a proclamation offering freedom to enslaved and indentured servants who agreed to fight for the British, Black women responded. They ran away from their enslavers and fled to the British Army. Although most of the records reveal the presence of Black men, two women are mentioned accompanying "a party of nine slaves [who] were seized in mid-December after putting out to sea in an open boat in an attempt to reach Norfolk[, Virginia]."[11] Dunmore had issued his proclamation aboard the *William* in Norfolk harbor, which explains why this group of runaways took to the water trying to reach the port city. Their attempt to reach Dunmore was unsuccessful, and they were captured by the Continental Army.

As enslaved people answered Lord Dunmore's call, they were utilized by the British military service. The "Negroes who reached the British were generally able-bodied men who could be put to many uses." Dunmore needed soldiers, and he armed Black men and immediately supplied them with "muskets, Cartridges &c."[12] It is believed that by December of 1775, the British had approximately three hundred enslaved men who formed the "Ethiopian Regiment." Their roles among the military are not well documented, but scholars argue that this regiment gave the British certain advantages. However, American colonists fighting against them had mixed feelings about officially extending enlistment to Black people.

Few if any references to women appear in the military records on both sides, but we know that they contributed to the war effort. Some Black women were so eager to fight for General George Washington that their enslavers had to petition for their return. In May 1777, James Burton of Virginia requested that the Fifth Virginia Regiment return the eight enslaved people he had allowed to serve in the war. This group included one woman.[13] One wonders what kind of labor she performed during the war. Was she a cook, a laundress, a nurse, a spy, a soldier? Did she labor or serve with the seven enslaved men in her regiment? Did she survive the war? Even though we do not know her name or how long she and her comrades served, it is clear that by the spring of the second year of the war, Burton wanted his enslaved laborers returned. The Fifth Virginia Regiment was formed in December 1775 as part of the Continental Army. In 1776 Commander Robert Howe led the brigade, where the regiment served in Virginia, North Carolina, South Carolina, and Delaware. This group was then assigned to Stephen's Brigade and moved north to New Jersey, Pennsylvania, Delaware, and Maryland, as part of the Main Army led by George Washington.[14] It is likely that the eight enslaved people Burton sought received their discharge on May 22. The enslaved woman served the Continental Army in some capacity long enough for her enslaver to summon her back to his service. Was this a setback in an attempt to gain her liberty? We do not know, but enslaved people faced obstacles, hardships, and challenges to their status on a daily basis. The war years were no exception.

As the military on both sides found ways to utilize enslaved and free Black people, domestic work represented the bulk of duties performed by women. Some enslavers rescinded the option to sell enslaved people because they were needed in the war effort. General William Smallwood suspended the sale of "Two Negroe women" in July 1781.[15] He believed that their valuable services benefited him as well as the soldiers because the women could work in the kitchen. Women also served in the Hospital Department of the military through hiring contracts that compensated their enslavers during their absence.[16] One of the greatest outcomes of aiding the British was the opportunity to evacuate to Canada at war's end.

ONE ASPECT OF ENSLAVED PEOPLE'S STRUGGLE that never disappeared was their continued efforts to secure freedom, even if it meant leaving the country. Many of those who made it to the British lines boarded ships to Canada at the end of the war in 1783. This group of about three thousand enslaved and free Black people first traveled to New York, the home of the British headquarters. There they waited to cross unfettered waters and claim their liberty in Nova Scotia. From April to November, Black people embraced a journey that led to what they hoped would be "liberation" in Canada. However life in this snowy climate was not always the freedom they imagined. They went seeking new lives and were promised land and freedom, but "of the 3,550 blacks transported to Canada, only one-tenth ever received land," and many were treated like the enslaved in America.[17]

Travel to Canada took place well before the formation of the nineteenth-century Underground Railroad. Embarking upon a voluntary migration, Black people now traversed the Atlantic seaboard on ships that emancipated rather than ships that enslaved. For too long, the maritime experience had involved forced migration and enslavement. When we think about people of African descent on ships during this period, we automatically think about the transatlantic slave trade, which devastated the lives of millions of people. At the close of the war, however, enslaved Black people liberated themselves on vessels. Free Black people went as well, and both groups left Virginia, Georgia, South Carolina, New York, New Jersey, and New England, searching for a place of deliverance from slavery and racial discrimination. Some of them escaped their enslavers before looking for opportunities to embrace voluntary migration to Canada, West Africa, and the Caribbean. The number of Black women who chose this avenue is astonishingly high.

Starting in that year of 1783, they embarked on ships bound for Nova Scotia in order to start new lives as freed and free people. Four women, Lucy, Hannah, Phoebe, and Dinah, are known to have boarded the *Mary*, on its way to Port Roseway, Nova Scotia. They traveled with thirty-four others and their families. Hannah (twenty-one) and her husband, Joe (twenty-six), traveled with their two small children. They had been away from their enslaver for three years. Lucy Whitting, a thirty-six-year-old free woman described as a "stout wench," had served Andrew Calder (likely through an indenture agreement) for six years. Phoebe Patrick (twenty-nine) and her husband, Thomas Patrick (forty-two), chose to leave their Virginia enslavers perhaps to live together in freedom. The couple had different Norfolk enslavers and left them at the same time, five years before boarding the *Mary*. Dinah (twenty) traveled solo and had been away from her enslaver for three years. The whereabouts of these women during the time they were away from their enslavers is unclear. However, the fact that they managed to escape for multiple years suggests that they may have fled to British hands. Regardless of their status as free women, the nomenclature used to describe them was still derogatory, for example, "wench" instead of "woman." Dinah was called a "stout black wench," a generic, often racialized descriptor given to Black women.

There were many other enslaved women and girls on this ship, including thirteen-year-old Charlotte Plumb, a mulatto offspring of her enslaver; fourteen-year-old Hannah, described as a "fine girl" from South Carolina; and Sarah Fillifitas, a fourteen-year-old "mulatto" girl who was born free in Pennsylvania. The 636-mile journey from New York to Nova Scotia takes two to three days today and was probably twice as long in the eighteenth century.

Those who navigated on the *Esther* traveled in a group of thirty-six men, women, and children. A handful came from Virginia and had run away from their enslavers. The Godfrey family voyaged together after being enslaved by Colonel Godfrey of Norfolk. Elizabeth (thirty) left for Canada with Ned (forty-two), likely her husband, and their children, Jeffry (seventeen) and Betsy (one and a half). Joining them was the family matriarch, Abigail (seventy-five), described as "nearly worn out."[18] This multigeneration family had been away from their enslaver for four years prior to boarding their vessel to freedom. One can only imagine how difficult the war years were for little Betsy and her grandmother Abigail. The uncertainties of weather and travel had to be taxing on their fragile bodies. However, it did not prevent them from making their way to Canada in 1783.

Some vessels contained small groups of ten to twenty people, while others were large and brought more than two hundred people to freedom, including infant children and new mothers. The *Clinton*, for example, brought 227 enslaved and free Black people to Annapolis County, Nova Scotia, as part of this mass migration. In this group were 90 women and girls and 137 men and boys. Their ages ranged from five-month-old Agnes Reddick to eighty-year-old Adam Way. Many of the mothers with young children liberated themselves from slavery and gave birth "within British lines." In fact, it seems as though some mothers made the deliberate choice to have their babies in spaces they believed guaranteed their offspring liberty. Agnes's mother, Pleasant Reddick, was twenty-nine when she fled John Tatum of Crane Island, Virginia, in 1778. When she left, she traveled with Elsey, who was two years old. It is hard to imagine the travel experience of this new mother. Somehow she left the secluded barrier islands of Virginia and made her way across three hundred miles to New York during the five years she fled from her enslaver. We do not know if she had a partner or any travel companions to assistant with baby Elsey, but at some point, Pleasant became pregnant again. She had her second child, Agnes, sometime after her arrival to the British forces. What was her pregnancy like and how did she care for her two children? We don't know the identity of the children's father(s) or whether her partner(s) joined Pleasant and the children on the ship. Pleasant was not the only mother of young children and babies when she boarded the *Clinton* with 5 month old Agnes. Her other daughter Elsey was now seven and had other young Black girls to interact with on the voyage to Canada.[19]

Nancy Johnson (forty-four) traveled with her five children or grandchildren between the ages of six and eighteen; Nanny Johnson (seven) and Fanny Johnson (six) would have been perfect companions for Elsey. Jane Halladay (twenty-two) brought her eighteen-month-old son, Peter, with her. Like Pleasant, Jane gave birth to Peter "within the British lines," and he was a "healthy child." Another Nancy (twenty-eight) fled her Norfolk enslaver in 1776 and gave birth to all three of her children "within the British lines," including eighteen-month-old Betsy and her siblings Polly (three) and James (six). Giving birth under British occupation was probably preferred over giving birth under enslavement. A mother imagined the possibility of liberation for her children, and it is clear that these women traveled for years and risked their lives to free themselves and their young progeny.[20]

Free Black people also immigrated to Canada and parts of the Caribbean, but they had slightly different motives and avenues. They filed petitions confirming their status and requested support for land acquisition. Hannah and her husband, Thomas Williams, lost their "free pass" and "all of their possessions in a shipwreck," but they confirmed their status and applied for fifty acres of land in Halifax, Nova Scotia.[21] Imagine the excitement the couple had as they embarked upon a new life in another country. Though tragedy struck and they lost their possessions, that did not stop Hannah and Thomas. They kept moving forward, first by protecting their free status and then applying for land.

The story of another free Black woman and her quest to secure freedom outside the American colonies helps to illustrate the diverse range of experiences during the Revolutionary Era. In October of 1782, Phillis Thomas, "a free Black woman," received permission from the British government to go "to the Island of Jamaica or elsewhere at her own option."[22] Such evidence suggests that there was greater flexibility for free Black people than enslaved.

Black women sailed waterways, estuaries, and the Atlantic to create passageways to freedom during the American Revolution. Their movement highlights a level of mobility at sea that few Black women experienced in the years preceding the war. They boarded ships and emancipated themselves or confirmed their free status in other parts of the world. Their journeys involved life-threatening risks, but it is likely that their determination overcame their fear. Not all women were as fortunate as Hannah and Phillis, however, as colonial legislation placed restrictions on Black lives regardless of their status.

As noted in the previous chapter, American colonists modeled early slave codes after those of the Caribbean. Such legislation stipulated the movement of enslaved people and included harsh regulations for conduct and behavior. In 1705, for example, the Virginia General Assembly created "An Act Concerning Servants and Slaves," one of the first comprehensive slave codes passed in the colony. This act contained restrictions on movement, marriage, religion, and payments that would be considered reparations. It governed the lives of the enslaved and of indentured servants who came to the colonies on a contract that would grant them freedom at a later date.

This legislation made clear distinctions between "servants" and "slaves." The law required that "all servants imported and brought into this country, by sea or land, who were not christians in their native country . . . shall be accounted and be slaves, and shall be here bought and sold notwithstanding a conversion to christianity afterward." The link between Christianity and freedom was clear and offered a slight justification for the enslavement of Africans (under the assumption that they were not already Christian). Non-Christian servants would be converted. Masters and "owners of servants" were to "provide for their servants, wholesome and competent diet, clothing, and lodging," but there was no similar stipulation for the enslaved. The law also made space for enslavement of certain groups of people. In act XI, the assembly noted that "no negros, mulattos, or Indians, although christians, or Jews, Moors, Mahametans, or other infidels, shall at any time, purchase any Christian servant." Yet they could purchase a person who was "of their own complexion" and those "declared slaves by this act." If those on this list of people purchased "any Christian *white* servant, the said servant shall . . . become free." The racial distinction of slavery and freedom is clearly articulated here, and so is the reservation of enslavement to specific groups of people. To prevent intimacy among the races, the law fined a "free christian white woman" who gave birth to a "bastard child, by a negro or mulatto." If she could not pay the specified fine to the church, she was "sold for five years" and the "child" would remain a "servant" until age thirty-one. Likewise, any "English, or other white man or woman, being free, who shall intermarry with a negro or a mulatto man or woman, bond or free," will receive a six-month prison sentence *"without bail."* Once again, the boundaries of slavery and freedom fell upon racialized lines, and early legislation focused on the separation of the races.[23]

The punishment for running away, and the compensation given to enslavers for the loss of their enslaved people, confirms the complex ways enslaved people's quest for freedom conflicted with the ongoing commodification of their bodies. Runaways were sent to jail, and their enslavers had to pay fines for their release. Runaways often received "corporal punishment" in the form of whippings while in jail, but if the "slave . . . shall happen to be killed in such correction, it shall *not be accounted felony,*" and the person who killed the enslaved "shall be free and acquit of all punishment and accusation . . . as if such incident had never happened." Clearly, this legislation allowed for the death of Black people in prison without any consequences, and it served as an early precedent for contemporary cases involving Black women who die or are killed while in custody. Enslavers whose human property were murdered received reparations according to the Virginia Assembly as they were compensated for the death of their enslaved people. Article XXXVII said, "For every slave killed . . . or put to death by law, the master or owner of such slave shall be paid *by the public.*" Payment was determined by a court hearing with testimony to establish "the value [of] the slave in money."[24]

Nearly one hundred years later, in 1801, a South Carolina enslaved woman named Mary committed arson. She was valued at $300 as part of her sentence, and it appears as if the estate of her deceased enslaver benefited from compensation. Likewise, in 1814, at fifteen years old, Hannah of Newberry, South Carolina, allegedly robbed, then burglarized and burned the home of Nicholas Summer, her enslaver. She, too, received a monetary value for her body prior to sentencing, $350, the payment of which went to her enslaver.[25] Thus, making a case for reparations and contemporary conversations about it will find evidence supporting the fact that the first set of reparations in America were given to enslavers.

No legislation was as important in the Revolutionary Era as the code that passed in 1793 as part of the US Constitution. On February 21, 1793, in Article IV, Section 2 of the US Constitution, the federal government issued its first federal Fugitive Slave Act. George Washington, president at the time, signed "An Act Respecting Fugitives from Justice, and Persons Escaping from the Service of their Masters," which stipulated that "any state in the Union" and "territories northwest or south of the river Ohio" shall treat fugitives as "having committed treason." This legislation gave state representatives and citizens the executive authority to arrest, charge, and commit the alleged offender to prison. Enslavers claiming their human property had to pay for all of the "costs or expenses incurred" in apprehending and sending the enslaved person back to their home state. Anyone who tried to help a fugitive gain their freedom in the transfer process would receive a fine up to $500 and jail time "not exceeding one year."[26] This legislation essentially called for white citizens in the Union to police enslaved people who ran away. However, this proved difficult and would be revisited in the next century.

Like legislation, labor was an important component of Black women's lives in the Revolutionary Era. It governed their day-to-day activities and controlled the amount of time they had to spend with their families. Black women worked in all kinds of settings, from Northern industrial factories to university campuses, to Southern agricultural plantations and small farms. They also labored in the rural and urban homes of their enslavers or guardians. In homes and private mansions, they served their enslavers by cooking, cleaning, grooming, and tending to their enslavers' needs. Work in this space involved greater scrutiny and created a different set of challenges than those faced by enslaved people who labored in the fields—a dynamic that will be discussed in greater detail in the next chapter, given the contemporary misunderstandings around the benefits and liabilities of enslaved labor in these spaces.

Decades before the American Revolution in 1732, Black women worked in the iron, coal, and ore industries. Enslavers saw that with training, enslaved people could be useful in factories. In offering advice to a prospective iron industry investor, a Mr. Chivers reassured William Byrd of Virginia that one could successfully carry out the iron business with "120 slaves including women."[27] At the Oxford Iron Works in Virginia, laborers helped outfit items for the war, including "shot and shell, bar iron, nail rods, camp kettles, horseshoes, and other iron supplies." After the war, the workers produced "bar iron for plantation and blacksmith trades" and cooking utensils and pots "for domestic use." Women and girls worked in several different areas of the forgery. For example, on the eve of the War of 1812, ten women worked in the furnaces and forges along with one "girl," age unspecified. Three women worked in coaling grounds, one woman at the ore banks, fourteen served as plantation hands, and one woman and one girl served as house servants.[28] Work in these settings offered different kinds of challenges than working in plantation homes and fields.

Industrial labor included work in sugar refineries, tobacco factories, textile mills, lumber mills, salt works, brickyards, and turpentine distilleries. These are not locations that people imagine when thinking about slavery and the labor of enslaved and free Black women. Yet, these are spaces where Black women and men worked and contributed to the fabric of American society. Here they worked with water- and horse-powered machinery, with saws, boiling vats, and furnaces. Enslaved women who worked in the coal industry at Oxford also raked leaves to "cover smoldering wood while it was being converted into charcoal." Labor at blast furnaces and ore banks generated different kinds of responsibilities and tasks for women. They had to clean and pick over the ore so there would be no impurities when sending it to the furnace. Three women, Betty, Phillis, and Judy, conducted this labor at Oxford. Their enslaver, David Ross, bragged about the versatility of his laborers and noted that all of his enslaved people could easily maneuver between industrial and agricultural labor. He paid attention to women's pregnancies and reduced their exposure to heavy lifting when necessary. He also punished women and sent them to the mines for bad behavior. Susan, a weaver, received a punishment and had to dig and rake iron ore, but Ross believed that it "enlightened her weaving talents."[29] Despite his calculated management and detailed structure, women like Fanny rebelled.

Ross discussed "little Fanny" ad nauseam because of her attempted infanticide of her sixth child, which occurred when she abandoned "the infant in the woods." To his delight, the child was "preserved." This pleased him "because had the innocent child perished," he explained, "I would have prosecuted [Fanny] until the ignominious death of the Gallows." Ross could not fathom why little Fanny left her child in the woods. "What then would induce her to such an inhuman act," he queried in a letter to his friend Richard Richardson. Fanny's actions led him to think carefully about pregnant women on his plantation and in his industrial settings.[30] This story shows the level of resistance enslaved women maintained despite location, work site, and time period.

Geography and soil composition dictated the kinds of crops women labored over in the fields. In this early period they worked in the tobacco fields of the Maryland and Virginia Chesapeake, the rice and Sea Island cotton fields of the South Carolina and Georgia Lowcountry, and the sugar fields of the Louisiana bayou. Their work involved rigorous conditions and backbreaking labor from sunup to sundown. They used machetes to cut sugarcane, sickles to cut rice stalks, and their bare hands to pick cotton. Field work pushed women to their physical limits under the task and gang labor systems. On farms and plantations that utilized the task system, individual enslaved people were assigned a particular task based on their physical strength and skill. Once they completed their task, they were given other tasks and/or spent the balance of the day laboring for their families or the families of their enslavers. The gang system involved working in groups of enslaved people with similar abilities. A lead worker, also known as a "slave driver," controlled the pace as the gang moved through the fields. Enslavers, overseers, drivers, or managers were always nearby with a whip to threaten the gang to continue working at a particular pace. Even when women left the fields and went to their cabins at night, they often had sewing or other tasks to complete with quotas for the planter family. Enslaved children recalled their mothers working well into the night and some had fond memories of the sound of the spinning wheel as their mothers made blankets and other items for the plantation community. Enslaved women who labored in agricultural fields worked for most of the days and in their cabins at night cooking, cleaning, and sewing; their labor sometimes took eighteen hours per day, giving them little time for rest.[31]

Some enslaved and free Black women worked for city governments, universities, and organizations. Their labor was often overlooked until recently. At the University of Virginia, for example, enslaved women accompanied students to the university and worked in the hotel (dining for faculty and students) and in kitchens across campus.[32] They appear in university records through complaints from students and professors alike, but they were on campus from the university's inception. Thomas Jefferson, who founded the university, assigned ten enslaved people to help construct the campus in 1817. Other universities, such as Emory, Harvard, Dartmouth, and Rutgers University at New Brunswick, and the University of North Carolina, Chapel Hill, allowed enslaved laborers on campus as well, and not just as field workers. Knowing that they populated universities forces us to think about slavery infiltrating many spaces.[33]

In Northern communities, enslaved women labored in mills in New York's Hudson River Valley and the homes of their enslavers in urban communities. Hough Caine advertised the sale of a "Negro Wench" whom he described as "healthy and strong, about 18 years old, that can do all sorts of house work."[34] Another woman was sold in a public auction after the death of her enslaver. She, too, was referred to as "a Negro Wench," but she was a skilled cook and housewife and had three young children on the auction block with her.[35] The domestic skills of these women are clear, and their roles as mothers also appear in the records.

Another nameless enslaved woman who appeared in the advertisements was described as "likely" and able to do all kinds of housework, "honest and sober, with a male child of 18 months old."[36] If she had so many good qualities, why were this woman and her young son for sale? Prior to the closing of the transatlantic slave trade (1808), some enslavers chose not to keep pregnant women and young mothers because their labor was disrupted by the responsibilities of motherhood.[37]

Black women who worked in the homes of their enslavers faced deep scrutiny. We know more about the lives and experiences of those who worked in presidential homes such as Ona Judge and Sukey. Judge served as the enslaved servant of Martha Washington and lived and traveled with the Washingtons during the first American presidency. Sukey served Dolley Madison at Montpelier during the presidency of

James Madison, the fourth president of the United States. Their labor reflects the type of work domestic workers performed in the homes of some of the most influential citizens of their time. Both women were exposed to travel, journeying to cities such as Washington, DC, Philadelphia, and New York. They also served key influencers at political meetings, social soirees, and family events. Labor for these women involved the very personal care of First Ladies. Ona and Sukey tended to Martha and Dolley's hair, laundered and cared for their "fine garments," dressed and groomed them, and were attentive to their needs during travel.

Despite their lives and labors in presidential mansions, these two women resisted their enslavement. Ona ran away and was never caught, while Sukey stole from her enslaver on at least one occasion. According to Dolley, Sukey was too valuable to be punished.

Enslaved women who worked in the homes of their enslavers were on-call twenty-four hours a day. Even those who worked in the most high-profile homes were under great scrutiny and lived under very challenging circumstances.[38]

Free Black women found work in urban areas as vendors, laundresses, and seamstresses, to name a few occupations. They also operated taverns and hotels, and some even held enslaved people in bondage. Their numbers were small during this Revolutionary generation, but as the new nation took shape after the war, gradual abolition in the North and manumission (release from slavery) legislation fueled the growth of the free Black population, adding to those who were already born free. According to the first census, collected in 1790, free Black people consisted of 7.9 percent of the total population. The majority of this small percentage resided in the North (40.2 percent), and a small minority lived in the South (4.7 percent). The highest concentrations settled in Upper South or border states such as Delaware, Tennessee, North Carolina, and Virgina.[39] No matter where Black women lived, labor was a significant part of their lives and for some, so was slaveholding. The term "slaveholders" is deliberately used to represent African Americans who held other African Americans in bondage. This word choice is different from "enslavers," which we use throughout to represent non-Blacks (i.e., whites and Native Americans) who enslaved African Americans. The term "enslaver" refers to someone who forces people into the system of slavery. The term "slaveholder" refers to someone who holds another person in slavery without the full power of a system to support the practice.

Black women made all kinds of choices to guarantee their freedom. Some turned away from their communities and became involved in relationships with white men. Others "married" (despite laws that forbade interracial unions) into white families and became slaveholders. Still another group of free Black women used slaveholding as a means to free their families by living in a space of makeshift slaveholding until everyone had their papers. Then there were Black women concubines forced into "relationships/marriages" with white men against their will. From where we stand, it is difficult to untangle these interactions and exchanges, but as noted, in colonial Virginia, the law supported people enslaving people "of their own complexion." These were the experiences of some Black women in the United States. Purchasing enslaved people was a financial decision that solidified their own freedom; it made them appear supportive of the system and was also a path to wealth.

This is a difficult history to report, as many of those who read it will place blame on Black people for contributing to slavery. But it is important to note the complexities involved. First, at every historical moment there have been Black people who positioned themselves to benefit and even profit from the oppression of others, including other Black people. During the transatlantic slave trade, there were Africans who sold other Africans. This is often cited as justification for enslavement, even though many involved in this practice did not see themselves as part of the same community as those they were selling. In some cases, their only commonality was the color of their skin. They often came from different countries, communities, and ethnicities; their language differed as well. They did not see those they sold as prisoners of war as "their own people."

One wealthy African family from the Congo shared an oral history of their role in preserving their freedom during the peak of the transatlantic slave trade. The living descendant told Harvard University professor Henry Louis Gates Jr. in an interview on PBS that Africans had two choices: "you either trade or be traded." The former was the answer for her relatives. This historical fact has often been highlighted or distorted to justify and blame Africans for the slave trade. Similar patterns exist for Black slaveholders, who strategically participated in slavery as a way to buffer themselves from being captured and enslaved.

In 1772 Fenda Lawrence, an African woman, boarded the *New Britannia*, a slave ship that left a region somewhere near the Gambia River for colonial Georgia. Lawrence was a free African woman who traveled in a privileged space while 220 souls who looked like her suffered in the belly of the same ship. She came to the New World to profit from slavery, and she did so as a free Black female enslaver and trader. Lawrence was widowed to an Englishman trader and upon his death made the decision to relocate to the Georgia Lowcountry. She was not quite an anomaly. Some African women chose to become intimate with European traders as a way to protect themselves from the horrors of slavery. But what was it like to travel to the colonies as an African trader and slaveholder? How did she fare during the Middle Passage? Why did she leave the Senegambia River region? What was life like for a free African trader in Savannah?

Lawrence traversed the Atlantic with five enslaved people of her own. They included "'a Woman named Camilla and her Child Nancy, one Woman named Morria and her Child Tony, also one Boy named James Lawrence.'" Bringing mothers and their children with her to serve as Lawrence's enslaved laborers suggests that her domestic staff included partial families and no fathers. Given that it was rare for African merchants to cross the Atlantic, we know that her gender made "her passage even more exceptional." The Senegambia region she came from had great diversity, and it is possible that African captives on her ship included "Mandinka, Jakhanke, or Juula" people. The Middle Passage took thirty-six days before the *New Britannia* "docked in Charleston harbor." When Lawrence arrived, the acting governor of Georgia, James Habersham, "issued a certificate granting her residency." Like most free Black women in the era of slavery, she had to carry papers confirming her status. Lawrence was described as "a free Black Woman and . . . Considerable trader in the River Gambia on the Coast of Africa [who] . . . voluntarily came to be and Remain for sometime in this province."[40] She migrated to the colonies in hopes of educating her children. Although she came from a region where there were other female traders, her presence in colonial Georgia was unusual. The community she became a part of in Georgia, under the protection of the governor, included "15,000 people of African

Ancestry" where "Two-Thirds of all enslaved Africans lived within twenty miles of the coast," and the free Black population probably had less than a hundred people.[41] Although we do not know much else about Lawrence's life in Georgia, other African women offer interesting perspectives regarding slavery and slaveholding among women.

Anna Madgigine Jai Kingsley, born in Senegal in the early 1790s, represents another example of an African trader and enslaver. Unlike Lawrence, she traveled across the Atlantic in the belly of a slave ship and was purchased in Havana by Zephaniah Kingsley of Spanish Florida. In the spring of 1811, at eighteen years old, Anna received her freedom when Zephaniah manumitted her. She was the mother of three of his children (George, three; Martha, twenty months; and Mary, one month) and to some considered his "wife." By manumitting her, he noted, "I have as my slave a black woman named Anna, about 18 years old . . . [and] I recognize [her children] as my own." Her service to him in "truth and fidelity" and his declaration of his intent "to give her freedom graciously and without other interest" confirm that he intended to live with her as a couple in marriage.[42] Their connection explains Anna's freedom at this young age, but her status as his wife also raises questions about the power dynamic involved. Anna was most likely his concubine and had no choice in the matter. She gave birth to three of his children starting at age fifteen when Kingsley was about twenty-eight years older than she was. Anna clearly did not have the consent to refuse a sexual relationship with her forty-three-year-old enslaver. However, it is clear through her life story that she remained with him, gave birth to a fourth child, and later purchased land and enslaved people. Just two years after she received her freedom, Anna Kingsley "petitioned the Spanish government for land" and she received the "title to five acres on the St. Johns River." She also purchased "goods and livestock . . . and she purchased slaves." Anna remained loyal to the Spanish when Americans tried to take parts of East Florida and was rewarded with a land grant of 350 acres. She and Zephaniah settled at Fort George Island and built their four-plantation empire "producing sea island cotton, rice, and provisions." But life proved difficult for a free Black woman, even though she was "married" to a white enslaver, and when Florida became part of the United States, Anna and most of her family relocated to Haiti "with more than fifty former Florida slaves."[43]

The stories of free African enslavers such as Fenda Lawrence and Anna Kingsley suggest that connections to white men enabled these Black women a set of choices not available to all Black women at this time. As slavery progressed in the antebellum era, patterns of Black slaveholding changed depending on avenues to enslavement and freedom. The experiences of African Americans who held other African Americans in the mid-to-late nineteenth century reveal other patterns and will be discussed in the following chapter.

Black women fought against the restrictions placed upon them through violent and clandestine means. Considering both day-to-day resistance and more overt acts such as rebellion, it is clear that they continued to demand justice in the eighteenth and early nineteenth centuries. How they made those demands were extreme in some instances and subtle in others. As noted, some women committed acts of infanticide, suicide, and murder. Others fled to maroon communities, committed arson, administered poison, and became literate. Just as they did during the American Revolution, some fled to British freedom. Many of them paid heavy consequences for their actions, including severe whippings and death.

In 1773 the Brunswick County, Virginia, Court of Oyer and Terminer established a value for an enslaved woman named Sall. Her enslaver, John Loftain, believed that Sall had "feloniously" murdered "her own child." However, from Sall's perspective she probably chose this action to spare her child a life of enslavement. Many Black women who carried out acts of infanticide believed they were expressing "a higher form of love" than most could imagine. For the court to establish a monetary value for Sall's life suggests that if found guilty, she would receive the death penalty and Loftain would receive compensation for the loss of his human property.[44] In the summer of 1809, Patty, another enslaved woman, "struck" her "child's skull with a stone" causing death.[45] Milley chose to smother her infant to death by burying the child with the head facing downward.[46] From a contemporary vantage point, it may be difficult to consider these actions as "love," but we cannot fully comprehend the circumstances of enslaved women and the limited choices they had at their disposal. Some mothers wanted to save their children (and themselves) from the pain of their child's enslavement; other mothers were overburdened by childbearing/rearing and did not want offspring; and some wanted to spite their enslavers by depriving them of the profits accruing from the sale of the labor of their children. Regardless of how we reflect on the occurrence of infanticide during slavery, one fact is certain: some enslaved women saw liberty for their children in death.

In addition to taking the lives of their children, enslaved women risked their own lives by murdering their enslavers. Juday poisoned her enslaver in 1772 and was publicly hanged for doing so. After she died, her enslaver received compensation for this loss of property.[47] In August 1808 an enslaved woman named Flora murdered William Whittenton by striking him over the head and in the stomach with a club. She was so clear about her motives that she told Whittenton's wife that "she had long owed him a spite, [because] . . . he was always going at her like a dog at a [*sic*] opossum." Moreover, Flora said she "intended to kill him, and was ready to be hung tomorrow for doing so." Whatever abuses Whittenton inflicted on Flora, she clearly was in desperate straits and could no longer tolerate his abuse. Flora was willing to die and suffer the consequences of her actions. Her resolve is astonishingly clear and a testament to her determination to end the abuse, just as the court ended her life via hanging.[48]

Maroon communities served as an alternative to slavery for some Black women who fled to swamps, forests, mountains, caves, and other seemingly uninhabitable settings to live in isolation. In the Great Dismal Swamp of Virginia and North Carolina, self-liberated enslaved people found refuge. It is believed that they lived in this region for "twelve, twenty, or thirty years and upwards," and women gave birth there to generations of offspring.[49] Maroon communities were so common that they appear in Frederick Douglass's novella *The Heroic Slave*, in which he introduces readers to Susan, who visits her loved one who lives in the swamp. For five years, she sees her partner once a week in secret meetings in the woods.[50]

The presence of maroon communities has appeared in contemporary archaeological excavations that have resulted in the discovery of more than three thousand artifacts and two hundred inhabited islands. Some of these discoveries include "arrowheads, pottery, and manufactured items like nails." Researchers also found "footprints of seven cabins" at a nameless site that dates between 1660 and 1860.[51]

We know that these sites were the makeshift homes of enslaved people who chose to live in the swamps rather than on plantations, on farms, and in industrial settings.

In addition to self-liberation, Black women found ways to express themselves and experience pleasure. In Northern communities like upstate New York, they participated in Pinkster Festivals, where they mocked their enslavers, dressed like Europeans, gave political speeches, told stories, and participated in festivities involving dance, music, and food. During these festivals, "African men and women enjoyed temporary independence, made money, and purchased goods." It was a time for celebration, including reuniting with loved ones and embracing African traditions, despite the fact that they were still enslaved. These festivals began around the same time that Haiti became the first independent Black nation after the Haitian Revolution, which lasted from 1791 to 1804. It is plausible that news of the independence fueled the joy and celebration in the new nation.[52]

Black women had a way of taking restrictions and refashioning them into new traditions. One of the best historic examples of this stems from legislation that attempted to restrict the creative ways Black women styled their hair. In 1786 Creole women of African descent in Louisiana were forced to cover their hair as a way to suppress their individual sense of style and dampen the desires of men who might have found them attractive. Established by Governor Esteban Rodriguez Miró during the Spanish period, the law noted that free "negro and quadroon women" spent their time seeking "carnal pleasures," and in order to police them, they were required to cover their hair with a "handkerchief." The governor noted that these women had an "extravagant luxury in their dressing" that some felt was excessive. Black women responded by using different kinds of headdresses and finding creative ways to tie and cover their hair. As they did, throughout their history, they found a way to express themselves in the midst of repression.[53]

THE WOMEN BORN in this generation continued Isabel de Olvera's demand for justice and protection. They challenged their enslaved status by filing petitions for freedom, escaping by running away, liberating their offspring through infanticide, serving in the Revolutionary War, and taking pleasure in festivals and adorning their hair with scarves in opposition to restrictive legislation. They saw ships as pathways to freedom during the Revolution, and many chose to immigrate to other parts of the world, such as the Caribbean and Canada. They witnessed two wars for independence from the British and saw their bodies become more important to the institution of slavery. Although some Black women received their freedom during these years, and others like Lawrence and Kingsley became enslavers, most experienced acts of commodification that were intensified in the antebellum era.

CHAPTER FOUR

MILLIE AND CHRISTINE'S PERFORMANCE AND THE EXPANSION OF SLAVERY, 1820–1860

We possess a natural independence of soul,
and feel a love for liberty within our breasts.

— MARIA STEWART[1]

JACOB AND MONEMIA McKOY, an enslaved couple from North Carolina, became parents in 1851, when Monemia gave birth to twin girls. As was the case with most enslaved families, the arrival of children was often met with both joy and trepidation. The two had seven children prior to the twins and understood very well the threat of family separation. "Aunt Hannah," the midwife, was there to comfort thirty-two-year-old Monemia through the delivery of the seventeen-pound twins. But there was something special about the girls, as the single birth weight suggests. They were conjoined twins. Named Millie and Christine by their parents, they had a typical first year and a half and reached the usual milestones of walking by twelve months and talking by fifteen. However, before they reached their second year of life, the girls were taken from Jacob and Monemia. Their enslaver sold them for $1,000 (some accounts say $10,000) to Joseph P. Smith of Wadesboro, North Carolina, who allowed a Mr. Brewer to take them to be viewed by medical faculty in New Orleans. This was likely the first medical examination and "digital rape" (penetration with fingers) the girls experienced. Over the course of their sixty-one years of life, they were physically examined by more than thirty physicians in major cities throughout the United States and Europe. They were also put on exhibition and drew large crowds: 150,000 in Philadelphia for eight weeks; 70,000 in Boston for three weeks; 10,000 in New York for a single day. Their European tour lasted for several months and was filled with drama because the girls were stolen by greedy showmen and craven medical professionals who wanted to profit from the commodification of their body.[2]

Nineteenth-century enslavers, traders, physicians, businessmen, and showmen were obsessed with Black women's bodies for many reasons. The closing of the transatlantic slave trade in 1808 ended the legal supply source of enslaved laborers directly imported from parts of West Africa and the Caribbean. It meant that natural and forced reproduction would be key to maintaining the system of slavery with additional sources of labor. It also meant that medical professionals became more interested in the female body. From the auction block to medical schools, women and girls faced sexual assault and exploratory surgeries on a regular basis.[3]

During the expansion of slavery and the growth of the institution through Black women's bodies, Black women continued to resist in their own ways. Some used avenues of freedom to escape the hardships of slavery and many were able to achieve liberty due to the gradual spread of abolition in the North.

Coming out of the Revolutionary Era, Black women continued to traverse the rough waters of the Atlantic and traveled around the Florida Panhandle into the Gulf of Mexico. Many of them were born in this new nation and experienced being transferred to the Deep South, where the slavery industry thrived until Emancipation, in 1865. Others continued to experience forced removal from their ancestral homelands in West Africa and arrived via slave ships until the official closing of the transatlantic slave trade, in 1808. Regardless of how Black women came to the United States or from where they were transferred, the antebellum years marked a period of expansion, commodification, and freedom—a unique mix of trials and tribulations as well as successes through struggle.

ENTERING THE NINETEENTH CENTURY, a fortunate group of Black women claimed their free status from gradual abolition legislation created in the eighteenth century, and they worked hard to help others gain their liberty. Those less fortunate labored in the fields, factories, farms, universities, and forgeries of their foremothers. In order to understand the four decades that led to the Civil War, it is important to begin with abolition and freedom.

Starting in 1777, Northern states began to abolish slavery, allowing some Black women to enter the nineteenth century as freed people. However, depending on the state, their freedom came with a price and, for many, a huge sacrifice. Some states placed age restrictions on freedom, others postnatal regulations that connected freedom to the enslaved women's womb, just as earlier legislation had anchored them to slavery. Regardless of the constraints, it is clear that by 1804, gradual abolition was in place in all Northern states. Vermont abolished "adult slavery" in 1777 in its constitution, stating that "no male person, born in this country, or brought from over sea, out to be holed by law, to serve any person, as servant, slaver, or apprentice, and he arrives to the age of twenty-one years." Then, as a follow-up, women are added to this clause: "nor female in like manner, after she arrive to the age of eighteen years." Notice that women in this state received their freedom, at age eighteen, three years before their male counterparts, who did not become free until the age of twenty-one. Thus, enslaved people remained in Vermont well into the nineteenth century depending on when they reached these key age markers.[4]

Pennsylvania was the second state to develop gradual abolition legislation in 1780. Like Vermont's, Pennsylvania's legislation also carried age restrictions and other limitations. Enslaved and formerly enslaved people had to pay close attention if they wanted to claim free status. For example, the act stated, "All persons, as well as Negroes and Mulattoes as others, who shall be born within this state from and after this passing of this act, shall not be deemed and considered as servants for life, or slaves." To address the *partus sequitur ventrem* legislation of the seventeenth century, this act clarified the following: "all servitude for life, or slavery of children, in consequence of the slavery of their mothers," shall be free unless born to an enslaved woman, then their freedom would not be granted until age twenty-eight. Like Vermont's, Pennsylvania's gradual abolition of slavery came with restrictions that forced some enslaved people to remain enslaved until they reached their late twenties. Moreover, as historian Erica Armstrong Dunbar explains, "The law stated that any person born in bondage on or before March 1, 1780, would remain enslaved for life." With the prospect of greater Black freedom, Pennsylvania legislators busied themselves with overhauling criminal justice. In moving from corporal punishment to confinement, the state that served as the birthplace of the nation would also give birth to the country's first penitentiary, in 1790. Black women may well have enjoyed emancipation in the state, but this liberty would be tempered by their subsequent disproportionate incarceration.[5]

Following Pennsylvania, other states created legislation that offered degrees of freedom for enslaved people: Massachusetts (1783), New Hampshire (1783), Connecticut (1784), Rhode Island (1784), and New Jersey (1804). Enslaved people in many of these states served as catalysts for emancipation after submitting petitions similar to those of their predecessors Dorothy Angola, Elizabeth Keye, and Belinda Sutton. Likewise, postnati emancipation provisions (legislation after 1780 that provided freedom at specific ages) were created in Connecticut and Rhode Island with clauses that guaranteed freedom after a particular date and at a specific age. For example, in Connecticut, children born to enslaved women after March 1, 1784, would be free after the children provided twenty-five years of "uncompensated service to the owners of their mothers." This clause remained "valid" until 1848, and those over age sixty-four were exempt.[6] New Jersey was the last Northern state to create gradual abolition legislation. All those born after July 1, 1804, were declared free, but this freedom was more like a "gradation of unfreedom" or "slaves for a term." Even if they qualified for freedom, children in New Jersey were required to serve their mother's enslaver until the age of twenty-one for women and twenty-five for men.[7] In fledging, free enclave communities, Black people built their own houses of worship, learned trades, and continued to become entrepreneurs. For example, before being displaced by an influx of European immigrants in the 1830 and the 1840s, Black men in Philadelphia dominated the barbering and catering fields, and many were also skilled in tanning, carpentry, and blacksmithing. Black women labored primarily as domestics and cooks, but a number also worked as pushcart vendors selling pepper pot stew in the city's public squares. One pioneering Black businesswoman, Rachel Lloyd, ran a restaurant in the Walnut Street Theater from 1808 until 1850, when she retired.[8] Yet in spite of the strides gradual abolition supported in the North, westward expansion reinvigorated the institution of slavery in the antebellum years.

The 1793 invention of the cotton gin; the 1803 Louisiana Purchase, which doubled US territory; the ideology of Manifest Destiny; and Native American removal in the 1830s bolstered slavery in the Deep South and in the West. Southern planters and their families moved to Alabama, Mississippi, Louisiana, and Texas, creating an empire where cotton became king and sugar became prince. Those from the Carolinas moved their homesteads further west and established new properties dependent on enslaved labor. The westward expansion of slavery occurred at a time when debates about slavery were popularized by abolition activists and societies. However, to understand early-nineteenth-century life in the distinct regions of the United States, one must first consider the domestic slave trade.

Elizabeth Keckley, an enslaved girl in North Carolina, vividly recalled the day her father was taken away from her and her mother, Agnes. The family had just been reunited on the same estate after a separation during which they only saw each other twice a year, but their joyous reunion was short-lived. Keckley's enslaver informed the family that "in two hours my father must join his master at Dinwiddie, North Carolina, and go with him to the West, where he had determined to make his future home." This news "fell upon the little circle in that rude log cabin like a thunderbolt," Keckley recalled in her memoir. She saw her father crying out "against the cruel separation . . . his last kiss; his wild straining of my mother to his bosom; the solemn prayer to Heaven; the tears and sobs—the fearful anguish of broken hearts."[9] Keckley's father was not alone in going to the West, as African Americans were being moved throughout the states as part of the domestic slave trade. Nearly one million African Americans parted ways with family and friends via the traffic on US soil, some via sale, others via the relocation of the plantations, farms, and estates they served. The domestic traffic moved more people throughout the United States than the transatlantic trade had brought to the country by nearly three to one.

Newspapers throughout the South contained advertisements about trade and westward expansion. Some advertisements show planters selling their land in order to move west. Others feature plantations in the Deep South available for purchase. For example, just a year after the Louisiana Purchase, in 1804, the plantation of an M. Rivera, located not too far from New Orleans along the Mississippi River, was for sale to any prospective buyer. This was valuable land containing nearly one hundred acres close to Lake Borgne with "two vast fields planted with sugar canes," as well as all the necessary equipment to cultivate and process the cane such as "a purger [draining house] . . . 6 sisterns, 20 . . . each capable of containing . . . above 300,000 lbs. sugar" and "a refinery capable of containing 2000 sugar loaves." In addition to these buildings the property included "a sugar house . . . calculated for two sets of boilers . . . a gallery with two chambers of the sugar works" and a "saw mill with cables, chains, &c." It was "situated upon a superb canal which leads from the river and communicates with the lake, and is abundant supplied with salt water fish." This was such a large estate that it had a plantation house, an overseers' compound consisting of "three apartments," a hospital, a kitchen, and a blacksmith's shop ("with all the necessary tools"), as well as "a dairy; two large poultry houses, a sheep fold; a spacious shed, a lime house, two covered ovens and 3.5 negro cabins." Enslaved people were included in this large sale: "Fifty slaves, the greater part of whom are capable of almost any kind of labor."[10] Those looking to migrate west had full plantations such as this one available to them.

In addition to sugar plantations, cotton plantations were also up for sale in the late 1830s. A Mr. Edwards advertised the sale of a plantation along the San Bernard River in Texas in the fall of 1837 with "three or five thousand acres of land . . . [and] under a high state of cultivation, with a good cotton gin and grist mill; good dwelling house and comfortable negro quarters." Edwards intended to sell the land along with "ten to one hundred negroes," depending on the purchaser.[11] With these types of offers, planters in the Upper South left for the Lower South with land and fully equipped plantations available during the antebellum decades of the nineteenth century.

As people moved west, soil exhaustion became a problem by the 1840s and 1850s. "Good and desirable lands" were less available in Alabama, Mississippi, and Louisiana, so people turned to Texas. According to newspaper propaganda, "There is an absorbent character in the soil of Texas" that makes it an attractive place to move. "Texas is more healthy than the other Southern States" and the perfect place to "employ ... slaves," claimed a local newspaper.[12] Some enslavers went to scout the new land first and then brought their families and enslaved laborers shortly afterward. Sarah Ashley, a Mississippi-born enslaved woman, recalled being sold on the auction block in Louisiana to work on a cotton plantation in Texas. Her family was separated and when she was put on the auction block, she was scared and cried, "but dey put me up here anyway." Her first journey on the domestic slave trade was a 520-mile journey to Georgia, where she was also up for sale. She recalled that "day didn't sell me for a long spell" until a "Massa Mose Davis" of Cold Spring, Texas, purchased her. Ashley then traveled 820 miles to her new home in Texas, where she remained enslaved until age nineteen, when freedom came.[13]

Ashley's experience in the domestic slave trade confirms that it was a complex system involving public and private sales, transfers, deeds, gifts, and mortgages, as well as long-distance travel. Simply defined, this trade moved enslaved people from plantation to plantation, farm to farm, and state to state, from as early as the 1760s through the end of the Civil War. One of the most important facts about the domestic slave trade is that "its birth coincided with that of the nation itself."[14] Washington, DC, was the Northern capital of the trade until the early 1850s, and New Orleans was the most significant market in the Deep South. At some locations, enslaved people were kept in "pens," jails, or other small holding facilities until the day of sale. Newspapers advertised upcoming auctions with detailed information about those available for purchase.

Some of these facilities were simple jails that had the capacity to harbor up to three hundred enslaved people. Others were more elaborate, with courtyards between individual cells. Many were in close proximity to hotels, taverns, banks, and courthouses and sometimes were even connected to them. In Richmond, Virginia, one former enslaved man recalled that the "gaol" he spent time in had a tavern and hotel to accommodate the "guests/buyers" who attended the auctions. He described it as "one of the most gloomy places I ever had been in before."[15] The "living conditions" were extremely poor in that there were no beds. According to this enslaved man, those being held there "have to lie or sit by night on boards. The food is of the coarsest kind [and] Sales take place every day." Continuing, he noted, "Husbands sold, and their wives and children left for another day's auction; or wives sold one way, and husbands and fathers another, at the same auction. The distresses I saw made a deep impression upon my mind. My attention was diverted from myself by sympathy with others."[16]

While enslaved people were in pens, potential buyers inspected the "goods for sale." Former North Carolina enslaved woman Harriet Jacobs recalled that her "mother was dragged to jail, there remained twenty-five days, with Negro traders to come in as they liked to examine her, as she was offered for sale."[17] Jordon Smith remembered the "trader yard[s]" in Virginia and South Carolina where "sometimes a thousand slaves was waitin' to be sold." "When the traders knowed men was comin' to buy," he explained, "they made the slaves all clean up and greased they mouths with meat skins to look like they's feedin' them plenty meat." After preparing them for sale, "they lined the women up on one side and the men on the other." Potential buyers walked in between these two rows and sometimes "grab a woman and try to throw her down and feel of her to see how she's put up." He added, "If she's purty strong, he'd say, 'Is she a good breeder?'"[18] At a different yard, on Cedar Street in Nashville, enslaved people were forced to "tek all of de Clothes off en roll down de hill so dey could see day you didn't hav no bones broken."[19] These testimonies offer firsthand accounts of the days and hours before the auction.

On a balmy mid-November day in Charleston, South Carolina, C. Abner wrote to his friend Mr. Kingland in New York. He bragged about the surprisingly beautiful weather noting that it was "one of the finest days that we observed upon the earth" and that "the trees & shrubs are in full foliage & the flowers are blooming in the gardens. It is more like June weather than the middle of November." In the same letter he described the slave pens in Virginia: "At Richmond, . . . I have never looked upon a more disquieting sight. . . . Young girls are first on the stand, & undergo the most indecent examination and questioning, they are made to march up & down the room, with their clothes above their knees, so that a gang of slave traders can see the motion of their limbs, dirty fingers are put into their mouths to see if their teeth are good, and if they are pronounced 'Sound & Kind' the bidding commences, & the girl is sold to the highest bidder."[20]

Upon being sold, the commodification of Black women's bodies continued. They were used in the fields and homes of their enslavers, as well as in industrial spaces, universities, and city governments.[21] They performed productive, reproductive, and scientific labor for enslavers and medical professionals throughout the nineteenth century. The field of gynecology emerged at the expense of three enslaved women: Anarcha, Betsy, and Lucy, who underwent experimental surgeries administered without pain medication by physician and planter J. Marion Sims of Alabama. They were exploited for the benefit of science and should be recognized for their contributions to our knowledge of the human body, including, in particular, the treatment of vaginal fistulas, for which Sims became an expert.[22] However, no two enslaved women experienced more medical examinations, separations, and kidnappings than the McKoy twins.

Their story has as much to teach us about African American women, slavery, disability, and nineteenth-century medicine as it does about what one scholar calls "critical feminist disability praxis."[23] An analysis of these women through the lens of critical feminist disability praxis would focus on the ethical issues surrounding their representation as differently abled Black women with particular attention given to their perspectives regarding their lives and their body.

The conjoined twins were considered "genealogical wonders" because they had a unique bodily configuration. They were displayed as "freaks," part of a traveling show, and put on tour throughout the world. In different countries, teams of white male physicians, "leading surgeons and medical men of Russia, Austria, Switzerland, Germany, Spain, France, Italy, and Belgium," examined them and marveled at their body. These physicians certified their examinations and all focused on their "anatomical curiosity," which centered on the fact that "the spines are united, having rectum and vagina in common." The twins were described as having "two heads, four legs, four arms, but one body, and one consolidated pelvis."[24] But how do we consider life from the twins' perspective as differently abled Black women during slavery? How did they experience the constant scrutiny and attention when they had little or no power to reject the examinations? What was their family life like and how did they respond to being digitally raped by white male doctors all over the world?

One window into the twins' lives is through the lens of their mother, Monemia. The agony she experienced from the time her children were sold away from the family as toddlers until they returned as adults offers a perspective on Black women's history like no other. Monemia was the mother of nine children, two of whom were famous because of their unusual body. She had no avenues of protection to prevent them from being sold into a system that exploited them for the examination and pleasure of others. Millie and Christine were put on stage and made to sing and dance before audiences that gaped at them. Simultaneously, there were private viewings of their most intimate parts. Monemia had no rights to her children as an enslaved parent, but her position as their mother saved them on one important occasion.

The girls were kidnapped more than once, stolen by greedy men who wanted to manage their appearances and make money from their shows. Each time Millie and Christine went missing, Monemia, naturally, experienced extreme distress. The first time they were toddlers, and Monemia was "frantic" for days, refusing to eat or sleep until she knew her girls' whereabouts. Not long after this first kidnapping, the girls were taken again, this time out of the country. The Smith family, with the assistance of a detective, Mr. Vestal, searched for them all over the world and ended up traveling to Europe with Monemia to locate her children. When they found the exhibition where Millie and Christine were to perform that night, they purchased tickets and quietly attended. However, when the girls saw their mother they screamed and Monemia passed out. It was quite a scene. When she came to, Monemia said, "My own child! O! Give her to me! Do not take her away again; she needs my care!" Referring to the girls as one person, Monemia was reunited with them, and "for the first time in three years, she slept with it [*sic*] in her arms."

Days later the family faced a hearing before the Court of Admiralty in Birmingham, England, and the case took a remarkable turn that could not have happened in the United States. Monemia was identified and valued as the girls' mother, and she was granted full maternal rights because her children were minors. The court ruled, "The child should be given into the custody of its [*sic*] lawful mother." For a rare moment in nineteenth-century history, a Black mother was reunited with her daughters because she was their mother, rather than taken away from them through the yoke of slavery. This could only happen in a country that did not recognize slavery.[25] The story of the McKoy twins offers just a glimpse into Black family life in the nineteenth century. The experiences of other families suggest that slavery and freedom were inextricably linked and that Black families had a wide array of structures and realities in antebellum America.

This is no surprise given gradual abolition legislation in Northern states and because free and freed Black people lived all over the country. For the most part, scholars note, Black families were as stable as they could be during an era when the separation of families reigned supreme. Those who were enslaved, as noted in previous chapters, followed the status of their mother. Given this clear lineal connection to status and slavery, it is no surprise that many large plantations gave food and clothing rations to mothers. Paternal lineage was not always recognized or acknowledged. Thus when one makes judgments about Black families in the twentieth century that essentially blame Black dysfunctionality on Black women, it is clear that the centuries of enslavement have not been considered. This will be addressed in chapter 10.[26]

Black family life in nineteenth-century America was fraught because of slavery. Those fortunate enough to establish families used these relations as a form of survival and support. On plantations and small farms, enslaved people courted one another, fell in love, married, albeit in ceremonies not legally sanctioned by the state, and started families together. In 1822 Frances "Fanny" Gordon married Paul Jennings of Montpelier. Their marriage complied with Virginia law in that "each master gave consent." The two "were given a marriage supper at her master's home . . . and they lived together over thirty years [and had five children] until she died as husband and wife."[27] Countless other enslaved couples had similar wedding ceremonies, which often involved "biblical scriptures and witnesses" and sometimes a community of people in attendance.[28] In small regions socializing among enslaved people crossed county lines, but many partners found each other on large plantations. Their marriages were complex, and their family lives often disrupted by enslavers and the law, "but despite all that African Americans suffered, they created meaningful bonds of wedlock."[29]

Not all couples lived on the same plantation or farm, and these "abroad" relationships were challenging and often dependent on how flexible enslavers were regarding visitation for the couples. Enslaved men (mostly) were granted passes twice a week to see their partners on nearby estates. However, if they "misbehaved," overseers and enslavers used the visits as bribes to control them. If a laborer completed his or her work according to the manager's liking, then the enslaved couple could see one another. If for some reason the manager or overseer was not pleased with the enslaved person, the visitation could be canceled. Some enslaved people preferred not to live in the same place as their loved one because they needed the emotional distance of not witnessing punishments and other abuses. Women like Harriet Newby, on the other hand, longed to see her husband. "I want to see you very much," she wrote in a letter to him, expressing that she could not wait until that moment arrived. "I want to see you so much," she repeated. "That is the one bright hope I have before me." She signed the letter, "Your affectionate wife." In a second letter dated eleven days later, Harriet expressed the same desire to see her husband: "You cannot *imagine* how much I want to see you. *Com* [*sic*] as soon as you can, for nothing would give me more pleasure than to see you." Clearly Harriet felt love and passion for her husband, and she expressed it through a series of letters, which were found on his body at his death.[30] Other couples who lived apart also wrote to one another. At Montpelier, an enslaved woman named Rebecca received a letter from her husband, Peter Walker, who reminded her to "remember the solemn vow" of marriage they shared with one another. They were to "be faithful to each other until death," and he had no reason to doubt her. Sadly, in the same letter he mentioned that Paul Jennings's wife, Fanny, was near death.[31]

Families and communities like those at Montpelier were extremely important to the enslaved. The "quarters," where most enslaved people and some free Black people lived in one- or two-room cabins, represented a place where they could express love, joy, peace, happiness, pain, sadness, and sorrow. It was a space separate from their enslavers, where Black family life received nourishment. They celebrated births, practiced religion, attended dances, and participated in other communal activities in the quarters. But family life was not always pleasant. For some, domestic relations were violent, and there is evidence that abuse and neglect were also part of the Black family experience.

Forced coupling is just one example of an unwanted familial connection that often went awry. Rose Williams of Texas told her story of sexual abuse and forced marriage to interviewers with the Federal Writers' Project in the 1930s, part of the Works Progress

Administration (WPA), a New Deal program. Her enslaver forced her to live with an enslaved man named Rufus. When she refused Rufus's advances, Rose's enslaver made the following remarks: "'Woman, I's pay big money for you and I's done dat for de cause I wanted you to raise me chillers. I's put your to live with Rufus for dat purpose. Now, if you doesn't want whipping' at de stake, your do what I wants.'" When Rose reflected on her family life and that her enslaver allowed her to stay near her parents, as well as the thought of being whipped should she not comply, Rose conceded. "So I 'cides to do as de massa wish and so I yields," she said. Her reluctance is powerful, and her concession is even more telling. Some enslaved women yielded to unwanted relationships because of other external circumstances.[32] They weighed their limited options and made decisions that were not only difficult but at times compromising. Given that slavery involved open forms of physical and sexual abuse on plantations and small farms, it is not surprising that Black family life was fraught.

Ironically, one unique way African Americans tried to save and protect their families was through slaveholding. Due to the increasing number of free Black people in the population, blended families with enslaved and free members were common.[33] As discussed earlier, in the Revolutionary Era, African women like Anna Kingsley married white men and became enslavers. In the nineteenth century, as more African American women received their freedom, many became property owners and some held enslaved people. In Charleston City, South Carolina, between 1820 and 1864, the majority of Black people who held other Black people in slavery were female. For example, in 1820, 1830, and 1840, 70 percent of Black slaveholders were women; during the 1850s and the Civil War, the percentages fluctuated but did not fall below 48 percent. It appears that Black women were manumitted more than Black men in Charleston City, leading to a population of female property owners. However, "many of the slave purchases made by black women were their offspring who were owned by white masters," thus these slaveholding women were working to free their families.[34] If one partner was free, the second partner often tried to purchase him or her so the family could live together in freedom or pseudo-slavery until all members were freed. However, as in earlier periods, not all Black women freed the enslaved people in their possession.

Marie Thérése Coincoin Metoyer of Louisiana, who gave birth to ten children by Frenchman Claude Thomas Pierre Metoyer, helped her family become one of the largest Black slaveholding families in the United States. In addition to the enslaved people she held in bondage, many of her sons were also slaveholders, and over time, the extended family accumulated wealth in land and enslaved people. She was first hired to work for Metoyer, who then purchased and freed her and several of their children so they could create an empire. The family owned about fifteen thousand acres and more than four hundred enslaved men and women in Louisiana. Likewise, Margaret Mitchell Harris of South Carolina inherited "twenty-one [enslaved] males and females from her father, a free mulatto. . . . She [also] received sixteen more from her mother's estate." By 1860, Harris had $25,300 in human property. Another free Black woman, Betsy Sompayrac of Louisiana, made sure in her last will and testament that her children would have support from enslaved laborers. Although it is difficult to determine the mind set and attitude of these women, it appears that they were trying to find ways to secure economic stability for their children through slaveholding because some of their offspring were already free.[35] Thus, these women served as slaveholders seeking to make profits from their enslaved people.

Black women resisted slavery, regardless of the race and gender of the enslaver. Enslaved and free Black women fought oppression throughout the nineteenth century. Famous figures such as Harriet Tubman, Sojourner Truth, and Maria Stewart chose dramatic ways to fight the institution in order to help other Black people receive freedom and equal rights. Tubman's journeys to and from the South escorting her people to freedom are well known and documented. Truth's thirty years enslaved in the North sparked her activism at conventions and prayer meetings. Stewart's bold rhetoric as the first woman, Black or white, to speak publicly, guided and encouraged antislavery and women's rights activism. Other Black women, such as Lear Green, Ellen Craft, Harriet Robinson Scott, and Anna Murray Douglass, made great strides against oppression. Some of them worked directly with antislavery societies, and others worked alone or with family members to guarantee their freedom and the freedom of others.

Lear Green escaped slavery in Maryland in a crafty way: she shipped herself in a box to the Vigilant Committee of Philadelphia, part of the Pennsylvania Abolition Society. Accompanied by her soon-to-be mother-in-law, a free Black woman, Lear packaged herself and was put on a steamer to make the trip from the Baltimore to the Philadelphia harbor. The journey took eighteen hours, and she brought with her "a quilt, a pillow, and a few articles of raiment, with a small quantity of food and a bottle of water." Lear was fortunate that her future mother-in-law accompanied her on the life-threatening trip. James Noble, her enslaver from Baltimore, Maryland, advertised a $150 reward for her capture. In the ad he speculated, "I have reason to be confident that she was persuaded off by a negro man named Wim. Adams." Black abolitionist William Still admired her hunger and thirst for liberty and shared her story in his book. She made it to freedom and married William Adams, and the two settled in Elmira, New York, with extended family. Unfortunately they only enjoyed three years of freedom after her successful escape, as Lear died of unknown causes at the age of twenty-one. She had spent eighteen years enslaved and three years free.[36]

Anna Murray was the first of her parents' children born free, and like most other Black women of her day, she had strong connections to those who were enslaved, including her parents and some of her siblings. Murray met her husband, Frederick Bailey, named after his mother but who later self-liberated and took the name Douglass, who became the prominent abolitionist. They fell in love "at the base of a mountain of wrong and oppression, victims of the slave power as it existed . . . one smarting under the manifold hardships as a slave, the other in many ways suffering from the effects of such a system."[37] This description of their union came from their daughter, Rosetta Douglass Sprague, who reflected on her parents' lives in the early twentieth century in an essay. We know that Anna Murray financed her future husband's "flight to freedom."[38] He used her money to purchase a train ticket, and he "dressed in a sailor's clothing that she had made for him, carrying another seamen's papers" through Maryland, Delaware, and into free territory.[39] In 1838 the two moved to New York, where they were married; "a new plum colored silk dress was her wedding gown."[40] They lived in holy matrimony for forty-four years, and "whether in adversity or prosperity, she was the same faithful ally, guarding as best she could every interest connected with ... [Douglass's] life work, and the home."[41]

Ellen Craft also chose self-liberation to escape the bonds of slavery. Rather than ship herself in a box, she passed as a white male enslaver traveling with her Black male body servant. The person pretending to be her servant was actually her husband, William, and the two of them traveled a thousand miles to freedom. Ellen's disguise was almost detected at various points in their journey, especially on trains when she traveled in the car reserved for whites. The bandage over her face and the sling over her shoulder protected her from having to talk, but she did not want to part from William, who was asked to take a separate car reserved for the enslaved and free Black people. However, they made it to freedom and moved to England, where Ellen gave birth to five children outside the bounds of slavery. The couple left a narrative about their experience.[42]

Harriet Robinson Scott chose the courts to fight for her family's freedom, following in the footsteps of her Colonial and Revolutionary Era foremothers. Born into slavery in Virginia in 1815, Harriet spent the majority of her enslaved years at Fort Snelling, a military outpost and trading center in present-day Minnesota. She challenged her enslavement because the 1820 Missouri Compromise outlawed slavery in areas north of the Thirty-Sixth Parallel (36 degrees, 30 minutes), which included most regions north of Arkansas and certainly Minnesota. During her time at Fort Snelling, Harriet met and fell in love with Dred Scott. They exchanged vows at a ceremony performed by her enslaver, Major Taliaferro, a justice of the peace. From that point forward, Harriet and Dred Scott were both owned by Dr. and Mrs. Emerson, and the two moved about at their enslaver's will to states including Louisiana, Missouri, and Minnesota. On one trip from the South to the North, aboard the steamer *The Gipsey*, Harriet gave birth to the couple's first daughter. In 1846, after the couple had a second daughter, they each decided to take separate legal actions against the institution that enslaved them. It took years for the cases to be decided, and at one point they were combined. However, Harriet's name was left off the Missouri Supreme Court decision (1857), and many people think Dred Scott was the sole plaintiff, but his wife, Harriet, fought the courts for her freedom as well. During their nine-year wait, the Scotts were incarcerated by the sheriff of St. Louis, who hired them out for work while they awaited trial. On January 12, 1850, the Scotts won the case, and "Harriet and her family were free." But freedom did not last long, as one month later, the widowed enslaver, Mrs. Emerson, filed an appeal, and the case was renamed, removing Harriet as one of the plaintiffs. The final decision came on March 6, 1857, when the Missouri Supreme Court ruled that the entire Scott family and any other enslaved person taken to a free territory would remain enslaved. It was a blow to the enslaved and a victory for the system of slavery.[43]

Aside from the individual acts of resistance addressed above, Black women were involved in large-scale uprisings and group escape attempts as well. Women in the antebellum era boarded ships to freedom just as their counterparts in the Revolutionary Era had done. In the spring of 1848, for example, seventy-seven enslaved people attempted escape on the Potomac River by boarding a ship named *The Pearl*. Their destination was Philadelphia, but three days into their journey, they were caught and jailed. Among this group were several women including those with ties to Montpelier, a large plantation in Virginia.

Ellen, the daughter of Dolley Madison's enslaved woman Sukey, was on *The Pearl*, along with Mary and Emily Edmonson, runaways from Maryland who became abolitionists and good friends with Frederick Douglass. It is believed that James Madison's enslaved man Paul Jennings was one of the organizers of the escape. With people like this involved, it is no wonder that the Montpelier community paid close attention to the outcome of this failed escape. After being captured, the enslaved people were jailed, and Dolley decided to sell Ellen for $400. When Sukey heard that her daughter had been sold to a Baltimore dealer, she was "overwhelmed with grief" and spent the next few months trying to find out about her daughter.[44] A Baltimore physician, Joseph Snodgrass, purchased Ellen from the Campbell & Co. slave jail and freed her. Ellen settled in Boston and, from what we can tell from primary source documents, enjoyed her freedom. The Madisons sold Sukey to a Washington family shortly after Ellen ran away, and the family allowed her to work toward her freedom.[45]

With the prospect of separation from family or in the aftermath of a sale, grief led some to choose death or bodily dismemberment as their form of resistance.[46] One enslaved woman from Maryland, who was described as "a most faithful servant," attempted to kill herself after being separated from her husband. Francis Scott Key, writer of "The Star-Spangled Banner" and a well-known lawyer, provided the details in a deposition: "She was taken by the Trader into the City in a hack & I am credibly informed & believe that she attempted to kill herself by cutting her throat in the hack—The wound was sewed up in the city at George Miller's tavern—I was told this by two persons who saw her afterwards."[47] However, we do not know the fate of this woman or the extent of her injuries. But we have evidence from a nineteenth-century physician, Jesse Torrey, that *may* address the outcome of this suicidal act. We learn from Torrey that even after she "cut her own throat," and they mended it, "she completed her design of destroying her life, buy cutting it again [this time] mortally."[48]

Another woman chose bodily dismemberment to interfere with a pending sale. She took "a cleaver, or some such instrument" and "chopped off one of her hands" in order to prevent a slave trader from taking her away from relatives. This woman's tactic worked, and the "trader refused to take her."[49] A few decades later, an abolitionist traveling through Washington, DC, in July, 1835, wrote about a woman who attempted suicide after being separated from her husband. She was so distraught "she leaped from an upper window, falling upon the pavement, her limbs were broken in a shocking manner," and the fall was so hard that she became "a helpless cripple."[50]

The resistance story of a mother and her daughter on the auction block sheds more light on the choices and challenges Black women faced under slavery. Enslaved in Virginia, Di, like many enslaved women, had been pregnant and given birth to several stillborn infants. She served as the plantation wet nurse to her enslavers' thirteen children (which means that she nursed them all on her breast) along with her own when her daughter, Pricilla, was born and survived infancy. The girl brought great joy to Di and her husband, Jim. The joy ended when Pricilla turned ten and a slave dealer came to take her to the market in Petersburg. According to the narrative, "nothing could induce the girl to leave her mother's side; she fixed her eyes steadily on those of the dealer, and clung to the skirts of her mother's dress." The family had one more night together because the dealer was planning to leave the following morning. That night, Di and Jim "sat, hand clasped in hand, looking at the sleeping girl." Neither of them spoke, "they could only weep; but they stifled their sobs," allowing Pricilla to sleep peacefully. The next morning, Di kept the dealer waiting as she stalled to have a few more minutes with her daughter. She postponed dressing Pricilla because she "felt as if, in dressing her, she should be hastening and consenting to the loss of her darling." Her time expired when the overseer instructed Di to get Pricilla ready. Di "had felt keenly her own sorrows early in life, through the chilling effects of age in part, but still more from long experience of the hopelessness of all resistance." She "was able now, without having a muscle of her face disturbed, or shedding a single tear, with her withered hands to deck [prepare] for the auction-block the child who, for ten years, had been like a dancing sunbeam in that lowly household."[51]

Di dressed her "dancing sunbeam" and took the time to say good-bye to little Pricilla, but some Black women participated in more overt forms of resistance and were often severely punished. Their quest for freedom was not seen as a noble effort by enslavers. They were seen as property, and their "noble effort" was seen as an act of defiance. Enslaved people were not supposed to respond with violence, and free Black people were supposed to treasure their freedom. But a system of oppression like enslavement harms all parties, the enslaved and the free. When acts of resistance involved death via poison, arson, severe beatings, and other violent crimes, Black women went to jail and sometimes to the gallows.

In Galveston, Texas, Lucy Dougherty was arrested and jailed for the apparent murder of her female enslaver. Not too long after, Dougherty confessed to killing her mistress with an axe and told authorities, "I would do it again."[52] Dougherty's story sheds light on the complex relationship between enslaved women and plantation mistresses, interactions that could become volatile.[53] But we know little about Dougherty except her quick dash into the historical record and her vanishing after she was publicly hanged. We know nothing about why she brutally killed her mistress except that she would gladly do it again. Her lack of remorse suggests that she believed her actions were justified and was willing to die herself for committing this crime.

We may not know why Dougherty killed her enslaver, but some women murdered their enslavers because of physical and sexual violations. Fourteen-year-old Celia of Missouri represents an example of a young enslaved woman who took extreme measures to avoid sexual assault. Her enslaver, Robert Newsom, raped her shortly after she was purchased. After five years of unwanted sexual abuse and giving birth to two of his children, Celia had had enough. On June 23, 1855, she refused his sexual advances and warned him that she did not want him to touch her. When he tried, she hit him over the head with a club. The blows left him dead. In order to conceal her crime of self-defense, she burned Newsom's body in her fireplace and hid his remains throughout the property. She later confessed to the crime and went to trial, pleading "not guilty" to an all-white, proslavery, male jury. Celia was convicted of first-degree murder and gave birth to a stillborn child while in jail. She made one escape attempt prior to her scheduled hanging but was caught. The night before her execution, in an interview published in a local paper, Celia made the following remarks: "I struck him with a stick until he was dead, and then rolled him into the fire and burnt him up."[54] Celia was hanged on December 21, 1855.

During the antebellum period, the rate of incarceration among enslaved women grew along with the development of the penal system. Being enslaved and incarcerated meant that Black women in correctional facilities faced a double layer of control. We have much to learn about their experiences behind bars during this time, including the complex response some had to incarceration. Harriet Jacobs, a North Carolina enslaved woman, saw jails as "sanctuaries of a sort from the horrors daily visited on her by a lewd and lecherous owner."[55] But jails also represented a place where enslaved and free Black people were whipped, paddled, and punished behind closed doors. In Savannah, Georgia, enslavers "sent their workers to the Chatham County Jail to receive punishments ranging from incarceration to public whippings," as some did not want to tarnish their reputations for not beating their enslaved people.[56]

An enslaved woman named Phoebe, of Virginia, went to jail after being captured for running away. While confined, it appears that "Phoebe suspended herself by the neck with a handkerchief tied to a bar of the window "until her life was extinct."[57] Was this a case of foul play or did Phoebe take her own life? We have no way of knowing who else might have visited her in jail or her relationship with the staff, but we do have questions about who was responsible for her death. These types of cases will become quite familiar in the contemporary era.

Though Black women faced hardships throughout the nineteenth century, they found pleasure and moments of joy that were important to their survival.

The enslaved women in one Georgia community found unique ways to share their artistic abilities through the production of clothes, quilts, and dolls. Some women were so talented that their children bragged about their mothers' skills. Adeline Willis claimed that her mother "was one of the best dyers anywhere "round." She had the skill to make colors "by mixing up all kinds of bark and leaves," and Adeline's favorite was "the prettiest sort of lilac," which she herself made "with maple bark and pine bark."[58] Other enslaved girls boasted about their mothers who "dyed some blue and brown striped" fabric from indigo they harvested on the plantation. These women made dresses and wore them on Sundays when they went to church. They also made clothing for their enslavers, using fine cloth, piping, buttons, and special stitching. Given the talent and skill found in dressmaking, it is no surprise that when enslaved women ran away, they often took fine articles of clothing with them. The mother-daughter duo of Beck and Mariah, who left this Georgia community in 1834, "carried off five" of the enslaver's daughter's dresses, including some made of silk, muslin, and lace.[59]

Free Black women were also artists, poets, sculptors, dancers, dressmakers, and preachers. They used various forms of art and personal and religious expression to feed their souls and create beauty, despite their difficult circumstances. Many know of the poems Phillis Wheatley wrote and published in the eighteenth century, but few know of sculptor Edmonia Lewis, dressmaker Elizabeth Keckley, and preacher Jarena Lee. Jarena, a free Black woman born in New Jersey, was one of the most well-known preachers of her day. Separated from her parents at age seven, she went to work as a house maid sixty miles from her home. Her religious conversion came in quiet moments and she asked the Lord to "sanctify my soul for Christ's sake." When the Holy Spirit responded, she jumped to her feet and cried. Jarena found Richard Allen's preaching moving and was actively involved with African Methodist Episcopal Church in Philadelphia, Mother Bethel AME. For four or five years she spent time alone worshiping and did not share her calling to "preach the Gospel." However, when she did, the Reverend Allen was the first person she told: "I now told him, that the Lord had revealed it to me, that [I] must preach the gospel." Allen's first reaction was that women were not allowed to preach. Disappointed, Jarena knew in her spirit that "nothing is impossible with God" and that "the Savior died for the woman as well as for the man." She left Philadelphia and married Pastor Joseph Lee and had two children. Unfortunately, she suffered the loss of her husband and five other family members. During this time, she focused on God and continued to pray. Eight years after she first asked the Reverend Allen for permission to preach, she attended Bethel Church, and when the preacher lost his words and froze during the sermon, Jarena jumped to her feet and completed the sermon. After this, the Reverend Allen allowed her to preach, and she became the first female in the African Methodist Episcopal Church to do so. From that day forward, Jarena traveled all over the United States, delivering more than 178 sermons and using her ministry to support the abolitionist movement.[60] Though she started her spiritual journey in the African Methodist Episcopal Church, Jarena gravitated toward the Holiness movement, a form of Christianity centered around experience, the Scripture, and the power of the Holy Spirit. Holiness encouraged a measure of freedom and contained an arguably revolutionary nature. This doctrine helped Black women preachers like Jarena thrive and meet the Spirit outside of gendered confines. Historian Bettye Collier-Thomas credits Jarena Lee's 1836 autobiography as serving as the first evidence of a "black feminist consciousness of the holiness doctrine and its power to subvert religious sexism."[61] Jarena Lee's revelatory ministry would be matched by other prominent free Black women, whose faith and commitment to the antislavery movement would also find them advancing causes for women's rights.

Black women such as Sojourner Truth, Henrietta Purvis, Harriet Forten Purvis, and Sarah Remond were avowed suffragists as well as renowned abolitionists. Historians trace the origins of the female suffrage movement in the US to the women's rights convention at Seneca Falls, New York, in 1848. From there, early suffragists began to meet, writer letters, and slowly organize. As the late historian Rosalyn Terborg-Penn explained, "The number of suffragists grew slowly from a small group of reformers within the confines of abolitionist circles in the northeast to a more diversified, but still limited number of individuals and groups nationwide. Diversification occurred as individuals, both Blacks and whites, joined the movement from regions throughout the nation." African American women were among the first wave of suffragists as legendary freedom fighter Sojourner Truth took to the podium, despite some white women's efforts to prevent her from doing so, at the national women's convention in 1851, in Akron,

Ohio. At the 1858 convention in New York, Sarah Remond, together with her brother Charles, delivered pro-suffrage speeches that won them accolades from the audience. Even as some whites objected, because the antislavery movement and the women's suffrage movement were closely aligned, Black and white women episodically worked together for women's right to vote.[62]

DURING THE ANTEBELLUM ERA, slavery was losing hold in the North as a result of the gradual abolition legislation that followed the American Revolution. But in the South, where cotton was king, the institution was deeply ingrained. As a result, plantation slavery grew throughout the Lower Mississippi Valley. The importance of Black women's reproductive labor became the lifeblood of the institution, as rape and forced breeding fueled the domestic slave trade. Even in this exploitative climate, African American women found ways to thrive and survive. Activism marked a key theme for Black women in antebellum America. They worked in abolitionist movements with whites in an effort to end slavery, and they were relentless and creative in their efforts to gain freedom for themselves and their families. By the time the Civil War started, free and enslaved Black women were never more ready to claim their freedom.

CHAPTER FIVE

MARY'S APRON AND THE DEMISE OF SLAVERY, 1860—1876

Soldiers was around me very thick.

—RHODY HOLSWELL

MARY COLBERT WAS FRIGHTENED by the sounds of war. She was about ten years old and living on a small Georgia cotton plantation owned by Major John Crawford when the Civil War began. She recalled the loud "booms" of the cannons and the "pop-pop" sounds of rifles drawing louder and closer. She knew that the inevitable was coming as she watched the white women enslavers scurrying about, hiding their heirlooms and treasured possessions. All the male enslavers were off fighting the war. So, too, were Mary's brother and father, who went with their enslavers to serve as attendants. Mary was left alone and scared. Her mother lived and worked on a nearby farm for a different family, and the child probably longed for her protection.

One day Yankee troops burst through the front door and began tearing apart the house searching for money, jewels, or anything of value. Mary, an enslaved girl in the house, with other women, stood in utter fear. Moments before the troops entered, Mary's enslavers, Major Crawford's daughters, Fannie and Ann, handed Mary a "bag of gold and silver, and some old greenback Confederate money" to hide in her sleeveless apron. She was told to keep still: "'Now, be a good little girl and don't move.'" When the troops came in, Mary said, "They went all over the house searching everything with their guns and swords shining and flashing. . . . I was so scared the sweat was running down my face in streams." But when "they came to the bedroom where I was standing by a bed, holding that money inside my apron," Mary said, "they didn't even glance at me the second time. Little did they think that [a] little slave girl had the money they were hunting for."[1]

Starting with the Civil War memories of a "little slave girl" like Mary provides a different perspective on how to interpret the past. Mary Colbert's role in Civil War history was crucial, because without her story we would not know how she inadvertently helped her enslavers by hiding their money. However, historians, just like the Union soldiers, have overlooked her and many other enslaved women because they neglect to "glance" at them a second, third, or fourth time. They may have glanced at her once, but they did not actually see her. For other enslaved women, such as Rhody Holswell, the war years were stressful because of the Union military presence in the South, leading her to comment that "during de war de soldiers was around me very thick."[2] What did the war years mean for Black women, for those who remained on plantations and those who fled? How did Black women transition from slavery to freedom, and how did they make sense of their new lives? Black women feared for their safety from soldiers on both sides of the war. The sounds of cannons, the military men who abused them, and the uncertainties about the future made the war experience particularly difficult for women, enslaved and free.

WHEN ELEVEN SOUTHERN STATES seceded from the Union, most Black women in the region were working in the fields, homes, factories, and educational institutions of their enslavers. Those who were free often congregated in urban centers, where they mainly worked as laundresses, housemaids, hucksters, and teachers. In December 1860 South Carolina passed its ordinance of secession, dissolving its connection to the Union and creating a "separate and independent State; with full power to levy war, conclude peace, contract alliances." South Carolina secessionists complained about the federal government's attitude toward slavery, saying that the federal government has "permitted open establishment among them of societies, whose avowed object is to disturb the peace," by encouraging and assisting "thousands of our slaves to leave their homes." And, they continued, enslaved people who did not leave were "incited by emissaries, books and pictures to servile insurrection."[3] Mississippi, Florida, Alabama, Georgia, and Louisiana seceded in January 1861, followed by Texas, in February. From April through June 1861, the remaining six states seceded from the Union in the following order: Virginia, Arkansas, North Carolina, Tennessee, Kentucky, and Missouri. This political realignment had an impact on Black women's labor and on their political ideologies, which varied from region to region, state to state.

As laborers, Black women served in several official and unofficial capacities during the war. Their labor during the Civil War included serving as "spies, regimental cooks, nurses, and laundresses and as workers on hospital transports and naval gunboats." They served "on plantations and farms; in towns, cities, and factories; and on the battlefield." According to historian Thavolia Glymph, "Black women fought and prayed for the Union cause and the cause of emancipation."[4] But as the war continued, they grew weary of Union and Confederate soldiers who destroyed property and threatened their lives. During the Federal Writers' Project, with interviews collected in the 1930s, many Black women shared their traumatic and stressful experiences.

Pauline Grice of Texas described the Confederate and Union forces that converged on her enslaver's plantation: "Fust de 'federate sojers come and takes some mules and hosses, den some more come for de corn." However, not much later, "de Yankee sojers comes and takes some more. When dey gits through, dey ain't much more tookin' to be done." Troops rampaged the plantation where she and her family lived and labored, causing stress and strife including food shortages that lasted most of the war. In addition to her memory of hunger, the ear-splitting and bone-chilling sounds of war were etched in her mind. She vividly recalled hearing "de cannon . . . bang two whole days 'thout hardly stoppin'."[5] For Pauline, the Civil War and its deafening sounds wrought incalculable uncertainties.

Black women also went to army camps. Millie Forward of Jasper, Texas, recalled, "When de sojers go to de war, every man take a slave to wait on him and take care he camp and cook."[6] Harriet Barrett was one of those enslaved women. "Massa, he carry me to war with him," she said with a sense of pride and privilege, "'cause I's de good cook." In addition to sharing her culinary skills, she also "nuss de sick and wounded clean through de war and seed dem dyin' on every side of me."[7] Whether on the battlefield or the plantation, enslaved women like Harriet witnessed the casualties of war firsthand, and for some these scenes proved overwhelming.

One Black woman from Arkansas was distraught because she and her enslavers had to take shelter in the basement of the plantation home in order to avoid the cannonballs that pounded the house. This house servant decided to hide in a "large barrel" even after "Northern friends" offered to take her with them. She believed that "schools for colored children would not be allowed by white folks, and if attempted, the children would be waylaid and killed." Her enslavers said she "showed signs of mind failure which grew worse and worse." Shortly after, the woman took more extreme measures and committed suicide by jumping into a well.[8]

Free and enslaved black women also labored as medical practitioners in both Union and Confederate Army camps. Susie King Taylor of Georgia was one of them. A nurse and educator in Union Army camps, Taylor was the great-great-granddaughter of Dolly, who died at the age of 120. Dolly had seven children and "five of her boys were in the Revolutionary War." Taylor then acknowledges her great-grandmother Susanna, a midwife who "was the mother of twenty-four children, twenty-three being girls." Susanna lived to be one hundred years old. Taylor's grandmother, also named Dolly, had two children, and Taylor's mother gave birth to nine children, three of whom died in infancy. Recognizing the women who came before her was something Taylor thought important enough to open her memoirs.

Taylor's memories of the Civil War begin with "the roar and din the guns made."[9] She understood the magnitude of the events unfolding in front of her. "It was a gloomy time," she explained, especially for Black women, who were given limited choices: remain on the plantation, join the war effort, or go to Liberia as part of a colonization movement. She chose the former and nursed soldiers at camp. In order to protect herself from catching diseases, she received vaccinations and "drank sassafras tea constantly."[10] In addition to caring for the military officers, Taylor also "taught a great many of the comrades in Company E [of the 33rd US Colored Troops] to read and write, when they were off duty."[11] She traveled on various "military expeditions," including one where she witnessed white rebels in blackface trying to disguise themselves as the enslaved. It was a tactic that led to several deaths among her party.[12] In the face of death, deceit, and devastation, Taylor, like other Black women, had hopes for a better life, one that would bring freedom for Black people. While that was still far off, Taylor nevertheless did find a snatch of hope and support in the midst of war. It was in the camps that she met her husband, Edward King, an African American noncommissioned officer of the Union forces. The two supported one another during the war and stayed close to try to protect one another from harm.

Black women were also present in Confederate camps. Plantation mistress Ada Bacon of Florence County, South Carolina, left her plantation in 1862 to nurse soldiers in Charlottesville, Virginia. When she left, she brought an enslaved woman to accompany her. In Confederate hospitals, plantation mistresses hired out their enslaved women as cooks, laundresses, and chambermaids.[13] While enslaved Black women were expected to tend to wounded Confederate soldiers, some of them used their proximity to Confederate troops and camps to aid the Union. An unnamed enslaved woman laundress worked as a spy to support the Union Army. Her husband, Dabney, explained that they communicated information by Ada's use of a clothesline to track the movement of Confederate officers including Generals Robert E. Lee, A. P. Hill, James Longstreet, and Thomas "Stonewall" Jackson:

> Well, that clothesline tells me in a half an hour just what goes on at Lee's headquarters. You see my wife over there? She washes for the officers, cooks, and waits around, and as soon as she hears about any movement or anything going on she comes down and moves the clothes on that line so I can understand in a minute. That there gray shirt is Longstreet; and when she takes it off it means he's gone down about Richmond. That white shirt means [A. P.] Hill; and when she moves it up to the west end of the line, Hill's corps has moved up stream. That red one is Stonewall Jackson. He's down on the right now, and if he moves, she'll move that red shirt.[14]

It is no surprise that this couple found a unique way to share military secrets. Their story represents the clandestine ways that Black women helped move themselves one step closer to freedom.

Black women also served on warships like the *Nashville*. A "floating hospital," *Nashville* was the first vessel of the Union Medical Department (1862). Here, white women managed Black women, often assigning custodial chores and heavy manual labor. Black women also used their medical training and skills to care for the injured and sick. Because of their race and gender, nursing smallpox patients often fell to Black women, like fifteen-year-old Malinda McFarland Jackson, assigned to Knoxville's Asylum General in 1864. During the war, there were approximately 778 contract nurses of which 281, or 36 percent, were Black.[15] They also served as matrons, cooks, and laundresses on board warships.

Some Black women made blankets and clothes for the troops. Jane Harmon of Georgia recalled, "My Ma wiz a 'sport spinner an' weaver, an' she spun an' wove thing ter be sont her de soldiers om de War."[16] Similarly, Mollie Watson noted that her community of women "spun blankets durin' the war."[17]

Whether black women worked as matrons, cooks, laundresses, personal servants, or medical practitioners, their labors were critical to the war effort that endangered their lives. The promise of liberty, however, for some, tapped into a desire to do all they could—often by taking advantage of their undesirable circumstances. As with the clothesline spy in the Confederate hospital, so it was with Mary Bowser in Jefferson Davis's home.

Bowser served Confederate president Jefferson Davis and acted as a spy for Union general Ulysses S. Grant. Bowser, who had several aliases, worked in the Davis home, serving as a cook and housemaid. Because she was educated, she was able to read the plans and documents that were left on Davis's desk. Bowser had a photographic memory and shared the secrets with her former enslaver Elizabeth Van Lew, who passed on the information to Grant. Some say that this spy ring represented the origins of the US Secret Service, and a freed enslaved woman was at its helm.[18] Whether they made blankets or clothing, Black women found ways to contribute to the war effort, many with the hopes of attaining freedom as well as with a sense of patriotic pride. African Americans in every period of US history sought to prove their citizenship and loyalty to a nation that rarely respected or welcomed them.

Although Harriet Tubman is probably the most well-known Black woman in American history, some do not know about her brave efforts during the Civil War. After spending the early years of the war attending to the sick, Tubman received permission to create a spy network in 1863 to infiltrate the Confederate base in South Carolina. She quickly organized a group of men who knew the land and could navigate boats with ease. She became commander of her spy ring and developed a plan that led to the freedom of nearly eight hundred people.

In June 1863, Tubman and her comrades began their military operation of bringing three ships up the Combahee River. It was an expedition that would inspire activists in the late twentieth century. Upon entering the St. Helena Sound with 150 Black soldiers, Tubman "guided the boats to designated spots along the shore where fugitive slaves had hidden." Her response to what she witnessed that night is profound: "I never saw such a sight," she exclaimed.[19] Some of the women "would come with twins hanging around their necks. I never saw so many twins in my life." The women also had "bags on their shoulders, baskets on their heads, and young ones tagging along behind." Tubman witnessed Black women risking their lives to gain liberty for themselves and their children. Imagine what it took to bring young children to the banks of the water in the dead of the night. They had to keep quiet and wait for the ships to arrive and pray they would not be detected. In addition to their children, some women brought with them squealing pigs and screaming chickens.

Tubman and her crew successfully loaded everyone on the ships and went upstream to raid the homes of some of the most prestigious plantation families in the state. They stole goods from the mansions and set fire to approximately thirty-four properties. Although historians disagree on the number of people Tubman led to freedom in this summer raid, scholars confirm that at least 750 made it to freedom. Official Confederate reports noted that whoever led this "well guided attack" was "thoroughly acquainted with the river and county."[20] Once again, Tubman showed that she was the Moses of her people, shepherding them out of slavery, even during the Civil War.

AS IN OTHER TIMES OF STRIFE, enslaved and free Black people resisted their inhumane and unjust conditions during the Civil War era. The enslaved continued running away to the Dismal Swamp of Virginia and North Carolina. During the war, a woman named Larinda

White met and married her husband, Abraham Lester, in the swamp. Their makeshift ceremony celebrated a commitment to one another beyond the bonds of enslavement. We know that Abraham had been in the swamp three years before the war and decided to join the Union Army when they arrived in Suffolk, Virginia. Now the couple was hoping to claim their freedom once again, but this time outside the swamp. Imagine their potential life change as war brought the hope of freedom and the possibility of living beyond the swampland. What was it like for children born in the swamp to see white soldiers for the first time? How did people like Larinda and Abraham learn to trust and believe the troops who came to "liberate" them when they had already liberated themselves?

When Union Army officers surveyed the swamp, they were surprised to find so many maroons living in an area believed uninhabitable. This land originally covered "more than 1.3 million acres," and few parts of it were above water. With the exception of a few "dry ridges" that "rose from the muck," there were scattered places of "solid ground that became the territory of numerous wild cattle, bears, deer and wolves." It was believed that this area was reserved for "suicidal fools" who "dared to venture in."[21] Enslaved people had been living in this region since the seventeenth century, and it is probable that Larinda and Abraham came to a place with a vibrant community of self-liberated people. A visitor at Lake Drummond Hotel, on the outskirts of the swamp, shared that he saw a "beautiful, finely-dressed lady" come out of the woods one morning. Astonished, he watched her walk "out on a log about twenty feet into the Lake, with a fishing pole in her hand." The woman "bait[ed] her hook" and threw it "out into the Lake." The woman came to this spot "every day for several days, and at the same hour each day."[22] The example of this woman indicates the ways in which maroons normalized their lives in a region where so many believed people could not live and survive. It also shows a search for food at an appointed time and place where this woman likely had success. Outsiders are always trying to make sense of life in the swamp and rationalize enslaved people's desire to live there as an addiction to running away, but most men and women entered the swamp because of their "addiction to freedom." They wanted to live in a space where they could marry, have families, and try to enjoy life, even during the Civil War. The presence of Union troops, for some, assured them that a potential end to their life in the swamp was near.

During the war, free Black women, like Charlotte Forten Grimké, also worked to aid Black people in their quest and transition to freedom. In the fall of 1862 this educated woman from a Northern anti-slavery family had the opportunity to go to the Sea Islands to do aid work at Port Royal, South Carolina, where thousands of enslaved people lived after enslavers abandoned their plantations. On the island, some African Americans trained, became educated, and prepared for life as freed people; others were forced to labor in cotton fields just as they did on the former plantations. Grimké was the first African American teacher hired. She taught school along with two white women from Philadelphia, Laura Matilda Towne and Ellen Murray. The women taught approximately a hundred students "from noon until three o'clock" and then gave evening classes for adults who worked during the day. One of Grimké's goals was to encourage her students to take pride in their heritage, so she made a point to teach them about "liberators and heroes of African descent" such as Toussaint Louverture of Haiti.[23] Of her time on the island, Grimké wrote about her first view of formerly enslaved children "of every hue," who "were playing about the streets." They looked "as merry and happy as children ought to look—now that the evil showed of Slavery no longer hangs over them."[24]

On her first morning at Port Royal, Grimké was overwhelmed with the joy of seeing "women in bright-colored handkerchiefs, some carrying pails on their heads," and children playing near them. "On every face," she wrote, "there was a look of serenity and cheerfulness" that warmed her heart and made her grateful to God for allowing her to live "to see this day" when Black people experienced controlled freedom. Grimké was also pleasantly surprised to see that everyone was "bright and eager to learn." On Sundays she enjoyed seeing everyone "neatly dressed" for church. The women wore "clean, dark frocks, with white aprons and bright-colored head-handkerchiefs." The headdresses were so impressive that Grimké preferred them to the hats with feathers. Recall that Black women had been covering their hair for nearly a century, especially in places that enacted tignon laws during slavery.[25] But Black women adapted this seemingly restrictive legislation and fashioned it for themselves so much so that in the

1860s, a free Black woman commented on the beauty and creative expression of their headscarves.

As the war raged on, Charlotte Grimké witnessed acts of resistance and courage among the families on the island. She shared the brave story of two girls around ages ten and fifteen years old. When Union forces captured the islands and separated the girls from their parents, their enslaver took them into the country. However, the girls, desperate and determined to find their parents, ran away "at night, and travelled through woods and swamps for two days, without eating." Suffering extreme fatigue, the girls doubted whether they could continue their journey. However, their "brave little hearts" and something deep in their souls helped them persist. When they made it to the Port Royal ferry, "the boat was too full to take them in." Those on the ferry, however, told the girls' father, who "immediately took a boat and hastened to the ferry" landing. When the young girls saw their father, they "were almost wild with joy," and when they saw their mother, "she fell down 'res' as if she was dead." The entire family was overwhelmed with happiness.

After spending nearly a year on the island, Charlotte felt a sense of pride for the work she had done and the people she had met. "My heart sings a song of thanksgiving," she wrote, "at the thought that even I am permitted to do something for a long-abused race, and aid in promoting a higher, holier, and happier life on the Sea Islands."[26] Charlotte's life and labors also serve as an example of how free Black women wove their faith into their daily experiences and of their expanding political and public culture. In similar fashion, Sarah Jane Woodson Early used the skills she had acquired as a free, educated Black woman to assist formerly enslaved women and men at the same time that she continued to create a space for Black women to play central roles in racial advancement. Sarah grew up in a free Black community in Chillicothe, Ohio, and obtained her degree from Oberlin College in 1856. She secured a position at Wilberforce University in 1859, at which point Sarah became the first Black woman to serve on the faculty of an American university. At the close of the Civil War, she followed in Charlotte's footsteps and headed south to Hillsborough, North Carolina, where she taught Black girls at a school run by the Freedmen's Bureau. A few years later, when she was forty-three years old, she married a pioneering African Methodist Episcopal minister, Reverend Jordan W. Early, and actively supported her husband's ministry, though she would go on to assert her own right to speak. Sarah became a "pioneering black feminist involved in the early women's movement."[27]

Although Sarah's life, accomplishments, and commitment to social justice might seem exceptional, they are arguably matched by a fellow Black Oberlin alumna, Mary Edmonia Lewis. Edmonia, a sculptor, sold her creations to support abolition.[28] Part Chippewa and part African American, Edmonia was born in the middle of the century as a free woman of color. After college, she was heavily influenced by abolitionists. During the Civil War she learned how to sculpt by working with portrait sculptor Edward Brackett. She was most known for her "medallion portraits" of well-known abolitionists such as William Lloyd Garrison, Charles Sumner, and Wendell Phillips. She used the proceeds from the sale of her medallions and the "portrait busts" of abolitionists John Brown and Colonel Robert Gould Shaw to fully finance her first trip to Europe in the 1860s. Although Edmonia experienced discrimination, she found that Europe felt more like home than the United States, so she settled in Rome and made trips back and forth between Italy and the US. Her time abroad not only offered a respite from American racism, but it also allowed Edmonia to maintain intimate relationships with European women. Known for sporting "her own androgynous dress," Edmonia was part of a lesbian artists collective in Rome. She breached racial and sexual boundaries in her life and art, and was renowned for her provocative marble statues. Edmonia Lewis would become the first Black woman to receive widespread, international acclaim in the fine arts.[29]

As Charlotte and Edmonia performed their work in education and art during the war, slavery's legal end was on the horizon and occurred in April 1865. Enslaved people throughout the US recalled the first time they were told they were free. Many celebrated with jubilation when they heard the Confederates surrendered. Some had been waiting since 1863, when they thought Lincoln's Emancipation Proclamation had freed enslaved people in the Confederacy, but enslavers in those rebel states refused to recognize Lincoln as their president. Recall that Harriet Barrett, who worked as a cook with her slaveholder in New Orleans, was afraid when the war ended: "I's most scared to death when de war end. Us still in New Orleans and all de shoutin' dat took place 'cause us free! Dey crowds on de streets and was in a stir jus' as thick as flies on de dog. Massa say I's free as him, but iffen I wants to cook for him and missy I gits $2.50 de month, so I cooks for him till I marries Armstead Barrett, and then us farm for de livin'. Us have big church weddin' and I has white loyal dress and black brogan shoes. Us been married 51 years now."[30]

Legalizing their unions, earning a wage, and receiving an education were the top priorities of newly freed African Americans. Some fled the plantations and farms that represented the sites of their enslavement, others stayed and worked for their former enslavers. "After freedom come, us stays right on with massa and missus," recalled Millie Forward, of Jasper, Texas, who had labored in the army camps. She and her family were fortunate because their former slaveholder taught them "school at night." But the lessons did not last long. Just as they were learning their "A, B, Cs" and "how to spell cat and dog and n_____," their enslaver became frustrated with them and refused to teach any more lessons.[31]

Not all formerly enslaved women chose to remain on their enslavers' plantations. Take for instance the testimony of Sarah Ford, interviewed in Houston. "When freedom come, I didn't know what dat was," she explained. Her uncle came to the yard and yelled, "'Everybody free, everybody free,' and purty soon sojers comes and de captain reads a 'mation." She was tickled when the military officer quieted her owner. "Dat one time Massa Charley can't open he mouth, 'cause de captain tell him to shut up, dat he'd do de talkin'. Den de captain say, 'I come to tell you de slaves is free and you don't have to call nobody master no more.'" Despite the good news, Ford made an observation similar to one made by other formerly enslaved people: they were "turned out like cattle." Ford said, "Well, us jus' mill 'round like cattle do." Her former enslaver said they were all welcome to stay, except for Ford's father, who was a "bad" influence. So, Ford recalled, "Papa left but come back with a wagon and mules what he borrows and loads mama and my sister and me in and us go to East Columbia on de Brazos river and settles down. Dey hires me out and us have our own patch, too, and dat de fust time I ever seed any money. Papa builds a cabin and a corn crib and us sho' happy, 'cause de bright light done come and dey no more whippin's."[32]

The desire to live independently and have a space to work were obviously priorities of Ford's father. Molly Farrell, another enslaved woman in Texas, said, "Everybody talk 'bout freedom and hope to git free 'fore dey die." However, she recalled, "Me and my mother lef' right off. . . . Most everybody else go with us. We all walk down de road singin' and shoutin' to beat de band. My father come nex' day and jine us."[33]

When freedom came, in April 1865, not all enslaved people even knew they had been granted their liberty. At ninety years old, Betty Farrow of Fort Worth testified, "I don' 'member bein' tol' I's free. We'uns stayed right dere on de farm 'cause it was de only home we knew and no reason to go. I stays dere till I's twenty-seven years ole, den I marries and my husban' rents land."[34] After the last battle occurred in Texas, the Battle of Palminto Ranch near Brownsville, on May 13, 1865, enslaved people in the Lone Star State were not aware the war was over. Many did not know until June 19, 1865, when General Order 3 was issued:

> The people of Texas are informed that in accordance with a proclamation from the Executive of the United States slaves are free. This involves an absolute equality of personal rights and rights of property between former masters and slaves, and the connection heretofore existing between them becomes that between employer and hired labor.[35]

Sarah Ashley, interviewed in Goodrich, Texas, recalled that she "was 19 year old when de burst of freedom come in June and I git turn loose."[36] Likewise, former enslaved laborer Mary Edwards recollected the day she learned that she was free:

> One day my mother come after me, and she tol' me that I was free. This was durin' a June yes, June 19th. I can remember how glad I was. The people I worked fo' didn't have no slaves, and didn't believe in it. They paid me fo' my work, and my mawster got the money. The pusson I was workin' fo' tol me, Mary, you're free and I always believed the cullud folks should've been free long ago.[37]

This example echoes the mixed sentiment regarding slavery among Texas residents. The fact that enslaved people in the state found out about their liberty a few months after the war did not stop them from celebrating. The delayed date has become a state holiday known as "Juneteenth," and it is celebrated in approximately thirty-eight states and in other parts of the world. An early Juneteenth celebration in Austin was described as follows:

> About 11 o'clock the procession was formed in the lower part of the city and marched through the Avenue to the barbecue grounds. It was headed by the marshal of the day, two drummers, and a flag bearer, holding aloft the stars and stripes. . . . Many of the men and horses were decorated with bright colored ribbons. They marched as men who felt their importance and knew the day they celebrated was one to be ever held in remembrance by them and their children.[38]

Juneteenth became an official holiday in Texas in 1980, marked as a day to celebrate Emancipation. Akin to those on the Fourth of July, Juneteenth festivities focus on freedom and remembering the history of slavery. Celebrations involve picnics, parades, barbeques, speeches, essay contests, and a host of family activities.

Although April 1865 marked the end of the Civil War (1861–1865), slavery was not legally abolished until the ratification of the Thirteenth Amendment of the US Constitution, on December 6, 1865. This legislation contained the following language: "Neither slavery nor involuntary servitude, except as punishment for a crime whereof the party shall have been duly convicted, shall exist within the United States or any place subject to their jurisdiction."[39]

Slavery as an institution came to an official end in the United States but not in Indian Territory (parts of present-day Oklahoma, Arkansas, and Texas). In Confederate-occupied parts of these regions, Choctaw elders offered some comfort to laboring Black women, despite the fact that abolition was not in force. The Choctaw created a "Mammy's quarters," or women's room, used for enslaved women to prepare meals; in this case, the enslaved cook made "delicious venison and made some genuine Indian corn-bread." Black women's labor extended beyond the official confines of the United States into regions not considered sovereign because of the indigenous populations that were forcibly removed there at the beginning of the nineteenth century. The Choctaw chief noted that they had a "number of slaves," but more important, he boasted that the enslaved people "know nothing whatever of the prospects of early freedom, there were servants to attend our slightest want." When a small group of white women traveled to the area, including Mrs. Francena Martin Sutton, they noted that the region had been hardly affected by the Civil War. The women living there did not feel threatened, and they had few worries or chores. There was an active enslaved population there of about eight thousand because "the Thirteenth Amendment was not yet effective in those parts," and it would not be for at least one more year.[40]

In 1865 Congress passed yet more important legislation. The Bureau of Refugees, Freedman, and Abandoned Lands (the Freedmen's Bureau) was created to help *loyal* Southern citizens recover from the Civil War. This recovery would take a long time, because the war was one of the bloodiest in American history with approximately seven hundred thousand casualties.[41] Freedmen's Bureau agents were to help the Southerners, including the formerly enslaved, negotiate labor contracts, and they were charged with helping families recover from the property, personal, and financial losses suffered during the war. The bureau's work mirrored some of the work done at Port Royal by educators such as Charlotte Forten Grimké.

News of abolition brought former runaways back to the United States, even to the South. After going on an abolition tour in Europe and raising their five children in freedom, William and Ellen Craft returned to Georgia and established a school for newly freed enslaved people. Likewise, Susie King Taylor worked with other Black women educators in Savannah, Georgia, to create schools for students of all ages. African Americans recognized and understood the importance and privilege of receiving an education.

Just as Texans began celebrating Juneteenth in 1866, a turning point in post-Emancipation race relations occurred that impacted African American communities throughout the United States. This was the year that states issued the Black Codes and the Ku Klux Klan was founded, in Pulaski, Tennessee.

The Black Codes were a series of laws passed in most Confederate states. These restrictive laws were designed to limit the freedom of African Americans and to promote and maintain white supremacy. Some of the codes emulated the slave codes of the eighteenth century. Most African Americans were required to have jobs as agricultural workers and any violators could be imprisoned. If they wanted to have an occupation that did not resemble the labor performed during slavery, freed women and men had to purchase and apply for a license. Black Codes also restricted loitering and contained clauses that prevented freed people from assembling without the presence of a white person. Many forms of punishment for noncompliance resembled forms of punishment practiced during slavery.

In addition to the Thirteenth and Fourteenth Amendments, which abolished slavery and guaranteed citizenship by birth and equal protection under the law, respectively, the Civil Rights Act of 1866 eliminated the Black Codes. The act contained ten clauses that essentially guaranteed and protected citizenship for those born in the United States, "excluding Indians." It provided specific language that "such citizens, of every race and color, without regard to any previous condition of slavery or involuntary servitude, except as punishment for a crime. . . shall have the same right, in every State and Territory of the United States," including Indian territory.[42]

When Congress ratified the Fifteenth Amendment, in 1870, granting universal male suffrage, it also marked the steep decline of sustained, cooperative organizing between Black and white female suffragists. Although a number of Black female suffragists were also opposed to having only men obtain the franchise, white women suffragists unleashed racist diatribes as they vehemently opposed Black men being able to vote before them. Elizabeth Cady Stanton declared that she could not have "ignorant Negroes and foreigners make laws for her to obey." Bigotry aside, Sojourner Truth was herself deeply opposed to the measure as well. She believed in women's rights and feared enfranchising only Black men would make Black women subject to them, that somehow Black men would replace white masters. Truth said that she wished she could "sojourn once to the ballot-box before I die." Unfortunately, she would not get her wish. Sojourner Truth died on November 26, 1883, about forty years before the passage of the Nineteenth Amendment. Though her dream to vote was not realized, she had risen from enslavement "and found her level among the purest and the best."[43]

RETURNING TO MARY COLBERT, who hid treasured possessions in her apron during the war, we learn of a common experience of formerly enslaved people: their enslavers hardly respected them. Describing what happened after Union soldiers invaded the house where she was enslaved, Colbert stated, "After the Yankees were gone, I gave it all back to Miss Fannie, *and she didn't give me the first penny.*" Clearly Colbert and many other formerly enslaved people expected to be rewarded for their loyalty. "When news came that the Negroes had been freed," she later reflected, "there was a happy jubilee." In fact, her owner, John Crawford, survived the war and "explained the new freedom to his slaves." Colbert said, "We were glad and sorry too. My mother stayed with Marse John until he died. . . . It wasn't so long after the surrender before the schools for Negroes were opened." Mary went on to marry Isaac Dixon of Alabama, and after he died, John Colbert of Mississippi. Her final thoughts about freedom: "It was God's will that we should be freed."[44]

CHAPTER SIX

FRANCES'S SEX AND THE DAWNING OF THE BLACK WOMAN'S ERA, 1876–1915

None of your d___ business.

—FRANCES THOMPSON

IN 1876 FRANCES THOMPSON, a formerly enslaved Black woman, was arrested in Memphis, Tennessee, and fined $50. She had migrated to the area about a decade earlier—at the time, maybe full of hope and excitement as she began her new life as a free woman in the city. She made friends and lived in a booming Black community. She liked nice dresses, especially those in bright colors. In 1866 she would survive the extraordinary violence that decimated her neighborhood. Just a year after Emancipation, Frances would testify before a congressional committee. One of five Black women to tell their stories that day, Frances, who relied on crutches because of a foot malady, described how she had been robbed and gang-raped by a group of white men, at least two policemen among them. The men burst into the home she shared with another Black woman, Lucy Smith, and savaged them both. As Frances testified, "They drew their pistols and said they would shoot us and fire the house if we did not let them have their way with us." The Memphis Riot, sparked in part by white rage at Black Union soldiers, claimed over forty African American lives, as well as ninety-one homes, four churches, and twelve schools, the latter all set ablaze. Untold numbers of Black women and girls likely suffered the same fate as had Frances. But Frances and the other women followed in the footsteps of Black women who reported soldiers' crimes during the Civil War. Specifically, they went on record to state unequivocally that they did not *consent*.[1]

The published congressional report laid bare whites' cruelties, and locally, Frances Thompson became persona non grata. For the next decade she would endure police harassment, accused of everything from distributing "hoodoo bags" and telling fortunes to being responsible for "infamous traffic as a procuress and keeper of one of the vilest dens in the city." And there were more serious allegations. According to the *Memphis Public Ledger*, Frances had been "arrested several times on suspicion of being a man, and notorious lewdness, but always managed to escape the clutches of the law." However, in July 1876, she did not get away. Though Frances maintained that she was "of double sex," a local white doctor, doubtful of her claims, had her arrested and after subjecting her to a series of invasive examinations by four white physicians, told authorities that her true sex was male.[2] What did these examinations mean for Frances? One wonders how she coped with such violations.

Frances had lived at least twenty years as a woman, donning ladies' hats and gingham overskirts with petticoats—attire fashionable for her day. The finding that her sex was male forced her into men's clothes and onto a male chain gang. Whereas Frances had maintained a smooth face, in custody authorities denied her the ability to shave as the *Days' Doings* noted, "a thick black beard is coming out all over his face, to his great disgust." As a free woman, Frances had cleaved out a life for herself, weathering seasons that might find her "almost in rags" or draped in "the finest kind of loud-colored toggery." Behind bars, she suffered but never lost her fight, answering rude questions about her gender by responding, "None of your d____ business." When Frances worked the chain gang, large crowds gathered to ridicule her. So much so that officers had no choice but to remove her from the line. She was eventually forced to work as a "washerman" inside the stationhouse. Further, the news of her "male sex" was used to discredit her earlier testimony as well as that of the other women. Frances survived her months in custody, though she took ill shortly after her release and died later that year, in November 1876.[3]

Reconstruction died a year later, in the Compromise of 1877. Whites had grown tired of defending Black rights, and white hate groups like the Ku Klux Klan (KKK) continued a reign of terror to discourage African American men from voting. The political battle waged between Republicans and Democrats during the election fiasco of 1876 would end with the Republican nominee, Rutherford B. Hayes, taking office. As part of that agreement, however, Hayes withdrew federal troops from the South and allowed former confederate states to rejoin the Union, largely on their own terms—which for them meant a return to the wholesale oppression of Black women, men, and children.

It was a chaotic era. Enslavement had barely ended and Reconstruction proved fleeting, even though the government affirmed Black citizenship with the Fourteenth Amendment and gave Black men the right to vote with the Fifteenth. This period found Black women aiming to lay claim to freedom just as racist whites and various state representatives were actively doing everything to strip them of it. What were Black women's interpretations of freedom? Frances's life offers important evidence of Black women's strong desires to celebrate and define Black womanhood on their own terms—against white supremacy, patriarchy, and restrictive gender identities. Her story also lifts the veil on a hidden aspect of Black women's history, one that shows how race, gender, sexuality, and notions of freedom mixed in deeply complicated ways. The years after Frances's death are further inflected with the same spirit of courageousness, as Black middle-class women would come to regard this moment as marking a new era for African American womanhood. Beyond controlling their own wombs and choosing their own marital partners, Black women, whether preening in attention-grabbing outfits or wrapped in pristine white as holiness saints, seized upon citizenship. They established organizations, clubs, and businesses; some fought for reparations and the rights of workers, and a few even honed their creative talents to critical acclaim—all against a backdrop of shrinking rights and political access, intensifying sexual violence and criminalization, and, for many, crippling poverty.[4]

IN 1884 A YOUNG MEMPHIS RESIDENT, Ida B. Wells, physically fought the white conductor who ejected her from the ladies' car, later writing, "The moment he caught hold of my arm I fastened my teeth in the back of his hand." Just like her colonial and antebellum predecessors, Wells tried to use the courts to defend Black civil rights. She sued the railroad company and won. Wells's loss on appeal, however, was a gloomy harbinger of even more devastating verdicts to come. The landmark court decision *Plessy v. Ferguson* in 1896, ushered in Jim Crow segregation by finding that separate facilities for Blacks and whites did not violate the Constitution provided the accommodations were equal (though in practice the latter was never the case). The verdict occurred in tandem with stringent employment discrimination and relentless voter suppression tactics such as the poll tax, a hefty fee to cast a ballot that few Southerners (Black or white) could afford. Combined with a campaign of racist violence meted out by groups like the Knights of the White Camelia and the KKK, the turn of the twentieth century witnessed the implementation of a kind of lethal, second-class citizenship for African Americans.[5]

Prior to Emancipation, most lynching victims were white men—enslaved Black bodies possessed a monetary value, so one could not just go and lynch another white man's or white woman's property. Freedom, ironically, removed this deterrent, and without it, Black women and men suffered tremendously in the void. Black women like Mrs. Laura Nelson, who died at the end of a noose off of a hangman's bridge in Okemah, Oklahoma, in 1911, were lost to the terror. Laura died alongside her young son, after a group of white men kidnapped them from the jail where the two had been held awaiting murder charges for the fatal shooting of a white deputy. Authorities had come to their home believing that Laura's husband had stolen a cow, a skirmish ensued, and Whites accused Laura's son of killing the officer. Laura was also charged with murder because she allegedly grabbed the gun used in the shooting. Raped before she was murdered, Laura Nelson joined roughly 200 other Black female lynching victims and 2,500 Black male victims, primarily in the South. Over 3,500 African Americans were lynched between 1877 and 1950 nationwide.[6]

White men used false claims that Black male lynching victims had raped white women, but a number of Black female lynching victims met their end resisting white rapists. In the case of seventeen-year-old Marie Scott, in 1914, a white lynch mob murdered Marie and her brother after he killed one of the two white men who violated her in Wagoner County, Oklahoma. Such attacks, coupled with their alarming frequency, led thousands of African Americans to go west. Many successfully formed all-Black communities in places like Nicodemus, Kansas; Mound Bayou, Mississippi; and Langston, Oklahoma.[7]

But flight was not the only response to the racist tides of white violence. Ida B. Wells, who had grown into a renowned journalist and militant social justice activist, fearlessly canvassed the South, investigating lynchings and publishing the true facts surrounding the murders of Black women and men. In her newspaper, the *Memphis Free Speech*, and in two published reports, *Southern Horrors* (1892) and *A Red Record* (1895), Wells, the daughter of formerly enslaved Black people from Holly Springs, Mississippi, exposed the white lies undergirding mainstream excuses for mob violence. Wells found that often Black men and women who challenged white supremacy in some way, whether by creating businesses that rivaled those of whites or failing to adhere to brute white passions, were targeted for murder.

Further, Wells found that some of the instances labelled as rape were, in fact, consensual liaisons between white women and Black men. In an editorial in the *Memphis Free Speech* she wrote, "Nobody in this section of the country believes the old threadbare lie that Negro men rape white women. If Southern white men are not careful, they will overreach themselves and . . . a conclusion will then be reached which will be very damaging to the moral reputation of their women." For her scathing candor, whites placed a bounty on her head and destroyed her printing press.[8]

Death threats compelled Wells to leave the South, but she continued her work. Not only did she maintain her antilynching campaign, but Wells also worked together with other liked-minded Black women, helping to found organizations such as the National Association of Colored Women (NACW) in 1896. Regarded as the first national African American civil rights organization, in short order the NACW swelled to twenty-eight federations and over a thousand clubs, and boasted a membership that was fifty thousand strong. Black women also created clubs within churches such as the Women's Convention (WC), an auxiliary group of the National Baptist Convention. Black women founded Greek-letter organizations such as the Alpha Kappa Alpha sorority in 1908 and Delta Sigma Theta in 1913.[9] African American clubwomen worked tirelessly on behalf of Black women and Black communities. Elite and middle-class Black women such as Mary Church Terrell, who served as the inaugural president of the NACW, also protested lynching, routinely decried racist double-standards in the criminal justice system, and fought for female suffrage.

The NACW helped organize masses of Black suffragists who started voter-education clubs, created and submitted petitions, and volunteered on local campaigns. As historian Paula Giddings writes, "By the 1900s, Black suffrage clubs were to be found all over the country, including Tuskegee, St. Louis, Los Angeles, Memphis, Boston, Charleston, and New Orleans, and there were state suffrage societies in Delaware, Idaho, Montana, North Dakota, Texas, New York, and Maryland, among others."[10] Black suffragists' zeal and commitment would be matched by Black clubwomen's labors on behalf of those African Americans who were less fortunate.

Organizing food drives, creating settlement homes for women and children, Black clubwomen fund-raised to support charitable efforts for the poor. Their organizations also helped finance social justice campaigns such as the antilynching efforts of Ida B. Wells (after her marriage she would go by Wells-Barnett). They also made the protection and elevation of Black women a top priority. Imbued with Christian religious values, clubwomen pushed back against damaging national stereotypes about Black women's supposed lack of morality. They called out white hypocrisy, as well as what they felt was Black men's often inadequate defense of their honor.

Indeed, many were unabashedly critical of Black male leadership—leadership that some believed too timid and accommodating at a time that demanded fortitude and fight. In 1894 Victoria Earle Matthews, an editor for the Black women's newspaper *Woman's Era* promoted voices that challenged Black men to either "sell out, transfer their books, etc., over to the women, and a great change would come over us . . . or do better generally than they have done for the past twenty years." The paper also printed resolutions from the National Colored Women's Congress in 1896, which boldly declared, "We condemn every form of lawlessness and miscarriage of justice, and demand, without favor or compromise, the equal enforcement of the law for all classes of American citizens."[11]

The tensions embedded in their activism, however, existed not just with respect to racist whites or chauvinistic Black men. Black clubwomen sometimes, in their zeal to "uplift" their race, patronized poor and working-class Black people. The women practiced respectability, which was a blended social and political ideology that aimed to combat racism and Black women's sexual assault by embracing Christian morality and notions of chastity and purity, a strong work ethic, and proper social etiquette. However, in their adherence to the politics of respectability, clubwomen sometimes unwittingly affirmed negative stereotypes about African Americans. For example, members of the WC circulated leaflets, pamphlets, and even went knocking on doors to educate everyday Black folk about the evils of such things as chewing gum, talking loudly (especially on streetcars), wearing bright or otherwise gaudy attire, having messy front yards, and carousing to jazz or loafing on street corners or in jook joints.[12]

Clubwomen, like most African American women, labored to carve out a space for themselves as respectable wives and mothers but also as earners, writers, and political leaders. They made valuable intellectual contributions to ongoing discussions about racial advancement. Critical to that project was reclaiming Black womanhood. They acknowledged their history of enslavement at the same time that they affirmed their own humanity and equality. Fannie Barrier Williams's sentiments perhaps best embody this approach, as she wrote, in 1904, "I believe that the colored women are just as strong and just as weak as any other women with like education, training, and environment."[13]

Black clubwomen supported and encouraged each other as they gathered in packed halls, church basements, and each other's homes to read, talk, laugh, and practice speeches that documented their achievements, and pursued more ways to advance political causes. In her speech at the NACW biennial, in Detroit in 1907, Mary Church Terrell told a captivated audience, "Colored women need not hang their heads in shame. . . . There is scarcely a service which colored women can render their race that they are not actually performing or trying to perform."[14] Other speakers directly called for African American women to be the stewards of their own destinies, not only for their own sakes but also because Black women are the barometer by which the soundness of the race could best be measured. This philosophy is embedded in Anna Julia Cooper's pivotal book *A Voice from the South* (1892): "Only the BLACK WOMAN can say 'when and where I enter, in the quiet undisputed dignity of my womanhood, without violence and without suing or special patronage, then and there the whole Negro race enters with me.'"[15] Cooper's words were more than just aspirational platitudes.

The economic landscape for the masses of Black people meant that not only were African American women expected to attend to the overall well-being of their households but also that their labor was critical to their families' survival. In rural parts of the country, where Black families were concentrated in sharecropping, African American women hustled to bring in additional "side money." Whether taking in laundry, peddling homemade goods, telling fortunes, and possibly selling gris-gris bags, as Frances Thompson is alleged to have done, or doing day work as domestics, their supplemental income kept Black families afloat. It also likely contributed to the small percentage of Black farmers, roughly 15 percent, who owned their own land.[16]

Black women worked hard and consistently, often under unfair and degrading circumstances. In Louisiana, for instance, African American women endured grueling conditions for little pay as sugar plantation owners collaborated with one another to keep wages down. Black women earned only fifty cents a day for sweating it out in cane fields; Black men's pay was not much better, as they received a meager sixty-five cents per day. Because of Black women's and men's paltry earnings, most families—the majority of them two-parent households—continually lived on the brink of financial abyss. Agricultural yields varied across the South, and economic conditions between 1880 and 1915 were so precarious that any misfortune—drought, heavy rains, fluctuations in market prices—could easily move a family from poverty to downright starvation.[17] Black rural women were hardly alone in their financial misery.

Just as they did during enslavement, African American women laboring in urban centers in the South and North also vigorously tried to steel themselves against hardships. In Atlanta, Black washerwomen organized collectively for better wages, even going on strike as early as 1881. They networked to stabilize costs for their services, and they put the word out on harsh or unfair employers. Laundry work was among the most labor-intensive forms of domestic service, often requiring the use of homemade lye soap for scrubbing clothes against a metal washboard before pressing with irons heated over open flames. However, many Black women preferred it to housekeeping because it allowed them to work from their own homes, where they could enlist the help of children and other family members.[18]

Domestic servants, those working in white homes, were under scrutiny and subject to the more taxing demands of their employers. "I live a treadmill life," declared one Black woman in the *Independent* in 1912. As she detailed the hours she spent working at the beck and call of her young white charges, she also bemoaned conditions for most African Americans, noting the quality of life for "poor colored people is just as bad as, if not worse than, it was during the days of slavery. Tho today we are enjoying nominal freedom, we are literally slaves."[19] Sometimes responsible for everything from cooking and cleaning to childcare, those who lived-in missed their families and worked long hours for low pay. While opportunities in clerical work and even positions in factories were opening up for white and European immigrant women, African American women were systematically barred from these opportunities. White employers did not want to hire them, and those who attempted to do so faced heavy resistance from white female employees who refused to work alongside Black women.

For more skilled or educated Black women, opportunities for better-paying employment beyond dressmaking, nursing, and teaching were rare. Mary Church Terrell lamented how few career options were available to Black women, even in the nation's capital: "It matters not what my intellectual attainments may be or how great is the need of the services of a competent person, if I try to enter many of the numerous vocations in which my white sisters are allowed to engage, the door is shut in my face."[20] The rejection could be devastating, but Black women resisted these restrictions.

Small numbers of Black women even managed to break through, so that by the early part of the twentieth century, "160 Black female physicians, seven dentists, ten lawyers, 164 ministers, assorted journalists, writers, artists, 1,185 musicians and teachers of music, and 13,525 school instructors" existed in the United States. Some even moved into areas of finance, as Maggie Lena Walker did, founding in 1903 and heading the first Black-owned bank in the country, in Richmond, Virginia. The St. Luke Penny Savings Bank had Walker at the helm with several female board members. Historian Shennette Garrett-Scott explains, "As black women built, ran, and patronized the St. Luke Bank, they helped construct and alternately deconstruct discourses about race, risk, and rights."[21]

African American women also seized upon education in an attempt to escape low-skilled wage work and as a way to serve Black communities. A number of Black women either founded or headed Black schools. For example, famed educators Nannie Helen Burroughs and Anna Julia Cooper served as the principals of institutions that educated generations of Black students. In Cooper's case, however, her appointment was not entirely without controversy, as some initially doubted her ability to supervise male students and male faculty.[22] Though teaching held a great many rewards, and was regarded as a middle-class occupation, a number of Black educators struggled to make ends meet. Even as Black educators fund-raised tirelessly to support these institutions and themselves, it was not uncommon for Black teachers to also be the beneficiaries of the community's charity or to take on other work to supplement their incomes.

Black women preachers and wives of clergyman, too, strenuously organized relief efforts to sustain community members and their ministries. Often, Black female congregants worked long hours, usually without compensation, on behalf of religious bodies. Typically representing the majority of Black congregations in the early twentieth century (historians estimate that African American women accounted for anywhere from 60 to 90 percent of Black church membership), these women effectively shaped the Black community's social and moral development. As Nannie Helen Burroughs said of the Black woman: "She carries the burdens of the Church, and of the school and she bears a great deal more than her economic share in the home."[23] Those pressures and responsibilities made Black women's employment obstacles that much more of a hardship.

In response to their limited job prospects, thousands of Black women found economic and political autonomy in storefronts and the back parlors of their homes, where they ran their own beauty shops. Incredibly skilled at transforming their marginalization into opportunities for expansion, African American women turned their exclusion from mainstream beauty culture into a million-dollar industry that they dominated. Enterprising Black women such as Sarah Breedlove (also known as Madame C. J. Walker) and Annie Turnbo Malone developed beauty and hair-care products specifically for African American women and became self-made millionaires in the process. As historian Tiffany Gill has shown, by developing these products, Black female entrepreneurs created good jobs for other working-class Black women, especially those who could not afford to go to college or obtain nursing degrees.[24]

Black beauty culture also invented new avenues for Black women to love and adorn themselves, while also creating new spaces for political discussions and grassroots activism. Amidst the sound of hot-combs sizzling, masses of Black women used beauty parlors as sites to explore and share their ideological platforms. To be clear, these were dynamic and sometimes contested sites. When purveyors of straightened hair and skin-lightening creams faced criticism that they were conforming to white beauty standards, Madame Walker insisted, "I want the great masses of my people to take greater pride in their personal appearance and to give their hair proper attention."[25] Walker, who was also concerned about the health of Black women's hair, believed that a neatly coiffed hairdo might also improve Black women's chances at securing employment. Unconvinced, Nannie Helen Burroughs remained a critic of the industry and said, "What every woman who bleaches and straightens out needs is not her appearance changed, but her mind."[26] The friction pointed both to the tensions surrounding "colorphobia" within the Black community and to Black women's efforts to craft their own kind of modern style. It also marked social anxieties about African American women's growing visibility in public spaces.

A steady stream of Southern migrants settled in Mid-Atlantic, Western, and Northern cities, with single Black female travelers prominently among them. African American reformers worried about the implications, fretting about unwed Black women populating urban landscapes. Harsh rebukes came from Black men such as William Hannibal Thomas, who denounced African American women as "lascivious by instinct and in bondage to physical pleasure." Thomas further derided Black women as lazy and materialistic, and he accused Black mothers of raising their daughters under such lax moral conditions that they effectively hastened Black girls' "early transition from purity to concubinage." His stinging insults would not go unanswered, as Black women decried him as a traitor and an ignoramus who did the bidding of racist white men. Fannie Barrier Williams caustically noted, "How rare are the reported instances of colored men resenting any slur or insult upon their own women."[27]

Yet as the numbers of Black female migrants grew in cities such as Philadelphia and New York, as well as in urban centers in the South, Black clubwomen, along with well-known Black male leaders such as W. E. B. Du Bois, bemoaned their presence. Regarding Black female migrants as largely naive and uncouth, Black reformers worried that single Black women would be easily seduced by unscrupulous men who might lead them to the seedier parts of town—areas littered with bars, brothels, and gambling parlors, as well as into areas where they might engage in all manner of sexual activities—sex outside of marriage, adulterous sex, queer sex, and sex for money. Such behaviors would reflect poorly on the race, it was thought, and would potentially harm uplift efforts designed to show how African Americans fit into mainstream society.[28]

Black people were not the only ones worried. White middle-class reformer Frances Kellor founded the National League for the Protection of Colored Women in 1906, and prominent Black clubwoman Sarah Willie Layten served as the league's first field secretary. Representing a range of concerns, from those seeking to protect Black women to those aiming to protect the city from them, league members met Black women at bus depots and train stations. With chapters primarily in the Northeast, reformers, worried that Black female migrants might fall prey to dishonest employment agencies or fast-talking confidence men, worked to connect the women to legitimate jobs and decent housing. Reformers also harbored fears that newly arrived Black women would succumb to the sordid side of city life and choose urban crime.[29] However well-intentioned Black reformers might have been, such efforts nonetheless condescended to poor and working-class Black women. Moreover, the efforts did little to dissuade curious Black women from taking part in what reformers viewed as harmful urban pastimes.

Many Black women chose to frequent corridors with clubs that played ragtime and blues, that sold beer by the bucket, and that had scores of sweaty young women and men dancing until late hours. The dancehalls and jook joints were popular, as most Black women struck a balance between the drudgery of their work lives with the merriment of bars, parties, parks, and dime shows. Even so, concerns about "illicit sex" were not entirely without merit, as some urban haunts facilitated not only drinking and dancing but also allowed prostitution.

Some Black women did enter the sex trade, and there were many reasons for it. Some did so out of economic necessity, though other African American women preferred it to other work because it afforded more autonomy and better pay than scrubbing floors. Mostly working out of brothels in so-called tenderloin sections of cities, Black madams and Black prostitutes performed a variety of sex acts for cash. Black madams in Chicago and Philadelphia controlled much of the Black sex trade in the late nineteenth century. Such parlors were sporadically policed, running with little interference from authorities. But when social attitudes and urban geographies shifted in the early twentieth century, sex workers, especially streetwalkers, found themselves under heavy police surveillance and increasingly under arrest in vice raids. However, while some Black women prostitutes served time, the majority of Black women who landed in prisons and penitentiaries were there for crimes against property—a trend that occurred in all states.[30]

Even as inmates, Black women raised their voices against unimaginable conditions. Lulu Sanders, a former Texas prisoner, wrote begging the governor to investigate Black women's inhumane treatment explaining, "When they whip poor women they tie [their] clothes up over their heads and expose their [nakedness] to all the guards and in some cases I have seen some of the women during their monthly period have been whipped so bad until they have had to [scrub] the floor after them." After Reconstruction, across the South a system of convict leasing took hold, as local whites reconfigured criminal justice to curtail Black freedom. Using vagrancy laws to criminalize and limit Black mobility, thousands of African Americans, including disproportionate numbers of Black women, effectively found themselves in bondage to the state. Black women prisoners helped rebuild the South as convict labor pioneered modern business industries in the region. Working in camps or on chain gangs, as many Black female prisoners did in the South, proved particularly perilous. Georgia convicts worked "sun to sun, rain or shine," and as historian Talitha LeFlouria explains, imprisoned African American women worked in railroad camps, brickyards, chain gangs, lumber mills, plantations, washhouses, barns, and "big houses," in addition to being "terrorized, whipped, raped, and emotionally bruised."[31] Conditions in prisons and penitentiaries elsewhere in the country were also dire.

African American women served sentences in squalid, rat-infested cellblocks where they were vulnerable to violence and sexual assault. Further, nationwide, Black women and Black men were disproportionately imprisoned, though numbers proved especially stark for African American women. For example, although Black people only accounted for 2 percent of the Midwest population in 1880, they accounted for 12 percent of all state prisoners; 12 percent of male prisoners were Black men, while 30 percent of incarcerated females were Black women. In the Northeast in 1900, where, again, African Americans made up approximately 2 percent of the population, they accounted for roughly 13 percent of all state prisoners, with Black women accounting for 18 percent of female prisoners and Black male prisoners making up 12 percent of incarcerated males. Conditions were most severe in the South, where African Americans accounted for 30 percent of the population and 74 percent of the region's prisoners; Black men accounted for 73 percent of incarcerated men, and a staggering 90 percent of incarcerated women were African American.[32]

African American women's high concentration in unskilled work in particular contributed to their overrepresentation in the criminal justice system, as domestic service arguably operated as an early pipeline to prison. The work kept Black women impoverished at the same time that it placed them in proximity to ample food, warm clothing, and other valuables in employers' homes. Sometimes desperate housekeepers did steal. But Black servants were also especially vulnerable to false accusations of theft. As one Black washerwoman remarked, "White folks tend to lose what they ain't never had." And when said items went missing, if white employers called in the law, all too often Black women would be convicted by all-white juries and harshly sentenced by white judges.[33]

Moreover, though the justice system quickly served up lengthy sentences for African American women, it routinely failed to police crimes against them. Under the circumstances, an absence of protection left Black women particularly vulnerable. They often encountered sexual violence and sexual harassment but had few avenues for legal redress. As one Southern Black woman explained, "I have had a clerk in a store hold my hand as I gave him the money for some purchase and utter some vile request; a shoe man take liberties, a man in a crowd to place his hands on my person, others to follow me to my very door, a school director to assure me a position if I did his bidding." Given the climate, Black women had to be prepared to defend themselves, both against random attacks from lurid strangers but also in cases of domestic violence. Yet if that defense left would-be assailants or batterers grievously injured, the same system that denied Black women protection proved all too willing to punish them for self-defense. Frustration at the state of affairs could be paralyzing, as one Black woman decried the fact that, "on one hand, we are assailed by white men, and, on the other hand, we are assailed by Black men, who should be our natural protectors." The struggles, hardships, and dangers that awaited Black women were certainly palpable, and their despair about it was real.[34] Some Black women decided to live outside the law precisely because they felt there was no way for Black women to survive playing by fixed rules in a broken society. But the overwhelming majority of Black women did not.

As in the past, they worked together, they held to their faith, and some Black women turned to the arts to find and create beauty in their worlds.

OFTEN REFERRED TO as the "Black Patti," Matilda Sissieretta Jones's prolific musical career began in her father's African Methodist Episcopal church. Born in Portsmouth, Virginia, in 1868, she moved with her family to Providence, Rhode Island, in 1876. The family likely chose to exit Portsmouth as Reconstruction collapsed, though Providence was hardly free of racism. Yet through her rich musical gifts, Jones was able to study at the Providence Academy of Music in 1883 and, two years later, at the New England Conservatory of Music, in Boston. Her impressive vocal talents would find her soon performing before enchanted crowds in renowned music halls, prestigious venues, and even at the White House, where she would sing for Presidents Benjamin Harrison, William McKinley, Grover Cleveland, and Theodore Roosevelt. Jones traveled abroad and toured the Caribbean, visiting a number of nations, including Jamaica, Panama, Barbados, Venezuela, and British Guiana (now Guyana), with the Tennessee Jubilee Singers in 1888 and the Star Tennessee Jubilee Singers in 1890. She also performed in Europe, gracing stages in London, Berlin, Paris, Milan, and Saint Petersburg.[35] Popular amusements such as minstrelsy, vaudeville, and burlesque shows had mass appeal, though Jones maintained a passion for classical music and opera.

With her thick, straightened hair swept up, dressed in a fine gown, and bathed in jewels, audiences eagerly awaited Jones's performances, as she was adored for her beauty and vocal talents. By the 1890s, Black performers had cultivated a kind of "ragtime operetta," as well as musical comedy shows. Jones's career evolved, from singing in the Black Patti Troubadours, an ensemble company that sang, danced, and juggled, to headlining the Black Patti Musical Company in 1909. However, in 1915 Matilda Sissieretta Jones disbanded her company and returned to Providence to take care of her ailing mother. Jones stopped singing professionally but stayed active in her church choir until her death, in 1933. Though she traveled the world and graced stages in top venues, at the time of her death, Jones had few resources.[36]

If women such as Frances Thompson and Sissieretta Jones have anything in common with the masses of their sistren, it's that poverty stubbornly dogged Black women's best efforts at advancement. Economic instability remained a serious problem. To address it, some Black women threw themselves into fund-raising for their community, while others confronted poverty's structural roots. Callie House, who had been enslaved in Tennessee, was especially aggrieved by the abject living conditions of older formerly enslaved women and men. A widow and working mother of five, Callie was an early champion for reparations in the United States by urging the formerly enslaved to petition the government for pensions. She canvassed the South, raising funds to support the National Ex-Slave Mutual Relief, Bounty, and Pension Association, an organization officially chartered in 1898. The group relied heavily on the postal system to fund-raise and promote their advocacy. With Callie House's help, the association's membership ranks rose to 34,000, and by 1900, it had nearly 300,000 members nationwide.[37]

The movement for reparations gained some traction in the South among the freedmen and freedwomen, but middle-class Black people across the country tended to frown on the association's charge. Many among them had chosen to cast their lots with Black leaders such as

Booker T. Washington, whose prominence was aided by wealthy and powerful whites in part because he discouraged direct political challenges to white supremacy, favoring instead a politics of accommodation (publicly at least) and the belief that African Americans should pull themselves up by their bootstraps. Others believed reparations to be tantamount to some sort of scam. According to the *New York Times* in 1903, in an article that derided African Americans for expressing support for Senator Hanna's bill, seeking pensions for the ex-enslaved, it noted that "many intelligent negroes here are constantly warning the members of their race of the character of their scheme."[38]

Callie House's dedication to empowering poor and working-class African Americans and her advocacy for Black people's constitutional right to petition the government, also alarmed a variety of federal agencies. Though few seemed to seriously believe that the association's goal to provide pensions for "ex-slaves" would ever come to fruition, federal agents were nonetheless wary of the organizing taking place, as they regarded Callie and her ilk as troublemakers, even potential anarchists. Acting on these fears, the US Justice Department, US Treasury Department, and US Postal Service targeted and harassed the association. The postal service went so far as to deny the National Ex-Slave Mutual Relief, Bounty, and Pension Association their mail, claiming they had been using the mail to defraud already impoverished and vulnerable formerly enslaved citizens. These charges would find Callie House arrested in 1916 and, after refusing to take a plea, convicted and sentenced to one year in a prison in Jefferson City, Missouri. Callie's arrest largely curtailed the national reparations movement, though local branches remained active and attentive to the needs of its membership until the 1930s. House died of cancer in 1928.[39] Callie House's history helps reveal the diversity of Black women's political activism and the foundational role that Black women have played in the country's reparations movement.

Other examples of African American women's political diversity include women such as Lucy Parsons, the formerly enslaved progeny of a Black mother and a white enslaver. Parsons, who actually was an anarchist, defied restrictive notions of race, gender, and sexuality, and she was outspoken in her contempt for the wealthy and those authority figures who safeguarded them at the expense of the exploited masses of the working poor. Born in Virginia and freed in Texas following the

Civil War, Lucy began entertaining the affections of Albert Parsons, a white man and Confederate cavalry veteran. At age twenty-one, she, then going by the name Lucia Carter, married Parsons, who was six years older, in McClennan County, Texas, in 1872. Under mounting racial hostilities, the two moved to Chicago, and in the years to come Lucia would start using a new name and invoking a different racial heritage, one undertaken as her husband moved increasingly into the public eye because of his political labor advocacy. Lucy Parsons did not hesitate to embrace a historical narrative that erased her enslavement by claiming Mexican and Indigenous ancestry. Yet her radicalism nonetheless reflected her objections to the economic, social, and political imbalances brought about by enslavement.[40]

In Chicago, Lucy and Albert began roundly decrying "wage slavery," as well as adopting the rhetoric of far-left activists, particularly as the Parsonses gravitated toward socialism and advocated against the struggles of factory workers and immigrant laborers. Becoming increasingly militant, both Parsonses supported armed self-defense, and Lucy organized under charged slogans such as "No Masters, No Slaves." Historian Jacqueline Jones notes that Lucy began her lifelong writing career in 1878 when the *Socialist* published a series of her letters to the editor. In fiery rhetoric, she decried the "bloated aristocracy" and emerging "money-ocracy" that entrapped hardworking folk. Lucy considered the monied classes a thievish, greedy lot that had to be challenged and resisted. Outraged by the suffering of the working poor, the Parsonses incorporated anarchist ideologies, as Albert started writing for a radical San Francisco paper called *Truth*. He penned pieces such as "Dynamite: Plain Directions for Making It" and "Dynamite Will Be Used in America." As it turns out, the words would be prophetic ones.[41]

A bomb did go off.

On May 4, 1886, at a Chicago rally where both Lucy and her husband spoke, an explosion ripped through Haymarket Square. Eight policemen and several workers died, and nearly seventy more people were injured. The authorities immediately suspected the couple. In the end, Albert, along with three associates, would be tried and eventually hanged. Throughout her husband's trial, Lucy endured police harassment and vile charges in the press. Cursed as a "nigger" and characterized by a host of racist epithets, she battled harassment and constant scrutiny. Following Albert's death, Lucy remained active politically. She also had a number of illicit affairs with younger lovers, much to the chagrin of her fellow anarchists, who expected her to live the chastened life of a martyr's widow. Alas, Lucy hardly fit the bill. But she did keep up appearances. Emma Goldman considered Lucy a "hypocrite who followed free-love principles in her own life but spoke openly only of her desire for conventional respectability." Undaunted by the criticism, Lucy continued giving fiery speeches and engaging in free love. In 1893 the *New York Times* described her as giving an address "full of lurid pictures of famine and want, and thrilling exhortations to concerted action against the dominating capitalist that set her auditors in a frenzy of wild applause as she concluded." Living to the age of ninety-one, Lucy died in a house fire in 1942.[42]

FRANCES THOMPSON, everyday Black women, Black clubwomen, and activists like Callie House and Lucy Parsons resisted constricting opportunities and civil liberties. African American women effectively, if not miraculously, cultivated and applied a variety of social and political tactics to confront racial bigotry and to stake their own claims on what freedom and US citizenship would mean. African American women's migration would continue to transform Black communities. The year 1915 served as a watershed moment, as ongoing racial hostilities, dim economic prospects, and widespread crop devastation set millions more in motion. Yet the immediate decades after Frances Thompson's life witnessed African American women building institutions, industries, popular entertainment, and polities. Black women organized and published on a variety of topics and launched brave campaigns against racist tyranny. Demographic changes would also engender exciting new developments in Black thought, art, political action, and sexual attitudes, and African American women's voices would make their way into the public sphere in even more profound ways.

CHAPTER SEVEN

AUGUSTA'S CLAY, MIGRATION, AND THE DEPRESSION, 1915–1940

*At the mud pie age, I began to make
"things" instead of mud pies.*

—AUGUSTA SAVAGE

GROWING UP IN GREEN COVER SPRINGS, Florida, Augusta Christine Fells first began molding objects out of the red earthen clay found around her childhood home. "At the mud pie age, I began to make 'things' instead of mud pies," she recalled. Though her early talent for sculpting was evident, her father, a farmer and Methodist preacher, discouraged her art. Fearing it akin to making graven images, "father licked me five or six times a week and almost whipped all the art out of me." For a time, creativity would take a back seat to the womanly conventions of her day: marriage and motherhood. First wed at age fifteen, in 1907, Augusta lost her husband shortly after the birth of her only surviving child, Irene. In 1915 she married James Savage and also went to school in Tallahassee. Augusta planned to become a teacher, but a chance meeting with a local potter would set her on a different course entirely. By 1921, like masses of Southern Black women, Augusta had made Harlem her home. She had also shed her second husband, started studying at Cooper Union, and used the move to New York to reinvent herself. Augusta referred to her fourteen-year-old daughter as her little sister and pretended to be a decade younger. She never mentioned her two marriages.[1]

In the city, Augusta pursued her art with a fierce dedication, routinely battling through, around, and up and over racist obstacles. Sometimes whites were apprehensive about exhibiting her work. In 1923 they prevented her from participating in a tuition-free women's summer art school in Fontainebleau, France. An American, white-male selection committee felt that white women would not want to travel with a Black woman, much less share a room with one. In the shadow of World War I, the infuriating irony of the episode was not lost on Augusta. In an article in the *Amsterdam News,* an independent Black newspaper in New York, she commented, "Democracy is a strange thing. My brother was good enough to be accepted in one of the regiments that saw service in France during the war, but it seems his sister is not good enough to be a guest of the country for which he fought." Augusta also wondered how she could compete with other American artists if she was not to be given the same opportunity. Following the path trodden by so many Black women before her, Augusta continued to study, create, and strive. She would eventually go abroad, studying in France for two years on a Rosenwald Fund grant. By most accounts, she enjoyed her time in Paris, even as her artistic pursuits remained deeply tied to Black culture in the United States.[2]

In Harlem, Augusta's life was steeped in the blossoming African American cultural revolution taking place. She also wrote poetry, and her routinely overcrowded apartment hosted Harlem Renaissance literary dignitaries Dorothy West, Claude McKay, Langston Hughes, and Zora Neale Hurston. Augusta's sculptures included busts of leaders such as Marcus Garvey but also those of everyday Black people. Together with thousands of African American women, she had a profound appreciation for Garvey's message of race pride, a political affinity that may have cost her professionally. As the renowned artist Jacob Lawrence explained, "Savage was a Black Nationalist. And then being a woman, too, she didn't have it easy in the art world." Augusta also didn't have it easy in life. Her marriage to Garveyite Robert Lincoln Poston was short-lived. He died within a year of their wedding from pneumonia after returning from a trip to Liberia in 1923, where he had been working on the mass repatriation of Black people. Their infant daughter, Roberta, lived only ten days.[3]

These losses undoubtedly took their toll, however, few Black women were strangers to loss and hardship. Many found ways to channel their suffering and, in this sense, Augusta was no different. She grieved, picked herself up, and plodded a path forward. Among her many accomplishments, Augusta created a free art school, which, by 1934, was the largest in New York City. She organized Black artists and cofounded the Harlem Artists Guild. The guild pressed officials in the WPA, the federal agency that gave out-of-work artists jobs, for support for Black artists during the prolonged financial depression of the 1930s. The guild also secured funds for an arts center in Harlem in 1937, and Augusta served as its inaugural director. In 1938 she received a lucrative commission to show a piece in the New York World's Fair. Her sixteen-foot, awe-inspiring statue *The Harp* was among the most visited sights. One critic wrote, "Augusta Savage is a Negro sculptress, whose work has been outstanding, and who has in large degree exemplified, or rather interpreted, the emotional pathos and sensuousness of her race." Yet when she attempted to reclaim her position at the center, she was denied. The WPA regarded her acceptance of the commission as employment; under the circumstances, its obligation to her had been fulfilled. The maneuver was likely political payback for her leadership of the Harlem Artists Guild.[4]

Some women might have given up at this point, but Augusta continued exhibiting her work, showing at the Negro World's Fair in 1940, though she struggled to obtain adequate financial support. Renting an apartment on East 119th Street with her daughter, Irene, who was by then thirty-two-years old and working as a laundress, the two eked out a living. These difficulties were compounded by other difficulties, not the least of which was the unwanted affections of a white writer, Joe Gould. Gould met Augusta at a function in 1923 and became obsessed. In 1926 he had begun to write her letters, which she asked him to stop doing; he then told people they were having an affair, which she denied; he wrote about her in his notebooks, which she also asked him to stop. At one point he proposed to her; she said no.[5] It's likely that this, her ongoing financial struggles, and growing rumors about her purported cooperation with the FBI, which had been investigating Black communists in the Harlem arts world, all factored into her decision to relocate to upstate New York in 1945. Upstate, Augusta lived on a small farm, where "she raised pigeons, and grew flowers, and mulled wine." Friends from Harlem and family would take the train up and visit from time to time. Augusta lived there until her death, in 1962.[6]

While Harlem's cultural scene drew unconventional types and Black artists including Augusta Savage, thousands more Black people moved to New York to escape the worsening economic landscape of the South resulting from the invasion of the boll weevil. About one-quarter of an inch in size, the insect devastated crops in the region between the late nineteenth and early twentieth centuries. It first appeared in the Southwest, wreaking havoc in Texas in the 1890s, for example, before making its way through the Deep South to reach Georgia's farming communities by the 1920s. Dated farming practices, a lack of pesticides, and limited crop variation left fields especially vulnerable to the bug's insatiable appetite for cotton. As farm yields dropped by nearly 50 percent, the stark ripple effect led to the widespread dispossession of Black sharecroppers.[7] Just as this period is punctuated by Black people's unprecedented migrations and the legendary Harlem Renaissance it helped launch, war, entrenched racial violence, and catastrophic economic instability also powerfully impacted Black women's history and tested African American women's aptitude for both perseverance and resistance.

BEULAH NELSON, a migrant from South Carolina, detailed a web of interrelated financial and social factors that shaped her move north in the early twentieth century. As tenant farmers, even when her family produced "enough cotton to get money back at the settle—they wouldn't give you but so much money. And that's how they was." white store clerks even cheated Black customers outright, as Beulah described intervening when she saw a white merchant deceive her grandfather and father. She announced that the clerk counted wrong, but neither her father nor her grandfather reacted, so Beulah described saying it "louder and louder—two more times. Then my older brother said something too. Nobody said nothing. But they looked at me; then Brother. What happened? I got the worst whipping—got beat for telling the truth! My brother was sent away that night. Then I had to go away for school." Given that 90 percent of African Americans lived in the South, with 80 percent of that number residing in rural communities prior to the boll weevil, the kinds of theft Beulah witnessed were probably widespread. It was not uncommon for Black sharecroppers to be indebted to white landowners at the end of crop cycles. Like their foremothers, Black women and Black girls often adapted to suit the needs of their families, which were often large, with as many as eight to ten children. Black mothers and Black women in general did everything from household chores and helping extended family to pitching in during planting and harvesting cycles, taking in laundry, and doing domestic work on the side. In the Cotton Belt, life for many Black women was almost frozen in time—they worked exactly as their enslaved ancestors had, both because of racism and also because many farming techniques had remained unchanged. Tractors were not introduced until 1930, and mechanical cotton pickers not until the 1950s.[8]

Black women sought better opportunities wherever and whenever they could, though the search was not without repercussions. Their enterprising efforts could find them at odds with white local landowners whose main goal was to have a stable Black workforce that they controlled. African American families seeking to obtain a better economic foothold might get a visit from "riders," white men hired to oversee and intimidate aspiring and ambitious African Americans. Even local Black schools would be shuttered if whites felt Black children's time was better spent in the fields alongside their parents. But sometimes "the very measures used to subordinate black farmers served as an impetus for them to move away." Some Black families shifted (moved to different plantations), while others elected to journey much farther.[9]

Black women swept up in the race's massive migration were largely motivated by the new jobs the war effort created, after millions of men enlisted at the start of World War I, in 1917. Labor shortages opened up otherwise off-limits industries to women, especially manufacturing. To reach these jobs, Black women braved costly and dangerous travel given white hostilities, to say nothing of having to contend with the filthy, dilapidated conditions in segregated bus depots, bathrooms, and railway cars. However, companies anxious for workers issued travel passes to cover ticket costs on the front end with the expectation that Black passengers would pay it back through deductions on future wages. Southern whites used countermeasures to stop Black women, including station agents refusing to accept the passes. Such attempts ultimately failed to stop the movement of 1.5 million African

Americans to New York, New Jersey, Pennsylvania, Ohio, Illinois, Michigan, Missouri, and elsewhere between 1916 and 1935.[10]

African American female migrants usually had personal reasons for wanting to escape domestic service as well, particularly in the South, as rape remained a constant threat in white homes. Black families did their best to prepare young women, as Odessa Minnie Barnes recalled: "Nobody was sent out before you was told to be careful of the white man or his sons. They'd tell you the stories of rape . . . hard too! No lies. You was to be told true, so you'd not get raped." Historian Elizabeth Clark-Lewis's interviews of Black Southern migrants revealed several accounts of Black families trying protect Black women and girls, as Weida Edwards explained, "You couldn't be out working 'til you knew how people was raped. You'd know how to run, or always not be in the house with the white men or big sons." For Ora Fisher: "My daddy just gave me a razor and he said it's for any man who tries to force himself on you. It's for the white man."[11] Black women and girls went north with a cleared-eyed resolve, but that didn't necessarily mean they were prepared for what they would find.

For Mamie Richardson, her first view of Washington, DC, was startling: "It was just smelly and people busy hollering this or that. And your eyes jumped from one sight to the next. All I had seen was a Carolina farm! But I tell you soon as you hit land things was moving. And fast too! Get this and do that, run to and fro, you up and gone."[12] Whatever their initial shock, Black women quickly recovered and seized the new opportunities available to them, which, in addition to factory work, included jobs in the garment industry and greater representation as nurses and social workers. Some Black women even found work as correctional officers. However, they earned between 10 and 50 percent less than white women, and on shop floors white women refused to work with Black women, leaving them with onerous tasks regarded as unsuitable for white women.[13]

The war also gave Black women a chance to demonstrate their patriotism, which would shape their political activities at home and abroad. Not only did they labor on behalf of the war effort, but they also worked specifically to support Black servicemen, who after enlistment were given subpar housing and menial labor tasks. African American women made comfort kits, championed rationing, and protested segregation in the armed forces. Addie Hunton and Kathryn

Johnson served in France with the War Council of the Young Men's Christian Association and sacrificed to support Black troops. In their book, Addie and Kathryn lauded Black men's efforts and noted how they guarded German prisoners: "Somehow we felt that colored soldiers found it rather refreshing—even enjoyable for a change—having come from a country where it seemed everybody's business to guard them." The two also wrote of "warning sirens, air-battles by night and 'Big Bertha' bombs by day" in Paris, and they told of how "colored women who served overseas had a tremendous strain placed upon their Christian ideals." What were the strains? What difficulties did they encounter? How did they protect themselves abroad? The answers to those questions are largely unknowable since the two refrained from disclosing ugly or explicit details about incidents that tainted their service. Describing lurid events publicly ran counter to the ideals of respectable, Christian womanhood. Instead, Addie and Kathryn chose to thank those who helped them "keep their faith in the democracy of real Christian service." Further, Addie and Kathryn had accomplished something extraordinary as Black women by going abroad to do war work.[14]

Most African American women stateside, however, found that their lives blended better jobs and greater freedoms with the tumultuous fits, starts, and reversals characteristic of racial progress. For example, once the war ended and soldiers returned home, African American women were forced out of their new jobs. Meanwhile, growing numbers of whites started to prefer white ethnic immigrants as domestics over Black women. The shift in hiring practices likely reflected rising racial tensions that boiled over as increased Black urban migration, together with the return of Black soldiers at the end of the war, collided with racist whites. They were outraged at any hint of Black advancement. For their part, Black soldiers refused to accept racial intimidation and fought back. The summer of 1919, infamously referred to as the "Red Summer," saw bloody racial clashes occur in cities from Chicago to Washington and Omaha, with a total of twenty-six race riots nationwide.

But neither violence nor constricting employment opportunities, nor even housing discrimination, could stem the tide of Black women entering urban centers like New York, Philadelphia, and Washington, DC. Upon arrival Black women relied on kinship networks, clubs, and extensive faith communities to learn about jobs and to earn money in more informal ways. Whether selling plates of food, taking care of children, reading cards and palms, or running numbers to make ends meet, African American women in the city found ways to make money. And Black expressive culture expanded in unprecedented ways as the Harlem Renaissance birthed an awakening in Black art, music, entertainment, and literature. For example, writers such as Alice Dunbar-Nelson created genuine Black characters imbued with unprecedented intimacy. Prior to her renowned career abroad, dancer, singer, and future civil rights activist Josephine Baker shined in Harlem performing in nightclubs and eventually on Broadway. It was an era when Black women used their talents, creativity, and voices to redefine how the world viewed them and amplify how they saw the world.

African American female performers took to stages in cramped bars and grand halls alike, scenes awash in cigarette smoke, thinned gin, and explicit sexual entanglements. In cabarets, Black women engaged the personal in the blues to talk about issues such as domestic violence and incarceration but also to give voice to the erotic. Songs like Ma Rainey's "Black Eye Blues" told the tale of Miss Nancy, whose man beat her, cheated on her, and took all of her money. It also told of her efforts to fight back by warning, "You low down alligator, just watch me/Sooner or later gonna catch you with your britches down." Gertrude "Ma" Rainey's performances also brazenly flouted heterosexual norms. With songs such as her 1928 hit "Prove It on Me Blues," she crooned, "I went out last night with a crowd of my friends/They must've been women, 'cause I don't like no men/Wear my clothes just like a fan/Talk to the gals just like any old man/'Cause they say I do it, ain't nobody caught me/Sure got to prove it on me." The lyrics and performances exploded respectable concepts of how to be Black women and men in the world, and it opened up a space for a variety of sexual identities to emerge.[15]

Black lesbians like Gladys Bentley donned tuxedos and played before raucous crowds eager to drink in Bentley and bathtub gin by the mouthfuls. Headlining clubs such as the Clam House, in top hat and coattails, Gladys in particular had a commanding presence that made her a top-selling artist in Jazz Age Harlem. As renowned poet Langston Hughes described: "Miss Bentley was an amazing exhibition of musical energy—a large, dark, masculine lady, whose feet pounded the floor while her fingers pounded the keyboard—a perfect piece of African sculpture, animated by her own rhythm."[16] Hughes beautifully captured the essence of Gladys, who made no secret of her intimate relationships with women.[17]

Blues and jazz culture also created spaces for Black lesbians to find and socialize with each other outside an exclusively heterosexual gaze. For example, rent parties and buffet flats—essentially local parties and social gatherings that featured erotic entertainment, food, and alcohol—doubled as spaces for the Black queer community to celebrate themselves. But the scenes were not always harmonious; just as with the more mainstream parties, too much of a good time could quickly devolve. Jealous crime scenes erupted where lovers' quarrels ended with fists being thrown and razors drawn. As the *New York Age*, a Black newspaper, salaciously wrote in 1926, during a rent party at her Manhattan apartment Reba Stobtoff, "severed the jugular vein in the throat of Louise Wright after a fierce quarrel in which Reba had accused Louise of showing too much interest in a woman named Clara, known to underworld dwellers as 'Big Ben,' the name coming from her unusual size and from her inclination to ape the masculine in dress and manner, and particularly in her attention to other women."[18] The article's tone lays bare the biased conflation of lesbianism with violence and pathology.

The fact is, despite the open performances and the fairly expansive Black queer community in Harlem, discrimination remained firmly entrenched. Black lesbians like Mabel Hampton did not wear pants in public in an effort to avoid stirring the ire of men and police. Though the latter tended to be unavoidable for all Black women, as Hampton (largely known as a "woman's woman") was nonetheless arrested on a trumped-up prostitution charge when she went out on a heterosexual double date. She and many other Black women routinely found themselves accused of prostitution. Walking home late in the evenings from work might find African American women randomly arrested in police prostitution sweeps. Authorities used Black men to entrap Black women by asking them out on dates, only to later testify that the women had been soliciting.[19]

On the flipside, Beulah Nelson sought out extralegal gigs soon after moving to Washington, DC. Upon observing a nearby residence that was "jumping," Beulah approached the occupant directly and told her that she wanted to make money. The woman "was selling liquor, cigarettes, hot clothing, had gambling games, everything. In a day she taught me everything 'cause I'm quick—remember I been to school." Though her brother had saddled her with babysitting his two children, plus three from another family while he and his wife worked, Beulah was still in the streets. She reminisced, "Now here I am, with these kids, going around for numbers or helping her in this joint place. Making money all the time!" Even with her brother and his wife working, the couple still had major money troubles. When faced with eviction, Beulah's money proved long enough to cover back rent for the family and then some. Other Black women working informal rackets sold roots and dabbled in divining and mediumship.[20]

Though the fast life proved exciting and paid well for some, arrests, criminalization, and incarceration remained an ongoing problem for Black women, whether they participated in illicit activities or were netted in vice raids. Throughout the early twentieth century, African American women remained overrepresented in the justice system. And though the 1920s witnessed a pronounced move toward reformatories for women convicted of crimes, Black women and Black girls often went to custodial institutions, as administrators believed them to be biologically unredeemable.[21]

Black women languished inside prisons longer than white women, and their parole periods appear to have been more closely supervised. They were often released to work in white homes as domestics, and white employers and white parole officers effectively used the threat of incarceration to keep them working under exploitative conditions. Further, in New York and other cities, white parole officers believed that Southern whites knew how to control unruly Black people better. As historian Cheryl Hicks notes, in some cases, they shipped Black women south to serve parole, regardless of whether the women had any connection to the region.[22] Compared to Black life in Harlem, the South represented a backward mix of toxic racism, stubborn poverty, and entrenched political disenfranchisement.

THE RATIFICATION OF THE NINETEENTH AMENDMENT, in 1920, which granted women the right to vote, resulted from decades of suffragist organizing. Black suffragists such as Mary Church Terrell had actively lobbied in Washington, DC, and delivered passionate speeches connecting women's right to vote to broader notions of female equality. Despite their long history in support of the franchise, Black women rarely collaborated with white women. Many white suffragists harbored racist views, believing themselves better suited for the franchise, over both Black women and Black men. The same racial biases that prevented Black and white suffragists from working together also stalled their efforts to work effectively to combat voter suppression in the 1920s, though Black women soldiered on, independently.[23] Black women even ran for public office. In 1918, Mrs. Alice Presto campaigned for a state senate seat in Seattle, Washington. Presto lost her bid but achieved a place in history as the first Black female candidate to run for a state legislature. Her platform was robust and unabashedly feminist, as Presto championed equal pay for labor regardless of gender, called for a cost-of-living increase for widows' pensions, and held that taxpayer's children should not have to pay tuition at state educational institutions. Presto's audacity matched that of the masses of energized Black women. They were eager to make good use of the franchise, and many African American women despaired that their sisters in the South and elsewhere remained barred from exercising their constitutional rights.[24]

African American women organized voter registration drives in New York, New Jersey, Maryland, Illinois, Kansas, Colorado, and California. The South proved a challenge to voter registration, because the same tactics that had effectively disenfranchised Black men hindered Black women. Even those African Americans who could afford poll taxes and pass contrived reading tests still met other forms of voter intimidation—from loss of employment to loss of life. Pushing back against the tactics and racial terrorism, African American women organized through the NACW and the National Association for the Advancement of Colored People (NAACP) to canvass the region, gathering evidence and statements from Black people barred from exercising the franchise. The testimonies aimed to support the Tinkham Bill. The legislation, proposed by Massachusetts representative George Holden Tinkham in 1920, sought to use the number of votes cast, rather than population count, as the basis of congressional reapportionment. Perhaps unsurprisingly the bill was defeated, and the US

House of Representatives' census committee effectively added insult to injury by voting to increase the South's representation shortly after.[25]

African American women forged ahead, however, forming in 1924 the National League of Republican Colored Women (NLRCW), whose motto boldly declared "We are in politics to stay and we shall be a stay in politics." Mary Church Terrell served as treasurer, and Nannie Helen Burroughs was president. After assuring Black women that casting a ballot did not interfere with their Christian values, Nannie toured with Black and white candidates, visiting Black churches and fund-raising for upcoming elections. Yet even as the NLRCW tried to use Black women's concentration in the Republican Party (then still regarded as the party of Lincoln) as a voting bloc, they saw little benefit or acknowledgment for their party loyalty. Within the next five years or so, African American women would shift away from the Republican Party, which remained inactive on civil rights. By 1932 the NLRCW had disbanded.[26]

Voting was only one facet of Black women's political activism. With the influx of migrants from the South and some three hundred thousand Black immigrants from the Caribbean and South America between 1900 and 1930, new political philosophies and ideas began circulating, while older notions of Black nationalism witnessed a robust resurgence. The majority of these Caribbean immigrants settled in Harlem and would account for 20 percent of its residents by the 1930s. Some Harlemites identified with the notion of the New Negro, which regarded African Americans of the twentieth century as distinct from and more self-determining than their enslaved or even newly freed foremothers and fathers. Others were drawn to Marcus Garvey, a Jamaican immigrant, and to the Universal Negro Improvement Association (UNIA) because of its forceful stance on Black unity, resistance, and cooperative economics, and its proud affirmation of African heritage.[27]

Amy Ashwood Garvey, Marcus Garvey's first wife, cofounded the UNIA. A native of Jamaica, she took pride in her "Ashanti heritage" and revered dark skin as indicative of an "honorable lineage and beauty." She also had a nuanced, diasporic understanding of Blackness, shaped in part by her earlier experiences in Panama, when her family briefly moved to the Canal Zone, where her father opened a bakery. The family had returned to Jamaica by 1914, but the conditions in Panama impacted Amy, as she witnessed how hard Black women struggled financially and socially. She glimpsed how Black people suffered globally and realized the need for international, collective organizing. By the time she immigrated to New York, in 1918, to help fund-raise for the UNIA, which was then headquartered in Harlem, Amy was very much committed to the liberation of Black people. She and her husband toiled together to prosper the UNIA. However, the pair did not seem to be in accord in all areas. Marcus Garvey embraced patriarchy and believed that having Black men in charge would free Black women to assume their "natural" roles as submissive wives and attentive mothers. His wife, however, was in many ways steeped in the culture of Harlem in the 1920s. She drank in public, maintained friendships with other men, and seemed poorly cast for the demure role of helpmate. Marital tensions flared amidst the specter of a love triangle, and Amy Ashwood and Marcus Garvey would separate in 1920 and divorce in 1922. He took a UNIA secretary, also named Amy, as his second wife. Amy Ashwood subsequently traded New York for Canada and later went to London. She stayed active in Black diasporic social justice causes.[28]

Amy Jacques-Garvey was also a Jamaican immigrant and, like Marcus Garvey, advocated a Black Nationalist agenda that emphasized Black cooperative economics, education, and political activism.[29] The UNIA owned grocery stores in Harlem, acquired steamships to ferry Black people back to Africa, and operated its own newspaper, the *Negro World*. Amy Jacques-Garvey served as editor of the women's section, extolling such practices as teaching children race pride and thrift. She held in common with Black clubwomen the belief that Black women must command respect from all races. She also lobbied for more female leadership and criticized Black men for failing to acknowledge Black women's worth. She wrote, "White women have greater opportunities to display their ability because of the standing of both races, and due to the fact that black men are less appreciative of their women than white men . . . yet who is more deserving of admiration than the black woman, she who has borne the rigors of slavery, the deprivations consequent on a pauperized race, and the indignities heaped upon a weak and defenseless people? Yet she has suffered all with fortitude, and stands ever ready to help in the onward march to freedom and power." She also warned Black men to stand up and show courage lest they be displaced by Black women, who were poised to lead the race to victory and glory.[30]

The UNIA appealed to broad cross-sections of Black women, and though few formally occupied leadership roles in the organization, they played vital roles in its financial and political expansion. For example, Louise Little, Malcolm X's mother, herself an avowed Garveyite, served in the Omaha UNIA chapter. Her report, which was published in the *Negro World*, detailed information about the chapter's membership drive in 1926. Plus, as historian Eric McDuffie explained, Louise also "raised and instilled the principles of Garveyism in her eight children in the urban and rural Midwest." As a Caribbean immigrant who was born in Grenada, Louise's participation in the UNIA allowed her to be in conversation with like-minded, diasporic thinkers. Further, Black women's membership in the UNIA provided another avenue to participate in political activities, respectably, outside their homes. Still, it is important not to minimize that in joining this movement, Black women Garveyites cultivated and reveled in a deep love of Black people in the US and throughout the African diaspora. Even after Garvey's deportation, in 1927, and the organization's subsequent demise, the ideologies of the UNIA would influence future generations in critical ways.[31]

The UNIA's message of Black unity and collective economics had effectively fused methods that African American women had relied upon for decades to sustain their communities. Those practices would take on an even greater importance after the stock market crashed in 1929. The economic calamity stemmed from a convergence of factors—too little regulation, massive volatility, and reckless financial speculation. The national economy went from $81 billion in 1929 to $40 billion by 1932. Banks failed, and millions lost their life savings. Before the Depression, close to 40 percent of Black women worked outside the home, only 5 percent would be in manufacturing, another 5 percent held white-collar jobs, while nearly 30 percent worked in agriculture and another 40 percent in domestic service. As historians Darlene Clark Hine and Kathleen Thompson note, in contrast, almost 70 percent of employed white women held white-collar or manufacturing positions. By 1931, over 250,000 Black women would be unemployed, with their jobless rate soaring, as it did in Detroit, hitting 68.9 percent. The unemployment rate for Black women was far higher than for white women and was often higher than or equal to that of Black men. Moreover, cotton prices dropped by more than half by 1933, leaving the remaining Black sharecroppers in the region even more destitute. As Black women's employment fell by 50 percent, conditions in rural communities prompted another four hundred thousand Southern Black people to head north.[32]

Their long histories of self-reliance and collective organizing helped Black women keep their families afloat during the Depression. Black women grew their own vegetables, caught and sold fish as well as cooked goods, and rented out rooms. They also bartered for necessary household items and threw rent parties. In their churches, Black women helped provide needy families with free meals and warm clothing, and Black performers took to the stage for free for fund-raising events. In 1931, Harlem's Abyssinian Baptist Church, organized largely by women, served "28,000 free meals, gave away 525 food baskets, and distributed 17,928 pieces of clothing and 2,564 pairs of shoes."[33]

Even with families and friends pulling together, even with churches and other charitable institutions offering assistance, some Black women were in such need that they had to gather on street corners hoping to be picked up by white employers seeking day-laboring domestic servants. The practice was the subject of Ella Baker and Marvel Cooke's groundbreaking editorial, which first appeared in the *Crisis* in 1935. Likening the corners to new "Slave Markets," the authors condemned the degrading routine to which scores of poor Black women were now subject. With few viable options, though, destitute Black women did what they had to do to survive. Bargaining for their labor, African American women earned as little as twenty cents an hour for scrubbing floors, doing laundry, washing windows, and waxing woodwork. The arrangements led to the worst kinds of exploitation. After backbreaking labor, some "worked longer than was arranged, got less than was promised, were forced to accept clothing instead of cash." The scarcity of resources also intensified hiring discrimination, as unemployed whites demanded that any available jobs go to them first. Moreover, emerging governmental policies aiming to help struggling citizens essentially mirrored many whites' racist entitlement.[34]

These were not conditions that Black women intended to tolerate for very long, as the era found them protesting for workers' rights, organizing labor strikes, and joining unions. For example, in 1933

Connie Smith, a middle-aged Black woman, led nine hundred Black women pecan factory workers on strike in Saint Louis, Missouri. Fighting for better wages and working conditions, Smith worked across racial lines and got white female workers to support their efforts. Together, the workers forced a surrender from management. Not only did Black women's wages rise, one went from $3 a week to $9, but the pay between Black and white women was equal, and factory conditions improved. Black women workers also played pivotal roles in labor organizing in the International Ladies' Garment Workers' Union in the 1930s. Moreover, in 1938 a young Dorothy Height, who served as the "Negro representative of the Harlem Branch of the Y.W.C.A.," protested deplorable labor conditions before the New York City Council. Height decried the way young Black women were paid as little as "$1 a day or 15 cents an hour for domestic work at 'slave markets' in the Bronx and Brooklyn."[35]

These economic warriors could be found on gritty urban streets or in esteemed places of worship. Fannie Peck, the wife of a prominent pastor of an AME Church, started a grassroots movement in Detroit. As Fannie described it, the Black woman had an epiphany: she had been "making sacrifices to educate her children with no thought as to their obtaining employment after leaving school." Motivated by this concern, in 1930 Peck gathered roughly fifty other Black women to help found what would become the Housewives' League of Detroit. Harnessing Black women's spending power as the primary household consumers, the league enacted a kind of Black economic nationalism for the betterment of their communities. To join, Black women just had to commit to supporting Black businesses, products, and services to keep money circulating within the Black community. In short order, Housewives' Leagues sprang up in Chicago, Baltimore, Harlem, and Cleveland. Black women not only spent in their own neighborhoods but also boycotted businesses that did not employ African Americans. In a meeting with a bank head, in which they urged more opportunities for Black workers, a Mrs. Clara Bruce pointed out that "not only the economic . . . but the moral and spiritual welfare of the community is affected by unemployment."[36]

The Housewives' Leagues marked the dynamic process by which Black women's political, familial, and economic values blended with their extraordinary organizing abilities. Given the financial havoc wrought by the Depression, Black women taking matters into their own hands proved more than wise, especially when compared to how little assistance African Americans received from the federal government. Soon after taking office in 1933, Democratic president Franklin Delano Roosevelt ushered in a series of relief policies. Unfortunately, New Deal legislation largely failed to address the needs of Black workers. The Wagner-Lewis Social Security bill, for example, did not include farmers or domestics—together these occupations accounted for close to 65 percent of the Black labor force.[37] To take another instance, the Agricultural Adjustment Act provided subsidies to farmers to reduce output so that crop prices could rise and eventually stabilize. Though provisions existed for tenant farmers, racist and corrupt administration of the resources hindered African Americans' economic recovery, and Black farmers "endured the brunt of the production cutbacks." Further, WPA projects in the South pushed Black women into dangerous, labor-intensive public works, leading one doctor in South Carolina to observe: "The Beautification project appears to be 'For Negro Women Only'. . .Women are worked in 'gangs' in connection with the City's dump pile, incinerator and ditch piles. Illnesses traced to such exposure as these women must face do not entitle them to medical aid at the expense of the WPA."[38]

In 1933 the National Industrial Recovery Act established the National Recovery Administration (NRA) to regulate businesses by "setting minimum wages and maximum hours." Though NRA codes mandated equal compensation for Blacks and whites, enforcement was rare. In 1934, when a complaint was pursued against an Arkansas clothing company where Black women earned half of the white female employees' wages, the company opted to replace all the Black women with whites. Moreover, minimum wage laws and maximum hours did little for most Black workers since these policies did not apply to agricultural or domestic service work. It's no wonder that aggrieved African Americans denounced the National Recovery Administration, declaring that "NRA" really stood for "Negroes Robbed Again."[39]

Yet change was on the horizon. With so many African Americans now concentrated in urban centers in the North and Midwest, and with Black women's ongoing efforts to register Black voters, African Americans now constituted a powerful voting bloc in a number of cities and states. Whereas Black voters had been taken for granted by an unresponsive Republican Party, Northern Democrats had begun remaking their party's image. In efforts to actively court the Black vote, Northern Democrats ceded African Americans local political appointments. Moreover, it helped that Eleanor Roosevelt looked favorably on Black civil rights and had a personal relationship with Black women like Mary McLeod Bethune. Already a well-established powerbroker within the Black community, Bethune was also a renowned educator and activist who founded and led the National Council of Negro Women (NCNW) in 1935, which boasted five hundred thousand members.[40] Bethune effectively used her relationship with Eleanor to help alleviate the suffering of Black people and to help African Americans obtain a greater foothold within the White House.

Nearly 80 percent of Black voters cast their ballots for Franklin D. Roosevelt, marking a significant turning of the tide. Their support would not go entirely unacknowledged, as African Americans were vocal about their needs and the flawed relief policies thus far. Not only did Bethune become the head of the Negro Division of the National Youth Administration, effectively becoming the first Black woman to lead a federal agency, but Roosevelt established the Federal Council on Negro Affairs, also known as the "Black Cabinet," comprising twenty-seven men and three women, with Bethune at its helm.[41] This cabinet had limited power, though its existence in an advisory capacity was a crucial development, one that would contribute to the Black community's growing shift toward the Democratic Party.

However, during the Depression years, small numbers of African American women also joined the Communist Party (CP). As historian LaShawn Harris explains, "Conditions created by the economic collapse exacerbated existing employment problems," which found greater numbers of African American women gravitating toward leftist reform. In 1936, investigative journalist Marvel Cooke's CP membership was almost a natural extension of her reporting, which focused on the problems of New York City's poor and on her political ideals, which sought "working-class liberation and race and gender equality." Black women who had been plagued by socioeconomic inequities continued to turn to communist groups "for assistance in confronting the day-to-day problems of unemployment, unfair relief distribution, and persistent race-based discrimination."[42] The CP's message of uniting workers and aggressively fighting racism in relief efforts and employment practices was especially attractive. In communist organizations, Black women also found leadership opportunities. The League of Struggle for Negro Rights attracted ex-Garveyites such as Bonita Williams, a British Caribbean immigrant, who made Harlem her home. Williams helped organize "Flying Squads," which mobilized working-class housewives to agitate against high food prices.[43]

However, the CP's effective defense of the "Scottsboro boys" attracted significant numbers of Black women as well. The 1931 case, which saw nine Black teenagers charged with the rape of two white women on a freight train in Scottsboro, Alabama, brought national attention to the enduring consequences of the myth of the Black male rapist. The young men had been sentenced to death, but communists in the International Labor Defense took up their cause and helped fund mothers of the accused to go on speaking tours about injustices against young African Americans in the Southern justice system. Their plight resonated with many Black mothers.

The CP also attracted young radicals such as journalist Claudia Jones, who had a global critique of the oppression Black women faced. She knew that issues of race and gender, compounded by physical, economic, and state violence, lacked geographical boundaries. Moreover, as scholar Carole Boyce Davies explained, Claudia employed an integrated version of socialism that included "an anti-imperialist coalition, managed by working-class leadership, fueled by the involvement of women." A native of Port-of-Spain, Trinidad, Claudia immigrated to the United States in 1924, at the age of eight. Having passed through Ellis Island after stepping off the S.S. *Voltaire*, she followed in the footsteps of thousands of other Caribbean immigrants who undertook the journey. As a Black woman, she understood herself as both a member of the Caribbean diaspora and as an "African American under the oppression of U.S. racism." Highly critical of the United States' efforts to enter what would become World War II, Jones's work, *Jim-Crow in Uniform* (1940), championed socialism, charging that goals of equality would come about "by establishing a new social order in which working people will own and control all the vast natural resources and means of production, and use them for the benefit of all, instead of the few."[44]

That message should have resonated with many, because multitudes of Black women and men were broke and, for the most part, their financial outlooks remained grim. But rather than succumb to the gloom, African Americans found ways to laugh at their predicament. According to historian Joe Williams Trotter Jr., a popular joke among African Americans during the Depression revolved around two Black men taking pride in their wives' abilities to make do with next to nothing. Husband number one boasts, "My wife is smart. She don't waste a thing. Why, just the other day she took one of her old raggedy dresses and made me a tie." Husband number two replies, "Boy, that ain't nothing. Yesterday my wife took one of my old ties and made her a dress!" Combining dejection with the sardonic, Zora Neale Hurston's short play *Poker!* managed to sketch both the desperation and dark humor that sustained Black communities, as a group of Black men end up in a fatal fight over who claimed the pot. The play also uniquely showcases the wiry, wry resilience of Black women. Cramped around a tiny table in a shotgun house, the sense of too much booze mixed with stale tobacco and the scent of men's latent despair is palpable. The sole Black woman in the play, Aunt Dilsey, warns the men about the dangers of the game they're playing, ultimately to no avail. In the wake of their demise, as she remains the only one standing in a room full of dead bodies, she says, "It sure is goin' to be a whole lot tougher in hell now!"[45] Clearly, things were tough all over.

AS AUGUSTA SAVAGE LEARNED, even with the second wave of federal assistance, many of the intended programs administered by the WPA came up short. Through sheer will and collective action, Augusta's talent ultimately placed her at the vanguard of politically engaged Black artists and activists in Harlem. Other Black women managed to inspire social movements, continue to build institutions and organizations, and helped define new Black identities and cultures. Together, they survived the Depression. Augusta found ways to weather all that the era's groundbreaking heights and equally stunning depths extracted, though not unscathed. Her Black female contemporaries, too, went from exhilarating rides in one instance only to find themselves battered and abruptly stranded in the next. Yet African American women seemed to develop a rhythm for the upheavals. In the decades ahead, they would lay the groundwork to mobilize on behalf of themselves and Black civil rights on a national scale.

CHAPTER EIGHT

ALICE'S MEDALS AND BLACK WOMEN'S WAR AT HOME, 1940–1950

It was a rough time in my life.
It was a time when it wasn't fashionable
for women to become athletes,
and my life was wrapped up in sports.

—ALICE COACHMAN

EVELYN COACHMAN REMINDED her daughter, in 1939, "You're no better than anyone else. The people you pass on the ladder will be the same people you'll be with when the ladder comes down." Having won her first gold medal in an Amateur Athletic Union competition, eighteen-year-old Alice heeded her mother's advice. Hers had been a winding journey. The middle child of ten siblings, Alice had grown up on the rural outskirts of Albany, Georgia. Going to school but also needing to help supplement the family's income, Alice did everything from working in cotton fields and supplying corn to the local mill to picking plums and pecans. Like so many Black families, the Coachmans placed a premium on their children's education and initially did not approve of her extracurricular activities. Alice recalled how her father disciplined her "when she would leave the house to practice with the local high school basketball team or run to the playground." She explained that there was a sense that "women weren't supposed to be running like that." Plus, Fred Coachman wanted his daughters to be "dainty, sitting on the front porch." Track and field in particular was perceived as a masculine activity, and the Coachmans' harbored serious concerns that Alice's participation would place her beyond the margins of respectable womanhood. As she recalled, "It was a rough time in my life. It was a time when it wasn't fashionable for women to become athletes, and my life is wrapped up in sports."[1]

The middle child also had other serious concerns. Alice hoped that sports could lift her out of poverty; as she explained, "I was tired of picking cotton." She continued to play sports, leading her school teams to championships, and each win did open doors for her. By seventh grade she was such a phenomenal athlete that Cleveland Abbott, the renowned Tuskegee Institute coach, asked her parents if Alice could train with the institute's high school team in the summer. The connection would lead to Alice eventually enrolling in Tuskegee Institute in 1943. She continued her athletic pursuits, and as scholar Jennifer H. Lansbury notes, by 1945, Coachman had even bested a rival "for the 100-meter spring, adding that title to the 50-meter, high jump, and 400-meter titles, and winning the individual high-point trophy."[2]

Alice also dreamed about competing internationally, but she needed to earn a living too. So, in the late 1940s she made a number of key changes in her life, including leaving Tuskegee to enroll in a school in her hometown. Back in Georgia, at Albany State Teacher's College, she played for the women's track and field team. Though World War II meant that the 1940 and 1944 Olympics were cancelled, Alice trained intensively for the July 1948 Olympic trials. Her efforts were not in vain. Making the team, however, was only the start of Alice's high-jump accomplishments. At the games in London, she set an Olympic record for jumping to just over five feet, six inches. She was the only woman on the US women's track and field team to bring home the top honor, which also made Alice the first Black woman to receive an Olympic gold medal.

Mainstream press coverage of the historic victory ranged from mixed to decidedly bigoted. The *Atlanta Constitution* covered her victory but suggested that she was not a strong student academically. The dig was in alignment with racist thinking that lauded Black peoples' physical capacities over their intellect. Other press accounts suggested that Alice excelled in track and field because it was more a masculine activity, something that Black women were more suited to given their supposed overall lack of femininity.[3] African American presses aimed to use her victory as a means to highlight Black achievement abroad and at home. The *Chicago Defender*, an African American newspaper, noted, "Alice Coachman, the first American woman to be victorious in track and field events at London will become the first Negro in history to be honored by a parade," in Albany, Georgia.[4] Black presses also tried to counter stereotypes about Black female athletes like Alice by stressing their femininity and virtue.

Alice herself may have been feeling the pressure, because shortly after her win she stopped competing. She hung up her track shoes in 1949, telling reporters that she would spend her time "teaching others how." As far as she was concerned, "I had accomplished what I wanted to do. . . . It was time for me to start looking for a husband. That was the climax. I won the gold medal. I proved to my mother, my father, my coach and everybody else that I had gone to the end of my rope." For Alice, track and field was the key "to getting my degree and meeting great people and opening a lot of doors in high school and college."[5] Her words help frame the goals many Black women had during this period and the challenges they faced in trying to attain them.

African American women seeking to move beyond traditional gender expectations and activities experienced pressure from home and from the larger society. At the same time, for most, a lack of financial resources complicated their efforts, whether attempting to break into sports or trying obtain higher education degrees. The challenges reflected longstanding structural economic exclusion, as well as the lingering impact of the Great Depression. Even with relief efforts still underway and the installation of a Black Cabinet in Washington, DC, millions of everyday Black women, men, and children battled unrelenting poverty. Financial opportunities would improve, however. Defense industries expanded just as servicemen had to vacate jobs once the US entered World War II. The dynamics led to more lucrative income opportunities, though Black women's ability to benefit from the wartime economy would require significant action on the home front.

MABEL GILVERT, a Black woman from New Orleans, wrote to First Lady Eleanor Roosevelt in 1941, explaining, "I'm a Negro girl of 25 yrs. I'm sick. I been sick 4 months. I'm in need of food and closes. . . . I was working at the NYA. . . . I work there 10 month. They lad me off because I was sick and diden give me nothing to live off after." Gilvert, who was behind on her rent and without food, was not looking for a handout but rather pleaded, "You could give me some to do in the hospital or in a hotel or any where I will do it. I will take a day job are a night job anything. Please help me."[6] Gilvert's plea highlights something fundamental about African American women's relationship to the federal government.

Few Black women harbored delusions about America's racist double standards, yet they never stopped believing that they deserved better. They consistently fought to access the benefits that US citizenship was supposed to provide, including access to federal aid. As one resident from Mount Pleasant, Texas, wrote President Roosevelt, also in 1941, "Askin you is it fair or not for the white woman to do all this WPA work in titus county. Mr. Roosevelt I am a poor Negro widow woman and have 3 children to take care of. . . . Please turn us a helping hand by put us Negro woman to work on these WPA project."[7] Scores of entreaties pointed to the injustice of unfair hiring practices in projects administered by the government, and they called attention to the ways Black women were denied federal relief funds because Southern administrators had institutionalized Jim Crowism to the detriment of Black people across the region. Mary McLeod Bethune and other leaders worked tirelessly to help Black people.

Economic conditions in the US would eventually rebound with the country's entry into the war, on December 8, 1941, one day after the Japanese bombed Pearl Harbor. But even as production and manufacturing boomed, African American women encountered biased hiring practices.[8]

Black voters who had supported the current Democratic administration expected better results and chafed at the nation's continued inequalities. As Lutensia Dillard, of Michigan, explained in a letter to President Roosevelt: "We aren't getting a fair deal. Some of our boys are being drafted for service for our country and here we are in a free land are not aloud [sic] to work and make a living for their wives and childrens." The country's professed stance on upholding freedom and democracy, the double standard in justice, in notions of morality and decency, and in the administration of federal policies, particularly the earlier ongoing relief efforts—all of it had gone on for far too long. Why should Black people fight for democracy in Europe when it did

Millie and Christine McCoy.

Susie King Taylor, black educator and army nurse (1848–1912).

Edmonia Lewis (1845–1907).

Woman outside an Alexandria, Virginia, slave pen.

FRANCIS THOMPSON, THE MEMPHIS NEGRO WHO LIVED
FOR TWENTY YEARS AS A WOMAN.

FRANCIS THOMPSON IN FEMALE ATTIRE.

Frances Thompson, c. 1876.

Miss Nannie H. Burroughs
(1922).

Front row: Zell Ingram, Pemberton West, Augusta Savage, Robert Pious, Sara West, Gwendolyn Bennett; back row: Elton Fax, Rex Gorleigh, Fred Perry, William Artis, Francisco Lard, Louis Jefferson, Norman Lewis.

Women being transported from Memphis, Tennessee, to an Arkansas plantation, July 1937.

"Domestic servants waiting for a street car on their way to work early in the morning," Mitchell Street, Atlanta, Georgia, May 1939.

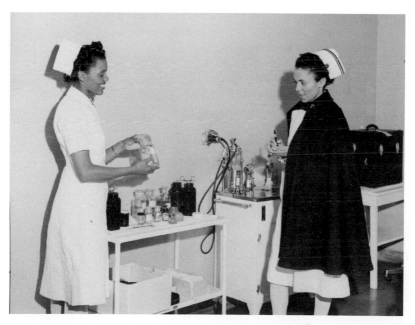

Captain Mary L. Petty, chief nurse, showing a bottle to Second Lieutenant Olive Bishop, who is writing on a pad of paper (c. 1945).

Members of the Women's Army Corps identifying incorrectly addressed mail for soldiers, Post Locator Department, Camp Breckinridge (1943).

Shirley Chisholm in front of microphones, c. 1972.

Gladys Bentley, "America's Greatest Sepia Player—The Brown Bomber of Sophisticated Songs, 1946–1949."

"Female Rappers, Class of '88": back row, standing or crouching (left to right): Sparky D, Sweet Tee, MC Peaches, Yvette Money, Ms. Melodie, Synquis; middle: Millie Jackson; sitting along the bottom row with legs crossed (left to right): unidentified, wearing jewelry reading "PAM"; Roxanne Shante; MC Lyte; Finesse.

not exist in the United States? The tension embedded in African Americans' political realities gave birth to an important political battle cry. The Double V campaign, called for democracy at home and abroad, and reflected the ways that the ground in Black America was shifting. African American women, seasoned activists as well as everyday Black women and girls, would be key actors in the dawning of the movement poised to break through.[9]

During a Chicago strategy meeting to confront employment discrimination in the defense industries, a Black woman delegate said, "Mr. Chairman, we ought to throw fifty thousand Negros around the White House—bring them from all over the country, in jalopies, in trains, and any way they can get there until we get some action from the White House." A. Philip Randolph, who was in full agreement, offered the support of his organization, the Brotherhood of Sleeping Car Porters, and spearheaded the charge. The proposed mass action, a march on Washington, planned for June 2, 1941, aimed to spotlight the nation's hypocrisy. How could such a country credibly claim to fight for democracy or stand against tyranny and antisemitism, while at home it remained submerged in racism, violent mob justice, and the treatment of African Americans as second-class citizens? Fearing the damage such a march would cause the country's image, the federal government moved to desegregate all industries affiliated with the war effort. Roosevelt signed Executive Order 8802 into law in 1941, and the Fair Employment Practices Committee was established to ensure that the order was upheld. It was a critical win. Still, African American women raised concerns that the order did not expressly include women, though it was taken for granted that the race provision would protect them."[10]

Against this backdrop, Black women rushed to fill vacancies left by soldiers headed to battle. To be clear, the shifts in policy did not automatically translate into a better quality of life for Black women and their families, as racist attitudes persisted. However, as historians Sharon Harley, Francille Rusan Wilson, and Shirley Wilson Logan explain, "World War II brought a brief exhilarating period when six hundred thousand Black women got industrial jobs with good salaries, making army vehicles, riveting aircraft and tank parts, working in ship and rail yards, in munition plants, and in the arsenals."[11] Even so, Black women battled white women workers who refused to share shop floors with them, and in Detroit, white women led hate marches to prevent African American women from obtaining jobs. Labor unions and the NAACP launched concerted efforts that finally opened ten thousand jobs for African American women, though another twenty-five thousand stayed unemployed. Yet Black women remained ready to seize new career options. For example, when the Army recognized and incorporated the Women's Army Corps (WAC) in 1943, even though the WACs would be segregated, four thousand Black women quickly signed up.[12]

If any Black servicewomen believed their primary adversary was abroad, events in 1945, the year the war ended, would have caused them to rethink the notion. Many enlisted Black women hoped to serve their country, earn money, and benefit from valuable job training. Alice Young, of Washington, DC, who already had a year of nursing school, joined the "colored WACs" after a recruiter said her experience would qualify her for more medical training. But when she arrived at Fort Devens, in Massachusetts, after basic training, Young and the rest of the Black female soldiers learned that they were there to "scrub and wash floors, wash dishes, and do all the dirty work." White WACs learned nursing skills, in addition to being spared the cleaning tasks assigned to African American women. Black women voiced their concerns, but the only available Black woman officer, Lieutenant Tenola Stoney, a supply officer for the Black WACs, had little power. The white officers, Colonel Walter Crandall and Lieutenant Victoria Lawson, isolated Black WACs rather than, as scholar Sandra M. Bolzenius writes, "incorporating them into the post's regular functions."[13]

Marginalized, degraded, and largely ignored, Black women at Fort Devens reached their breaking point and decided to strike. The decision reflected months of indignities, which were compounded by an especially cold, dreary winter and traumatizing events such as the attempted suicide of one of their ranks, Private Beulah Sims, in February 1945. When the women failed to report for duty, officers tried to reason with them. The exchanges became heated and negotiations broke down. On the second day of the strike, General Sherman Miles informed the striking Black WACs that if they did not immediately return to work, they would face a court-martial. He did add that he would investigate their concerns. Most then returned to work, reluctantly. But an upset and despondent Alice Young declared to Lieutenant Stoney, "I'm reporting back from my ward, and I feel like I'd rather take a court-martial than go back under present conditions, unless conditions are changed." She was not alone. Young was court-martialed along with Mary Green, of Conroe, Texas; Anna Morrison, of Richmond, Kentucky; and Johnnie Murphy, of Rankin, Pennsylvania. All four were found guilty and sentenced to a year of confinement with hard labor, loss of pay, and dishonorable discharge. The Black community was livid.[14]

African American fury, inquiries from members of Congress, and the NAACP's announcement that attorney Thurgood Marshall had agreed to represent Young, Green, Morrison, and Murphy on appeal, led the War Department to search for a swift way out of what was fast becoming a public relations nightmare. Invoking a procedural technicality about General Miles's role in the proceedings, the army proposed that Miles nullify the verdict and dismiss the case. He did so on April 2, 1945. Young, Green, Morrison, and Murphy returned to their posts, escaping imprisonment and dishonor by army standards, but their assignments remained unchanged. It was a sad, frustrating outcome.[15]

Though many Black WACs would confront unyielding institutionalized racism in the service, other African American women managed to crack barriers in the WACs. Charity Adams Earley, one of the first Black women to enlist, served as commanding officer of the Black WACs company at Fort Des Moines, in Iowa. Earley went on to command the 6888th Central Postal Directory Battalion, the first all-Black female unit overseas. Not only was Earley the first African American woman to be commissioned as an officer, but she was also the highest-ranking Black woman in the war. In her memoir of the period, Earley did not gloss over the humiliation of segregated service. Most Black WACs understood that it had to be confronted, but like so many other Black women, Earley also used every opportunity to conduct herself in a manner that would chip away at prejudiced stereotypes about her race. She wrote about how British papers commented, "These WACs are very different from the colored women portrayed on films, where they are usually either domestics or the outspoken old-retainer type. . . . The WACs have dignity and proper reserve." African American women also served in other branches of the military. The Women's Reserve of the US Navy (WAVES) accepted its first Black female member, Bessie Garret, in 1944, and by 1945 the number of Black WAVES had grown to fifty-six.[16]

Each stride African American women in the armed forces took was made possible only by their relentlessness and fortitude, and often each step met stiff resistance. Even as the war effort was in dire need of nurses, Black nurses battled to serve. At one point, the nursing shortage became so severe that in a message to Congress in January 1945, President Roosevelt suggested "nurse-draft legislation." Meanwhile, Mrs. Mabel K. Staupers, executive secretary of the National Association of Colored Graduate Nurses, had been lobbying on behalf of Black nurses and had even met with First Lady Eleanor Roosevelt to detail the obstacles they faced. For example, the army only allowed 160 Black nurses, while the navy barred their admittance altogether. Against the specter of a nurse draft, Staupers pointedly asked, "Why isn't the army using colored nurses?" The obvious solution to the situation finally prevailed on January 10, 1945, when the army announced that nurses would be admitted to the Nurse Corps "without regard to race," and the navy quickly followed. Within weeks, Black women were inducted. In June 1945, Captain Susan Freeman received the Mary Mahoney Medal from the National Association of Colored Graduate Nurses for being the "first Negro nurse to command Negro Army nurses overseas."[17]

Mabel Staupers did not limit her work to the plight of Black nurses. A key characteristic of Black women activists and leaders is that while their entry points in the struggle were always those areas that hit closest to home or their specific areas of expertise, they usually branched out and worked in broad coalitions on behalf of civil rights impacting the entire Black community. For example, Mabel also worked with other Black women, such as prominent attorney Sadie Tanner Mossell Alexander. Sadie, who was the first Black woman to receive a law degree from the University of Pennsylvania and the first Black woman to be admitted to the Pennsylvania Bar, represented the NCNW. She and Mabel joined A. Philip Randolph and others in ongoing efforts to hold politicians and the government accountable to the needs of African Americans. Leveraging the Black voting bloc, a constellation of Black activists issued a statement that warned, "Public officers who have not made a record of liberal or democratic action may expect Negroes to help remove them from office."[18]

Ultimately, whether combatting restrictive roles in the military or inactive public officials, African American women met challenges head-on at a variety of points, though sometimes their gains could be frustratingly fleeting. For example, as Black women pushed their way into the defense industries against racist protests and other discriminatory barriers, they received support from some major labor unions. The Congress of Industrial Organizations, in 1943, had initiated a committee to combat racial discrimination, and the United Auto Workers in Detroit and elsewhere worked in tandem with the NAACP and other organizations to call for employment opportunities for Black women.[19] Those efforts worked, for a time, but by 1948, most wartime gains had dissipated as Black women were forced out of the better-paying manufacturing positions they occupied in the defense industries.

CORRINE SYKES, a twenty-two-year-old African American woman, was put to death by "judicial electrocution" in Pennsylvania, on October 14, 1946, at 12:31 a.m. How Sykes, who possessed "the mentality of an eight-year-old child," would become the last woman executed in that state rests on a number of factors unique to Sykes's own historical moment.[20] Corrine was the youngest daughter of David and Alamena Sykes, Virginia migrants who in the early twentieth century made North Philadelphia their home. The city's racism differed in some respects from that of Southern cities, but it could be just as destructive, particularly for a child such as Corrine. She struggled academically and socially. Frequently fighting with peers, she ended up in a disciplinary school. Testing at age thirteen revealed that she had an IQ of sixty-three, roughly equivalent to the mental capacity of a seven-and-a-half-year-old. Social or educational resources for Black youth with special needs was rare, so in her early teens Corrine entered the workforce.[21]

Laboring as a domestic, she was arrested for theft and served eleven months in a county jail. Soon after her release, in May 1944, using the alias Heloise T. Parker, Corrine applied for another housekeeping position with an employment company. In December she started working for Freeda Wodlinger, a forty-five-year-old white woman who lived at 6305 North Camac Street, in the Oak Lane section of the city. On December 7, 1944, Wodlinger was found in the bathroom stabbed to death, and her home had been robbed of fifty dollars, three rings, and a fur piece. Fingerprint analysis would lead detectives to Corrine, who arrested two days later.[22] Over the course of her interrogation, her account changed a number of times, though she did implicate her boyfriend, Jayce Kelly. She told authorities, "I had Jayce on my mind. I know Jayce was speaking to me about some jewelry and stuff for him because he needed it. Before I know I struck her."[23] Kelly was arrested and charged as an accessory after the fact and for receiving stolen goods.

During Corrine's trial, which began in March 1945, all African Americans were successfully challenged for jury duty, and ultimately, an all-white jury consisting of eight women and four men convicted Corrine of murder. Her lawyer, Raymond Pace Alexander, spouse of Sadie Tanner Mossell Alexander, immediately appealed the verdict. Discovering evidence that the prosecution failed to disclose, Alexander argued that new evidence showed that Kelly had masterminded the crime and manipulated a mentally challenged woman.[24] Alexander appealed the case to the State Supreme Court and to the Supreme Court of the United States, to no avail. The State Board of Pardons also denied an appeal to commute Corrine's sentence. African Americans across the country followed the case, as it was covered locally but also by the *Chicago Defender*. Few believed justice was served. African Americans believed Corrine should have been punished, but they also felt that if she were a white woman in the same position, her life would have been spared.[25] It was yet another example of racist injustice, and it seemed that nowhere provided any respite, whether in the North, where all-white juries could sanction Black death, or in the South, where white lynch mobs committed racist murder with impunity.

The brutality and indignities of life in the South continued, but not without increasing contests. On one hand, African Americans were putting their lives on the line for the country serving in the armed forces, yet on the other, they were still being forced to sit at the back of the bus. The buses and segregated transportation in general had been an ongoing flashpoint, especially between Black women and white male drivers. For years Black women had been refusing to capitulate, and for years they had been punished for it. Viola white, a thirty-five-year-old widow and mother of three, worked at Maxine Air Force Base, in Montgomery, Alabama. In 1944 white refused to give up her seat to whites and was beaten, arrested, and fined ten dollars. After being found guilty, White appealed, and while the case stalled, police retaliated. An officer kidnapped and raped Viola's sixteen-year-old daughter. The young woman memorized the officer's license plate and bravely reported the crime. Under pressure to make an arrest, Montgomery authorities instead tipped off the officer, who left town. White died ten years later; her case never went to trial. Viola's experience, and that of her daughter, painfully illustrate just how high the stakes could be for Black women and girls who resisted.[26]

Pauli Murray, a legendary lawyer, writer, activist, feminist, and minister, perhaps comes closest to getting at the stifling ways that racism encapsulated African American women's lives noting that it "was the atmosphere one breathed from day to day, the pervasive irritant, the chronic allergy, the vague apprehension which made one uncomfortable and jumpy. We knew the race problem was like a deadly snake coiled and ready to strike, and that one avoided its dangers only by never-ending watchfulness." Pauli also noted racism's taxing effect on women, especially at moments of crisis: "The intrusion was unbearable, for no one had time to deal with it or to adopt the special behavior the racial code demanded. When piled on top of other troubles, race would be the sharp curve rising suddenly in the darkness, the blind railroad crossing, the fatal accident that happened when habitual wariness was momentarily relaxed." Or when Black women could no longer stomach supplication.[27]

Born in Baltimore, on November 20, 1910, Pauli was marked by two tragedies: her mother's sudden death due to a cerebral hemorrhage and her father's mental collapse after his wife's death and his bout with typhoid.[28] Pauli went to live with her maternal grandparents and two middle-aged aunts in Durham, North Carolina, when she was three years old. She attributed her intelligence and keen intellect to her father. Before his breakdown and subsequent commission to an asylum, he had been a teacher. Pauli excelled in school and planned to go to college, however, she did not want to enroll in a Black college because she refused to suffer the indignities of life in the segregated South. Instead, she saved up money and attended Hunter College, in New York City. Upon graduating she set her eyes on graduate school at the University of North Carolina, but segregationist polices thwarted her goals. Pauli fought the rejection, writing to the university president,

Eleanor Roosevelt, and the NAACP, threatening to sue. In the end, the NAACP passed on her case because she had not lived in the state long enough to claim legal residency.[29]

Pauli, a slim, androgynous woman, was emerging as an avowed activist, as well as a brilliant, creative mind. At the same time, she battled sometimes crippling depression and anxiety. Pauli also wrestled with her attraction to members of her own sex. She did not want to identify as a homosexual. For a time, Pauli had convinced herself that she was in fact intersex, possessing hidden testes—at least until an X-ray would prove her wrong. She then considered whether she had a "mother fixation" owing to the loss of her own mother at such a young age. Whatever the case, coming to terms with her sexuality, her penchant for dressing in men's clothes, and the emergence of "Pete, her 'boy-self,'" combined for a difficult journey.[30]

Her sexuality had the potential to collide with her civil rights activism in ways that could potentially alienate her from Black activist spaces. In 1940, Pauli and Adelene McBean, her roommate and school friend, were traveling on a segregated bus in Petersburg, Virginia. When the bus driver did not move the colored-section seating line so that they could sit in empty seats that were not broken, unlike the ones he had relegated them to, they did it for him. When he realized what they had done, the driver ordered them back to the broken seats. They refused. He summoned the authorities. The two women were arrested and placed into a filthy cell. Before their arrest, Pauli had written her name and that of a relative on a piece of paper. She had given it to another Black passenger on the bus and asked the passenger to have her relative contact the NAACP. As civil rights organizations and leaders got involved, the authorities dropped the charge of violating segregation against the women in order to avoid a legal constitutional challenge. The NAACP decided not to move forward with the case, once it was decided that Pauli only faced a disorderly conduct charge.[31]

But the NAACP's decision might have also been related to concerns about Pauli's sexual orientation and problems it would cause if the case proceeded. After Pauli's arrest, a curious story about it appeared in *Opportunity*, a Black journal. The story described the arrest, though in this version, the names were changed and the figures involved were described as a spirited Black woman (possibly Adelene) and her traveling companion, a "'slight,' light-skinned 'young man.'"

Pauli was light-complexioned. As historian Patricia Bell-Scott explains, although Pauli ultimately dismissed the story, she nonetheless "feared it raised speculations about her sexuality. That it had the same title and theme as one of her poems was a coincidence that added another layer to her aggravation."[32] Ultimately, Pauli Murray continued to challenge discriminatory laws by fighting both racism and sexism, but the stress she experienced trying to navigate the narrow gender expectations for Black women were common to many Black women, in every stratum and career.

African American actresses had long confronted restrictive gender codes, too, though the 1940s would add a new dimension to those struggles. Black women had been appearing in films since the early twentieth century, particularly in features made by Oscar Micheaux, an independent Black filmmaker. Some Black women had even been cast in early pornographic pieces, or stag films, as early as the 1920s and 1930s. However, as more African American women began to appear in mainstream white films, their roles were usually limited to playing housekeepers. Black domestics were scripted in line with the fictitious character of mammy, a stereotype that depicted them as fat, dark-skinned, asexual types who lived to serve and care for white families. Actresses such as Hattie McDaniel became famous in Hollywood for such roles, winning an Oscar in 1940 for her portrayal in *Gone with the Wind*. McDaniel was roundly criticized for playing such parts by members of the Black press and the NAACP. Ethel Waters and other actresses followed a similar career path, though the 1940s also witnessed Hollywood casting a new type of Black woman, such as Lena Horne and Fredi Washington, whose lighter skin and straighter hair allowed them to be cast as sexy and sultry albeit exoticized figures. The dynamic left older, darker-skinned actresses typecast as mammy-maids. During the making of *Cabin in the Sky*, Lena Horne recalled a vivid incident in which Ethel Waters unloaded on her and "the whole system that had held her back and exploited her."[33]

Waters, who had grown up dirt poor in Chester, Pennsylvania, had been rumored to be the product of a rape. Her father, a white pianist named John Wesley Waters, impregnated her mother, Louise Tar Anderson, reportedly when Louise was just twelve years old. Reared by her grandmother and always hungry, Ethel frequently ran errands for streetwalkers and pimps to earn money. She eventually took work as a domestic in a hotel where she was persuaded to sing, a move that effectively launched her career. She worked her way up from singing and acting on the vaudeville circuit to making it to Broadway and eventually into films, as was the case with *Cabin in the Sky*, in 1943. Based on the story of a drunken gambler given a second chance to redeem himself or face the fiery pits, the movie featured a bevy of Black actors with breathtaking vocals, vivacious dancing co-choreographed by the legendary Katherine Dunham, and the pulsating music of jazz great Duke Ellington and his band.[34]

Ethel's success and talents as a performer were unmistakable, but apart from her professional success, she endured a string of bad marriages, battled emotional volatility, and reportedly had a temper that could blow through sets like a hurricane. Perhaps because she experienced a great deal of racism and hardship, Ethel always held a space in her heart for poor and underprivileged Black people, stating, "My own people who despise Negroes who are poor and ignorant and condemned to live like animals arouse my fury as no white people can."[35] Given her own early circumstances, Ethel's alignment with poor and working-class Black people sketches the arc of Ethel's life, one that was complicated and etched with extraordinary highs and lows. She had lived the proverbial rags-to-riches story, but chafed at the limitations placed upon her as a Black woman, as someone who had come from the streets, and as someone who had run through husbands the way Alice Coachman ran laps in her youth.

The complexities of love, sexuality, labor, voice, and being able to live a full, satisfying life on one's own terms remained critical themes in African American women's literature. Building on her own breadth of work during the Harlem Renaissance, Zora Neale Hurston animated Black womanhood by diagramming the intersections of race, class, gender, and sexuality. Characters like Janie, in *Their Eyes Were Watching God*, first published in 1937, offered a rare sounding of Black female desire. In Hurston's work, Black women pursued love, sexual pleasure, and autonomy amid all their human frailties. Her work was joined by the unprecedented literary success of author Ann Petry. *The Street*, Petry's 1946 novel, would make her the first Black female writer to sell over a million copies. Drawing on the hardscrabble existence of Black women in the urban North, Petry wrote in haunting detail about her characters. Black people who lived in buildings crammed with an assortment of folks, some of whom "would be drunk and loud-mouthed and quarrelsome; given to fits of depression when they would curse and cry violently."[36] Black women writers resisted situating Black women's stories as solely about their troubles with whites or white supremacy, and they did not avoid Black women's personal difficulties. Rather, their words bridged, and likely reflected, African American women's desire to engage in pleasure and to be self-determining when it came to sexual intercourse and the potential consequences of those choices.

As Black women continued to take hold of their sexuality and erotic desires, not just in literature but in real life, they also became interested in learning about birth control methods. To be sure, the subject of birth control was especially charged for African American women, because so much of its earlier history had been wrapped up in racist advocacy. Eugenicists and white supremacists also took great interest in birth control as a means of curtailing the growth of the Black community and to potentially limit multiracial children. Under the circumstances, many African Americans were deeply suspicious of the methods. Some regarded birth control as tantamount to genocide. However, by 1941, the NCNW had commissioned a standing committee on the subject. The organization had even gone so far as to ask other Black organizations to add birth control to their agendas to stress that all Black families should only "have all the children it can afford and support but no more—to insure better health, security, and happiness for all." Marking the first time a national Black women's organization publicly advocated for birth control, the move also served as evidence of the ways that Black women were independently approaching the subject. It also pointed to Black women's embrace of more candid discussions about sex and procreation. Through the developments, the texture of Black life and potentially the tensions inside Black families and Black communities also come into focus. The shift also shows some of the ways Black women's activism continued to expand.[37]

Activism was growing in other ways, too, and African American women with radical and leftist views found themselves squarely in the crosshairs of the US government. These Black women challenged capitalism and liberal democracy—notions regarded as traitorous by a nation feverish with individualism and anti-communism. The government increasingly surveilled and criminalized those with political ideologies not in lockstep with American democracy. Against this landscape, long-time activists such as Claudia Jones were targeted and harassed. A series of laws essentially outlawed communism, beginning with the Smith Act in 1940 and intensifying with the passage of the Internal Security Act of 1950, which among its regulations required all communists to register with immigration and local police. In 1947 Claudia, who had immigrated to the US from Trinidad, was a secretary for the Women's Commission in the Communist Party. Claudia helped force the CP to acknowledge the "triple oppression" of Black women, and she popularized these ideas in works such as her essay "An End to the Neglect of the Problems of Negro Women!," which continued to draw the government's ire. She was arrested January 20, 1948. This arrest would be the start of a cycle of arrests, making bond, and attempts to fight a deportation order, as she was, according to the state, "an Alien who believes in, advocates, and teaches the overthrow, by force or violence of the Government of the United States." She was to be deported back to Trinidad. Activists rallied to her defense, and Claudia fought off deportation for years, but she was eventually incarcerated and deported in December 1955. Claudia went to London, where she was met by fellow Communist Party members. She continued organizing against racism and imperialism until her death in 1964.[38] Claudia and other Black communist women, however, were not the only Black women who held alternative political views to face federal persecution.

On September 21, 1942, Sister Pauline, national secretary for the Allah Temple of Islam, was swept up in an FBI raid. Though over seventy men would be arrested, she was charged along with two others from her Chicago mosque for sedition and allegedly advocating a "direct alliance with Japan." Sister Pauline was unabashed in her race pride, and she did not believe that Black people should support or serve US military interests, at home or abroad. Although the Black roots of Islam in the US stretch back to the Colonial Era, the communities became more visible in the 1930s. So much so that by the 1940s, the FBI had begun to surveil the groups, fearing that their religious activities might be subversive and undermine the war effort. Of particular concern was Black people's growing refusal to serve in the armed forces. During her interrogation, Sister Pauline allegedly told investigators that the white man was "grafted from the black man six thousand years ago" and that "black people have 7 ½ oz. of brain compared with the 6 oz. brain of the white devil." Though Sister Pauline was charged with sedition and described as a "top leader of the cult," the government regarded its case against her as the weakest and eventually dropped all charges against her in May 1943.[39] A few years earlier, Sister Pauline and many of the Black women in the mosque had begun to embrace more modest clothing. The shift in attire was religious but also political. On one hand, it offered a striking visual that reporters noted when the women packed courthouses to support other Temple members on trial. On the other hand, "wearing clothes that hid their outer selves protected them from roaming eyes on their body parts, visual assaults that plagued the lives of women after puberty."[40] But whether covered from head to toe or wearing their Sunday best, Black women remained targets of white sexual violence.

Untold numbers of African American women and girls were raped by white men and white youths, with few consequences. The outrages galvanized Black America and found everyday Black women continuing to mobilize and strike back. The rape of Mrs. Recy Taylor, a young Black woman returning home late one night from church services at the Rock Hill Holiness Church on September 3, 1944, in Abbeville, Alabama, struck many Black women to the core. Mrs. Taylor and her fellow parishioners were accosted by a group of white men in a car. The men—seven of them—kidnapped Mrs. Taylor, and six of them gang-raped her. She was twenty-four years old. The violent attack left her badly injured, and the nature of Jim Crow segregation meant that, as Mrs. Taylor explained, despite being ruptured by the attack, "not one of the townspeople came to see me or offered to provide a doctor."[41] Such assaults typically did not garner attention from local authorities or law enforcement, however, the crime was reported to the NAACP, which dispatched one of its skilled female investigators, a young Rosa Parks.

Parks, who already had extensive experience advocating for justice in sexual assaults against Black women, worked tirelessly after meeting with Mrs. Taylor. She would help form the Committee for Equal Justice for Mrs. Recy Taylor, with support from Taylor's family and other local African Americans. As they fought for justice in the case, the Taylor family received death threats from white supremacists, and their home was firebombed. Eventually, a grand jury, consisting of all white men, failed to indict any of the men involved, who had been readily identified by witnesses. Though justice was denied in Recy Taylor's case, the grassroots activism that developed as a result matured substantially.

Rosa Parks not only worked on the Taylor case but also on that of Gertrude Perkins, who charged that she had been raped by two white police officers in 1949. Perkins, twenty-five years old, was returning home on Sunday morning on March 27, when the officers drove alongside her and accused her of being drunk. As the *Chicago Defender* reported, "They said they were going to take her to headquarters . . . but instead they took her to an alley and at gun point, raped her." The NAACP, as well as local leaders and community groups including the Reverend Solomon Seay and the Women's Political Council (WPC), formed a coalition to agitate for justice, though they met with fierce resistance. The local authorities, steeped in white supremacy, took evasive measures to stymy the investigation, including denying the charges against members of the force. Perkins's legal counsel brought suit against the mayor, John L. Godwin, and sheriff, George A. Mosley, however, it was denied by circuit judge Eugene Carter. The attorneys had wanted to force "the sheriff to serve warrants against the policemen." Activists dug in and fought for two years for justice in Perkins's case, only to have the officers fail to be indicted.[42]

The outcome surprised few, though it spurred on the Black community, Black women especially, including Rosa Parks and those who joined the WPC, which helped lay the foundation for grassroots efforts in the 1950s.[43] In its earliest iteration, the WPC powerfully aided efforts to obtain justice on behalf of Black people in Alabama, including helping rape victims. Black women's central role in the WPC and the group's political evolution both mirror and foreshadow Black women's activism, not only during World War II but also the civil rights era and well beyond.[44]

———

AS AFRICAN AMERICAN WOMEN fought discrimination on multiple fronts, their victories helped change the country, particularly in sports and the armed forces but also in film and literature, and in activism. Black women never forgot what they were fighting for, even as they worked to create fulfilling personal lives in whatever ways were most meaningful to them. For Alice Coachman this included getting married (she would later go by Alice Coachman Davis) and having two children. She also remained in Albany, Georgia, where she taught and coached. In 1996, her achievements were honored at the Olympic Games in Atlanta, and she was inducted into the National Track and Field Hall of Fame in 2004. Alice died July 14, 2014. She was ninety years old. Before her death, it was clear that Alice understood her place in history and the importance of her legacy, as she explained to a reporter, "If I had gone to the Games and failed, there wouldn't be anyone to follow in my footsteps. It encouraged the rest of the women to work harder and fight harder."[45]

CHAPTER NINE

AURELIA'S LAWSUIT AGAINST JIM CROW, 1950—1970

We, the Negroes, request the Rev. King,
and not he over us.

—AURELIA BROWDER

AURELIA SHINES WAS BORN in Alabama in 1919. As a girl, she went to school and also helped her family with farm work. Aurelia loved to "put up fruits and vegetables." She wed Butler Ben Browder on May 12, 1948. Aurelia was a seamstress, a mother of six, and eventually a widow. In her thirties, she had worked hard to finish school, earning her degree from Alabama State College. Also a midwife, she often used the buses in Montgomery, Alabama, riding as much as four times a day. At age thirty-seven, in 1955, Aurelia was arrested for refusing to give up her seat. Though this act of defiance is most commonly associated with the brave action of Rosa Parks in December 1955, as noted in earlier chapters, Rosa was not the first Black woman to protest such racist treatment in this way. In fact, she was not even the first Black woman to do so that year. Aurelia refused to move from her seat on April 29, 1955, some months before Parks's action. Moreover, Aurelia's act of civil disobedience was not even the first time that Aurelia had refused to submit to racist segregation on public buses. She also refused to give up her seat in 1948. In that instance, the bus driver detained her, but rather than dragging Aurelia to the police station as his shift was nearing an end, he took her back to the stop where he first picked her up. She had to walk to her intended destination. Aurelia, who was herself pregnant at the time, had been headed to another delivery, which she missed.[1]

Experiences like Aurelia's spotlight the everyday heroism of Black women, and they allow us to glimpse their genius. Black women who later boycotted effectively transformed what white drivers intended as another form of punishment into a tool of resistance, one that would break the yoke of segregation on public transportation. Aurelia's actions further illustrate how the buses especially served as a flashpoint for Black women. Given their concentration in domestic service and the need to work outside their homes in general, Black women were routinely degraded as they traveled to and from work.

As in previous decades, they refused to be supplicants. Black women and Black girls fought back. When fifteen-year-old Claudette Colvin refused to give up her seat in 1955, she, too, was arrested before Rosa Parks. The NAACP opted not to bring a suit on her behalf because she was pregnant and unwed, and the organization feared the stigma that might incur. For them, Rosa Parks, who was forty-two, married, and a veteran activist, seemed like a better choice on which to base a strike against segregated busing.[2]

But before that strike was launched, two more Black women refused to give up their seats in 1955. Susie McDonald, a Black senior citizen, had been riding the buses for over seventy years, up to three times a day. Infirm and walking with a cane, she, too, had been mistreated on Montgomery's buses and resisted. Mary Louise Smith, aged eighteen, was riding the bus on October 21, 1955, when she refused to give up her seat. The driver asked her three times to move. She told him, "I am not going to move out of my seat. I am not going to move anywhere, I got the privilege to sit here like any body [*sic*] else." She was arrested and fined a total of $14. For Mary, the confrontation with the driver had been the last straw that day. A white woman she had been cleaning for failed to pay her the eleven dollars she was owed. Mary had gone to the woman's house seeking payment but was returning home empty-handed when she was ordered to move out of her seat.

All of these women had protested earlier than Rosa Parks. They also joined forces and sued. Aurelia, Susie, Claudette, and Mary would be represented by civil rights attorneys Fred Gray and Clifford Durr in a civil action brought against the mayor and the Montgomery Board of Commissioners. Their case challenged the constitutionality of Alabama state statutes and local city ordinances that required segregation on buses. A fifth Black woman was initially a part of the suit, but Jeanetta Reese withdrew amid intense racist harassment. And the risks were real; recall the terror and violence rained on Viola White and her young daughter in 1944. Still, the four women pressed on. Their testimonies would take place against the backdrop of the Montgomery bus boycott, which started in early December 1955, shortly after Parks's arrest. Each woman in the suit described her mistreatment on the city's buses, particularly at the time of arrest. For example, Claudette told of how she cried at the responses of whites as she was harassed and kicked by a police officer before she was dragged off the bus.[3]

Aurelia anchored the civil suit and served as the lead plaintiff. In her testimony, she described how she and two other Black people were asked to move: "I was sitting in a seat and another lady beside me. And the seat just across from me there was just one colored person in there. And he made all three of us get up because he said we was in the white section of the bus." Opposing counsel tried to suggest that Aurelia and her fellow plaintiffs were operating at the behest of the Reverend Dr. Martin Luther King Jr. and the Montgomery Improvement Association, a grassroots organization created to help guide the bus boycott. Aurelia said she did not answer any such demand, because "we, the Negroes, request the Rev. King, and not he over us."[4] Aurelia's words demonstrate the initiative of Black women in forcefully challenging racial segregation—they did not take their marching orders from Dr. King; rather the young charismatic minister answered the call of local people. Typically, when we think of the civil rights movement, the heroism and sacrifice of Martin Luther King Jr., as well as that of other key figures, is often at the fore. However, Black women and girls like Aurelia, Claudette, Susie, and Mary Louise represent the tireless commitment of lesser-known or otherwise nameless makers of the movement.

AFRICAN AMERICAN WOMEN played crucial roles in the civil rights movement at every level. Pauli Murray, who had obtained a law degree at Howard University, had, as a student, begun formulating a strategy for overturning *Plessy v. Ferguson*, ideas that she published in her 1950 book *States' Laws on Race and Color*. This work is credited with helping to lay the foundation for the arguments in *Brown v. Board of Education*, the 1954 case that ruled that segregation in schools is inherently separate and unequal. That landmark verdict was the culmination of legal precedents built up during the late 1930s, and 1940s, under the leadership of pioneer civil rights attorney Charles Hamilton Houston. Brave Black women plaintiffs such as Ada Lois Sipuel, who sued to desegregate the University of Oklahoma Law School in 1948, helped make *Brown v. Board of Education* a reality. It would help undo decades of Jim Crow laws and policies, and it served as case law cited in *Browder v. Gayle*. Filed in US District Court on February 1, 1956, *Browder v. Gayle* would wend its way through the courts as thousands of African American women resolutely walked to and from work. For 381 days, African American women walked and organized a network of informal carpools, pick-up and drop-off locations, while Georgia Gilmore and a cohort of other Black cooks like her, prepared and sold cooked goods to raise money to help sustain the Montgomery bus boycott. The women's actions were carefully planned and coordinated.[5]

Of course, history does not always allow for such pragmatic considerations. Sometimes events unexpectedly thrust Black women into positions that brought almost unthinkable responsibilities and consequences. Mamie Till-Mobley was one of those women. The horrifying murder of her fourteen-year-old son, Emmett Till, devastated a mother's heart, steeled her resolve to expose white supremacist injustice, and arguably served as one of the most significant sparks for the modern civil rights movement. Emmett Till's vicious murder by racist whites in Money, Mississippi, for allegedly making a pass at a white woman, shocked and enraged citizens, both Black and white, across the country. Yet Till's death would not have helped ignite the movement in 1955 were it not for the fearless maneuvers of his mother, Mamie Till-Mobley. Born Mamie Elizabeth Carthan in Webb, Mississippi, in 1921, two years later, she and her family would move to Argo, Illinois, just outside of Chicago. Her first husband, Emmett's father, Louis Till, died during World War II in Italy in 1945. She married "Pink" Bradley in 1951 but divorced him and then married Gene Mobley in 1957. The summer Emmett spent with his cousins down South set their family on a fateful path. Though most Black families took pains to prep Black children for how to behave in the South, particularly with respect to white authority, the young Emmett—who was a bit of a prankster—did not fully comprehend the grave nature of Jim Crow racism.[6]

After allegedly whistling at a white female store clerk, Roy Bryant and J. W. Milam kidnapped Emmett from his uncle's home. Days later, his badly beaten, mutilated corpse surfaced in the Tallahatchie River, despite having been weighted with a seventy-four-pound cotton-gin fan. The local sheriff sought to quickly bury the body. Mamie would have none of it. She described the racist runaround she experienced to an audience at Bethel AME Church in Baltimore on October 29, 1955: "We remark about the Iron Curtain in Russia, but there's a cotton curtain in Mississippi that must have a steel lining. When you make a telephone call, I don't know who signals whom, but the person that you want to talk to doesn't want to talk if the call is coming from Chicago. The people that you always knew as being great, wonderful leaders, suddenly had nothing whatsoever to say."[7] Mamie, who even telegrammed President Eisenhower asking him to personally see that her son received justice, would enlist the help of Chicago officials and she mobilized local relatives to recover her son's body and prevent his burial in Mississippi. In order to safely transport her son's remains, those relatives involved a white undertaker. The local Black undertaker felt that having the body in his establishment would lead to his business being destroyed and that he himself probably "wouldn't be alive in the morning." The white undertaker agreed to handle the body and prepare it for shipment, so long as Mamie's uncle promised "that this seal will never be broken and that nobody will ever review that body."[8] Whatever her uncle's intentions, Mamie was not bound to such an oath, though when she met her son's casket at the station, the pine box that held Emmett had been nailed shut. In the 2005 documentary *The Untold Story of Emmett Louis Till*, Mamie explained, "When I first saw that box, I just collapsed." Even so, she knew she had a job to do, and in stunning, heart-wrenching detail, she painfully catalogued for the filmmakers the litany of injuries she observed when she finally saw Emmett's body:

> I saw his tongue had been choked out and it was lying down on his chin. I saw that uh this eye was out and it was lying about midway to cheek. I looked at this eye and it was gone. I looked at the bridge

of his nose and it looked like someone had taken a meat chopper and chopped it. And I looked at his teeth because I took so much pride in his teeth; his teeth were the prettiest things I'd ever seen in my life I thought. And uh I only saw two. Well where are the rest of them? They'd just been knocked out. And uh I was looking at his ears. His ears uh were like mine. They curled; they're, they're not attached and they curled up. Uh the same way mine are. And I didn't see the ear. Where's the ear? And that's when I discovered a hole about here and I could see daylight on the other side. I said now was it necessary to shoot him? If that's a bullet hole was that necessary? And I also discovered that they had taken an axe and they had gone straight down across his head and the face and the back of the head were separate.[9]

At the funeral parlor, so many people attempted to see the body that Mamie contacted a local reverend and asked if the wake and service could be held at his church instead. The minister agreed, and the demand to attend was such that the actual burial was delayed for a few days. Thousands of people observed the violence visited upon Emmett Till's body. As Mamie recalled, "When they walked in that church, they had one feeling. But when they looked down in that casket, they got another. Men fainted and women fainted. I'm told that one out of every ten went to their knees and had to be carried out."[10]

Mamie's remarkable and indeed history-altering decision to show the monstrous face of white supremacy was, in many respects, only the start of her journey. While Emmett Till's disfigured image became a haunting symbol of the brutality of white racism, Mamie had to endure the trial and media coverage that sought to cast aspersions on her and her son's character. She carried herself with dignity and respect, yet she and her family suffered daily indignities and death threats. Those efforts failed to meet their mark because as Mamie explained, "They wrote: I'm glad that it was your n----- boy that was killed; that'll show some more smart kids in Chicago that they can't come down in Mississippi and get away with what they get away with in Chicago. I would like to tell those people tonight, that if it hadn't been for those letters, I probably wouldn't be standing here. I want them to know that every one of those letters gave me a new determination to stand up and fight that much harder."[11] And she did. Press accounts questioned her morality, and she faced criticism for speaking out about her son's death. Regardless, Mamie toured various parts of the country raising awareness about Emmett's murder and the case. She also had to face the acquittal of both of his murderers. Her son's death and her profound commitment in the face of unimaginable pain to seek justice on his behalf changed the course of the civil rights movement. To begin with, Rosa Parks cited Emmett's death, and her training at the Highlander Folk School that summer, as contributing to her decision to refuse to change seats. In 2017 the *New York Times* reported that Emmett Till's accuser, Carolyn Bryant, confessed that she had lied about what happened that day. Mamie did not live long enough to hear this admission, but she did live until age eighty-one. At the time of her death, on January 6, 2003, she had gone on to earn a degree from Chicago Teacher's College in 1960, where she graduated cum laude. She taught in that city's school system until her retirement, in 1983, and she also worked with youth on the history of civil rights and published a memoir about her son's murder and the harrowing events that followed.[12]

SHORTLY AFTER ROSA PARKS'S ARREST in Montgomery, on December 1, 1955, activists quickly followed with calls for action. Jo Ann Robinson, of the WPC, created a flyer that denounced the arrest and called for a boycott. She took it to the Albany State College campus where she worked and, with a colleague, stayed up all night to mimeograph thirty thousand copies. Moreover, the "WPC had planned distribution routes months earlier and, the next day, Robinson and two students delivered bundles of flyers to beauty parlors and schools, to factories and grocery stores, to taverns and barber shops."[13] Fifty thousand African Americans, mostly masses of Black women, heeded the call to walk rather than ride, impelled by righteous indignation and guided by the tireless grassroots activism of Jo Ann Robinson and the WPC. Unlike Rosa Parks, these were not seasoned activists but everyday Black women who had endured physical assaults, loss of work and wages, and daily threats and harassment.[14] The boycott, which lasted over a year, finally ended on December 20, 1956, after the Supreme Court ruled segregation unconstitutional in *Browder v. Gayle*. The grueling victory was one that Black women had collectively achieved through the courage of their convictions, incredible sacrifice, and a level of selflessness rarely seen. Mamie Till, Aurelia Browder, and other women never sought credit for their actions.

Perhaps they knew that getting the laws changed was just the beginning of the long journey to equality, since the end of the bus boycott did not end the dangers for Black women passengers. On December 28, 1956, Mrs. Rosa Jordan, a twenty-two-year-old Black laundress, was shot while riding a desegregated bus in Montgomery. Reportedly, though she was "shot in the legs . . . by a sniper," Mrs. Jordan survived, however her left leg was shattered. Despite such deadly threats, Black women and girls continued to ride the buses and continued to press for change, often confronting both racism and sexism in the process. For Rosa Parks, the costs of being the face of the boycott were also severe. She was fired from her job and contended with both unemployment and under-employment for the next decade. Threats of violence forced Rosa and her husband to move out of state, though even then they continued to receive death threats. At the end of her life, Rosa battled poor health and financial instability, but these challenges did not diminish her commitment to civil rights, and she remained active in social justice causes until her death, in 2005.[15]

Whether challenging segregation in education or in public spaces, Black women and Black girls were on the front lines where new laws were transformed into changed daily practices. But many were also beginning to combat gender disparities within their own communities. In the 1940s and 1950s Pauli Murray hotly criticized what she coined "Jane Crow," marking an early version of intersectional Black feminism. She was incensed by sexist ideas and practices at Howard University and within the civil rights movement that sought to limit women's leadership and intellectual contributions, especially as Black women were increasingly leading desegregation efforts. Black leaders such as Ella Baker, a seasoned grassroots organizer going back to the 1930s, had fought to move Dr. King and the Southern Christian Leadership Conference (SCLC) away from hierarchical approaches. Baker and King rarely saw eye to eye as she pushed for more broad-based coalition building that empowered everyday Black women and men. In addition to helping coordinate nonviolent social protest activities with the SCLC, Baker helped create a space for young people to organize themselves. Convening young activists at Shaw University in

1960, she effectively gave birth to the Student Nonviolent Coordinating Committee (SNCC). For Baker, having young minds play a central, independent role in the movement was essential, because she felt they enlivened the struggle and were less likely to be weighted with "scars of battle, the frustrations and the disillusionment that come when the prophetic leader turns out to have heavy feet of clay."[16]

Baker herself proved to be prophetic, because SNCC took grassroots organizing to a new level. SNCC members worked with local African Americans throughout the South and were committed to direct action. They fought for Black equality, which included exercising the right to vote. Ruby Doris Smith Robinson, a young Black woman, helped run SNCC's command center in Atlanta, which supported the organization's actions across the country. Black women in rural parts of the nation were equally engaged. Among the African American women who joined the organization were Unita Blackwell, born March 18, 1933, in Lula, Mississippi, and forty-four-year-old Fannie Lou Hamer, born in Montgomery County, Mississippi. Blackwell, who went from chopping cotton for three dollars a day in rural Mississippi to becoming a full-time civil rights organizer in SNCC, to later going on to become the first Black woman elected as a mayor in the state, in 1976, stands as a testament to Black women's ability to truly "specialize in the wholly impossible."[17] SNCC members brought vitality and a new kind of resolve to the movement.

When faced with the prospect of halting the Freedom Rides during the summer of 1961, after riders had been beaten and a bus set on fire in Anniston, Alabama, Diane Nash, a SNCC member, had strong objections. Freedom Rides, which involved Black and white activists attempting to use "whites only" bathrooms and water fountains in bus depots in the South after the Supreme Court ruled segregation in these areas unconstitutional, often ended in bloody clashes with local white racists. Diane recalled, "Some people said 'Well, why not let things cool off, and maybe, you know, try again in a few weeks or . . . or a few months?' And that was really . . . that would have been really a huge mistake because it's like metal. If the metal is hot, you can fashion it and shape it. Once it's cold, you can't shape it anymore." As she understood it, "We had to move at a critical time and we had to make certain that the Freedom Rides continued, especially since there had been a great deal of violence."[18]

Diane Nash was raised in Chicago, where she was born in 1938. The city had its own racial battles, but the world in which Diane was reared differed greatly from the one that she encountered when she enrolled at Fisk University in Nashville, Tennessee. Her arrival at the campus occurred just as that city became ground zero for the student sit-ins in February 1960. Although members of the Congress of Racial Equality (CORE) had engaged in sit-ins as early as 1942, in Chicago and in Southern and Midwestern cities, students undertaking the action in Nashville did so with a renewed sense of urgency.[19]

On the face of it, Diane might seem an unlikely activist. A former beauty queen from a middle-class family, she was seen by her relatives as having fallen in with the wrong element when they learned about her social justice activism. Yet, her dedication to the movement was principled, unwavering, and lifelong. Not only was Diane among the scores of students who valiantly sought to desegregate lunch counters, but she was among the pioneers when it came to SNCC's policy of sitting in jail rather than being bailed out. Her first stint, some thirty-eight days in a cell, along with three other SNCC members, was physically and emotionally grueling. It would be the first of many such actions. Another bid took place when she was pregnant with her first child. She was prepared to remain in jail, because she wanted to make a better world for her future offspring, even if that meant his being born in jail to achieve it.[20]

Diane's resistance represented many of the overlapping concerns for activist women in the 1950s and 1960s. Juggling marriages and children, while attacking Jim and Jane Crow, Black women had to make hard choices about how and when to actively engage, as they were often denied a public voice, and most enjoyed only limited leadership roles. Even when they obtained leadership positions, as Gwendolyn Zohara Simmons, a member of SNCC who worked on the Mississippi Freedom Summer Project, explained, that she "often had to struggle around issues related to a woman being a project director. We had to fight for the resources, you know. We had to fight to get a good car because the guys would get first dibs on everything, and that wasn't fair. . . . It was a struggle to be taken seriously by the leadership, as well as by your male colleagues." Gwendolyn added, "One of the things that we often don't talk about, but there was sexual harassment that often happened toward the women. And so, that was one of the things that, you know, I took a stand on. . . . There is not going to be sexual harassment of any of the women on this project or any of the women in this community. And you will be put out if you do it." For many Black women activists, their overall struggles existed at the cloudy intersection of the fight for liberation and the desire not to pad racist stereotypes about Black men. At the same time they confronted prevalent cultural biases that depicted them as less feminine than white women, many of whom touched off difficult rifts when they joined the civil rights movement. Negotiating these fault lines could be exhausting, but most Black women focused their attentions on directly challenging deeply entrenched social and structural racism in the South.[21]

Mississippi, the Magnolia State, which had the highest proportion of Black people in the US, was also the most repressive in limiting voting rights and Black advancement. The majority of the Black population were sharecroppers, and close to 83 percent of Black families in the state lived below the poverty line. As historian Vicki Crawford explains, "More than 40 percent of all employed black men were farm workers or laborers, and almost 65 percent of black women were employed as cooks, maids, servants, and in other service jobs."[22] Educational access was limited, and only 3 percent of African Americans in the state were registered to vote.

That number was about to change however. Fannie Lou Hamer was among the earliest of local African Americans to work with SNCC and to attempt to register to vote after attending a SNCC-sponsored mass meeting in Ruleville, Mississippi, in 1962. Her decision to try to access one of the basic rights of citizenship that year would alter her life trajectory. Upon her first failed attempt to register to vote, she returned home to learn from her spouse the news that she no longer had a job and that she was advised to leave the community where she had lived and labored. After the owner of the land where she and her family sharecropped issued Hamer an ultimatum—either withdraw your application to vote or leave—she decided that, despite having handled W. D. Marlow's time books, nursed his family, and cleaned his house, his demand was the final straw. As Hamer put it, "I made up my mind I was grown, and I was tired." She informed Marlow: "I didn't go down there to register for you. I went there to register for myself."[23]

Hamer would dedicate her life to activism; she continued to try to register to vote, finally attaining that goal on June 10, 1963. Any celebratory basking would quickly end, however. Shortly after, Hamer and a number of fellow organizers were arrested and beaten in a jail cell in Winona, Mississippi. She later said, "That man beat me—that man beat me until he give out." Hamer recalled that the beating had left her extremities swollen and blue, and that, at one point, she tried to fix her clothes to cover herself, as the violence had left them disheveled. She told how a white man who participated in the attack, and who had ordered other Black prisoners to beat Hamer, had "just taken my clothes and snatched them up, and this Negro, when he had just beat me until I know he was just [going to] give out, well, then, this state patrolman told the other Negro to take it."[24]

Despite that traumatic ordeal, Hamer somehow found the strength to continue to organize, whether working to feed the poor or decrying the state's racist 1964 sterilization bill, which, as historian Chana Kai Lee explains, was "immediately recognized as the legislature's pathetic attempt to repress the movement by scaring local folk, especially women." The bill would have made having a second child out of wedlock a felony, and mothers would have to choose between sterilization or prison.[25] Dubbed the "genocide bill" by SNCC and other local activists, the legislative effort reveals the profound threat to Black women's bodies. Hamer's testimony against the proposed legislation helped lay bare the frequency with which rural Black women in Mississippi were being targeted for sterilization; she herself had been the victim of such a procedure. In 1961, thinking she has having a cyst removed from her stomach, Hamer learned afterward that she had been given a hysterectomy without her consent. Hamer, along with fellow African American activists and Black women organizers such as Annie Devine and Victoria Gray, would help found the Mississippi Freedom Democratic Party (MFDP) to combat the all-white Democratic machine in the state. The MFDP challenged their exclusion at the Democratic National Convention in 1964, and, though they ultimately failed to unseat the all-white delegation, their actions continued to spotlight the virulent anti-Black policies in the state and the country. This episode, which led to a measure of disillusionment among MFDP members, also contributed to their radicalization. As Hamer explained it, "Even though we had all the laws and righteousness on our side—that white man is not going to give up his power to us. . . . We have to take it for ourselves."[26]

AFRICAN AMERICAN GIRLS, too, played major roles in propelling the civil rights movement, as they not only served as lead plaintiffs in *Brown v. Board of Education* but also took the lead in personally desegregating schools—from sixteen-year-old Melba Patillo helping desegregate Central High School in Little Rock, Arkansas, in 1957, to six-year-old Ruby Bridges desegregating an all-white elementary school in New Orleans in 1960. In her rousing memoir, Melba detailed her loneliness and isolation, as well as the daily harassments and assaults she and her peers endured that year. Melba also highlighted her betrayal by a teacher on the first day of school. The white woman who led the class did nothing as the boys called Melba a "nigger coon" and threatened to beat her up. Melba explained: "I waited for the teacher to speak up, but she said nothing. Some of the students snickered. The boy took his seat, but he kept shouting ugly words at me throughout the rest of the class. My heart was weeping, but I squeezed back the tears. I squared my shoulders and tried to remember what Grandma has said: 'God loves you, child; no matter what he sees you as his precious idea.'" The taunts were just the beginning, as Melba was tormented by white girls in the restrooms and in the cafeteria. Three white football players attacked Melba by first knocking her books and papers to the floor, and then, she recalled, "one of them pinned me against the wall. Someone's forearm pressed hard against my throat, choking me. I couldn't speak. I could hardly breathe." The young men delivered an ominous warning: "We're gonna make your life hell, nigger. You all are gonna go screaming out of here, taking those nigger-loving soldiers with you."[27] Even with a National Guardsman for protection, a white student managed to throw battery acid in Melba's face. The guardsman's swift action, immediately flushing her face with water in a nearby restroom, helped save Melba's sight. Melba survived her time at Central High School, though she sustained serious emotional trauma from the experience. Although Melba's story is marked by her adherence to nonviolence, not all Black girls followed those tenets in the strictest sense.

In 1963 Black girls in Baton Rouge strategically armed themselves and found ways to weaponize everyday items such as school bags, safety pins, and even books. Marion Greenup, a Black teen desegregating Baton Rouge High School, let white students believe she had a gun in her bag by warning them, "I don't think you want to mess with me, you don't know what I have." Freya Anderson, at Lee High, carried large, open safety pins in both hands, so that anyone who bumped into her got jabbed. Some Black girls physically fought back, but most actively chose nonviolent, direct action to defeat segregation. Clara Luper launched sit-ins to force desegregation at lunch counters and stores in Oklahoma, while college student Charlayne Hunter-Gault helped desegregate the University of Georgia in 1961. And young SNCC activist Diane Nash started out doing sit-ins before going on to organize voter registration drives and leading youth protests and marches. After students sought to desegregate by sitting-in at a lunch counter at Woolworth's in Greensboro, North Carolina, in 1960, masses of other students followed suit, leading their own sit-ins in fifteen other cities and in five states in the South. Within eighteen months, nearly 70,000 people, predominantly African Americans, had participated in sit-ins, and more than 3,600 were arrested. The impact was far-reaching, and national chains and stores in the North and South desegregated their lunch counters and places of business.[28]

Poor and working-class Black women also organized to desegregate public housing in Baltimore and other cities. Though this work had begun a decade earlier, the 1960s witnessed a new wave of activity. For example, in the 1950s roughly 45 percent of residents in public housing were working-class whites, but by the 1960s African Americans composed a significant majority. The transition was hardly smooth, as whites protested, lashed out at incoming Black people, and united against them. In cases where whites were more welcoming, they, too, faced a backlash from other white residents. As Rosalind Lundsford, a white resident, recalled that in the 1960s, for accommodating her new Black neighbors in Baltimore, she was labeled a "nigger lover."[29] If white women were called such ugly epithets, you know incoming Black female tenants faced an especially uphill battle.

Even as Jim Crow was slowly being dismantled, beatings, sexual harassment, and sexual assaults against Black women had largely continued unabated. In 1959 a Florida A&M University (FAMU) student, Betty Jean Owens, was viciously attacked during an evening out with friends in Tallahassee. Owens, along with another Black woman and two Black men, were felled by a group of white men who had made a pact to "go out and get a nigger girl" for an all-night party. The four accosted the group, pulled a gun, and separated the women from their male counterparts. The women were ordered into their car and driven away. Edna Richardson broke free and escaped. Betty Jean was beaten and raped seven times.[30]

Betty Jean's friends contacted the local authorities and, together, they spotted the assailants' blue Chevrolet. When officers stopped the car, they found Betty Jean, bound and gagged, lying on the floorboard. Her attackers reportedly laughed and joked all the way to the jailhouse. FAMU students undertook massive protests, demanding justice. In Black communities the sense was that "it wasn't just one Negro girl that was raped—it was all of the Negro womanhood in the South." The massive response forced circuit judge W. May Walker to call a grand jury for a special session on May 6, 1959. Two hundred FAMU students packed the segregated seating area. Betty Jean was brought to court with the aid of a nurse and her mother, as she was still being treated for her injuries and was suffering from severe depression.[31]

So unlikely was any sort of indictment or justice that a collective gasp escaped courtroom spectators when the panel voted that the men should stand trial. But African American women demanded justice. Ella Baker issued the following statement: "With memories of Negroes who have been lynched and executed on far less evidence, Negro leaders from all over the South will certainly examine every development in this case. . . . What will Florida's answer be?"[32] If Ella Baker was genuinely asking, Black Muslims believed they had the answer. Members of the Nation of Islam (NOI), at that time under the leadership of Elijah Muhammad, had also been following the case. The organization's membership had been steadily growing. Its message of Black Nationalism, together with its spiritual appeal, was powerful, but Black folks were also drawn to the mighty oratory skills of Malcolm X. As the trial of Betty Jean's assailants approached, the NOI decried the rape and announced, "We know there is no justice under the American Flag."[33]

For her part, Betty Jean Owens bravely faced her attackers and before a packed courthouse detailed how she had been stripped and assaulted. She told of how she begged to be released, and she also described her powerlessness: "I was so scared, but there was nothing I could do with four men, a knife, and a gun. . . . I couldn't do anything but what they said." She testified that she did not consent. The defense grilled her for an hour, alleging that the acts were consensual and asking whether she derived any pleasure from the encounter. The men were found guilty with a recommendation of mercy. The judge deferred sentencing for fifteen days. Rather than handing down a death sentence, which was customary at the time, the men received life sentences. Some African Americans took solace in the fact that there was an arrest and conviction at all, but other Black people were incensed at the double standard. As historian Danielle McGuire explains, "In the thirty-four years since Florida began sending convicted rapists to the electric chair instead of the gallows, the state had electrocuted thirty-seven African Americans charged with raping white women." Moreover, though the men were sentenced to life, they were all granted parole in 1965.[34] Still, the case marked an important turning point: the legal system had actually punished white men for sexually assaulting a Black woman.

For many African American women, civil rights was inextricably linked to respect for and protection of their womanhood. They fought for this acknowledgment in ways great and small. Even as justice was usually elusive, Black women kept placing a demand on the system, both in big cases like that of Betty Jean's and Aurelia's and in smaller but important cases as well. In 1963 Mary Lucille Hamilton was arrested at a protest in Alabama. She was thrown in jail for five days and fined fifty dollars because she refused to answer the judge until he addressed her as "Miss Hamilton" rather than "Mary." The NAACP took up her case, and the US Supreme Court ruled in her favor the following year, reversing the contempt judgement.[35]

However, progress in the civil rights movement was hardly a linear process. When Black children organized a mass walkout and protest in Birmingham in May 1963, local officials retaliated by turning on hoses and unleashing dogs, and arresting and imprisoning the youths. The images of the atrocities had a global impact, one that effectively turned an international spotlight on racial hatred in America. The

Children's Crusade also drew the wrath of white supremacists who, often with support of the state, cruelly targeted Black children for their retribution. Such was the case for at least thirty preteen and adolescent Black girls who protested segregation in Americus, Georgia, in July 1963. The children were violently arrested and transported twenty miles out of town, without their parents' knowledge. Authorities locked the girls in the Leesburg stockade. With one broken toilet and a broken shower, the girls languished in the sweltering heat, in filthy conditions, with inadequate food and no toiletries, for nearly six weeks. The girls squatted over the shower drain to relieve themselves, and they used the cardboard from sporadic burger deliveries as toilet paper. They tore strips off their dresses to use when they got their periods.[36]

This resourcefulness could not shield them from the suffocating odors or repel the ticks, roaches, and mosquitoes in the stockade. One old guard was posted to keep watch, and while he was himself a tormentor, he did run off two truckloads of drunken white boys who showed up one night looking for prey. As Laura Ruff, who was fifteen at the time, recalled, "They started yelling to Pops, 'Let us in there. We wanna have a little fun!'" Battling depression, dehydration, and bouts of diarrhea, the girls kept their spirits up by praying, singing freedom songs, and holding each other. A SNCC photographer, Danny Lyon, managed to obtain photos of the children, taken through the stockade's barred windows. Once exposed, pressure on the local authorities prompted the girls' release. It would be the first week of September 1963, just as the school year had begun.[37]

While the children were in captivity, a quarter of a million people marched in Washington, DC. The 1963 March on Washington, partly resurrecting an idea proposed a decade earlier, was the culmination of organizing by Black women, civil rights volunteers, and by the openly gay Black man widely considered to be its architect, Bayard Rustin. Rustin, a Quaker, from West Chester, Pennsylvania, was a lifelong nonviolent activist who played an influential role in shaping Dr. King's philosophies of nonviolence and civil disobedience. Under Rustin's stewardship, the historic march powerfully buoyed civil rights efforts.[38] But the march was a complicated event for Black women, whose ideas, bodies, labor, courage, and sacrifice had contributed mightily to the cause of civil rights. Their voices were largely muted. Josephine Baker spoke, though she did so before the official start of the program. Marian Anderson led the National Anthem, while renowned gospel singer Mahalia Jackson also performed a selection. The program included a hotly contested, utterly inadequate "Tribute to Negro Women Fighters for Freedom," in which a handful of Black women were seated on the platform, introduced and acknowledged, but they were not supposed to make any sort of speech.

Yet in the vein of so many sisters who had come before, shortly after A. Philip Randolph introduced her, Daisy Bates added her own inflection to a prepared introduction given to her and said,

> Our pledge to you, to Martin Luther King, Roy Wilkins, and all of you fighting for civil liberties—that we will join hands with you as women of this country. Rosa Gragg, Vice President; Dorothy Height, the National Council of Negro Women; and the Delta Sigma Theta Sorority; the Methodist Church Women, all the women pledge that we will join hands with you. We will kneel-in; we will sit-in until we can eat in any corner in the United States. We will walk until we are free, until we can walk to any school and take our children to any school in the United States. And we will sit-in and we will kneel-in and we will lie-in if necessary until every Negro in America can vote, [39]

The compressed statement commemorated the Black women's activist work and potentially positioned them as equals in the movement. It was a small concession in an otherwise momentous day.

Any sense of triumph would be short-lived, however, as the march was followed by a horrendous tragedy. On September 15, 1963, Robert Chambliss, a pathological avowed white racist, bombed the Sixteenth Street Baptist Church in Birmingham. The explosion claimed the lives of four Black girls: Addie Mae Collins, Denise McNair, Cynthia Wesley, and Carole Robertson. Denise was eleven; the other girls, fourteen. Their shattering deaths would inspire a rallying cry in the fight for equal rights and justice, as activists doubled down on their demands. The murders deeply tested Diane Nash's commitment to nonviolence. She vividly recalled the rage she and her then husband felt after the bombing. She told filmmaker Spike Lee, in his acclaimed documentary *4 Little Girls*:

> And we felt that in order to respect ourselves as an adult man and woman, we could not let little girls be killed. . . . We felt that there were two things that we could do; the first option is that we felt confident that we could find out who was responsible for having killed those girls, and we could make certain that they got killed. That was option one. . . . The second option was that if blacks in Alabama got the right to vote, they could protect their children.[40]

But for the parents who had already lost their children in the bombing, the pain was excruciating. One of the victim's fathers, Chris McNair, described seeing the girls' bodies in the morgue and his daughter, Denise, among them, "with this piece of concrete, mortar-like rock embedded in her head." After seeing her child's body, Denise's mother, Mrs. Maxine McNair said: "I couldn't stop hollering. I couldn't stop screaming."[41]

Some eight thousand people attended the mass funeral for three of the girls, while the fourth was buried in a private ceremony of family and close friends. The bombing lent urgency to efforts to secure voting rights legislation and ultimately helped usher in the Civil Rights Act of 1964, which banned segregation in public spaces and employment discrimination, and the Voting Rights Act of 1965, which struck down barriers to registration and implemented federal protections for all citizens aiming to cast a ballot. These legislative achievements were important, but they did little to quell the trauma and rage roiling in many Black communities.

When anger, depression, and grief became overwhelming, many African American women turned to their faith. Mamie Till-Mobley credited her strong belief in Christianity with surviving the tragic loss of Emmett, telling of how she pleaded with God for answers about why it had to be her son that died. She recalled that it was "as if He spoke to me and said: 'Without the shedding of innocent blood, no cause is won.'" She did not pretend that that answer stopped her regret or her pain and sorrow, rather, as Mamie put it, "He made me able to accept it."[42] Maxine McNair described how a pastor friend told her that "God has a will for everything, Maxine. You just have to go with it and you can't ask Him why, because He has a divine plan. And you know that so don't ask, just go on and do what you know is right to do." Alpha Robertson, whose daughter Carole also died in the Sixteenth Street Baptist Church bombing, said, "I worked hard not to feel anger and hatred. But um . . . I did. And I just had to work on it. And I kind of had to keep my spirits up so that I could help my husband to keep his up and you know, the other folks around me. And we had . . . good friends and family who gave us a lot of support. And I just had to work with it and pray."[43]

For many others tapping into the spirit through Freedom songs helped address their suffering. Born of the blues, Negro spirituals, and Black gospel traditions, these songs' rousing, harmonious, and, sometimes, haunting tones reached deep into the soul of a people at war. They acted as a restorative balm for the bruising rounds protestors faced. Sung in unison by large groups outside segregated establishments in the blazing heat, or drawn forth while activists were locked up, beaten and weary in decrepit, festering Southern jails. "We Shall Overcome," "We're Marching to Freedom Land," "Go Tell It on the Mountain," and other songs sustained protestors and taught listeners about Black history and the current journey. Songs like "Certainly, Lord," with lyrics testifying about going to jail and doing thirty days, helped African Americans draw on the Spirit, to remain in the struggle but also to exorcise trauma by *shouting troubles over*. The music points to the inextricable ways that the civil rights movement was rooted in Black Southern Baptist traditions, as well as in broad Judeo-Christian religious principles about justice, forgiveness, sacrifice, and suffering.[44]

Artists such as Nina Simone, however, were beginning to articulate something else. Described in 1960 as having "flair but no air. She has class, but does not wear it on her shoulders. She is unique," Nina was profoundly disturbed by the violent slaughter of Black girls and Black freedom fighters. In her words:

> The bombing of the little girls in Alabama and the murder of Medgar Evers were like the final pieces of a jigsaw that made no sense until you had fitted the whole thing together. I suddenly realized what it was to be black in America in 1963, but it wasn't an intellectual connection of the type Lorraine [Hansberry] had been

repeating to me over and over—it came as a rush of fury, hatred and determination. In church language, the Truth entered into me and I "came through."[45]

Though she initially considered turning to guns, because "even back then I wasn't convinced that non-violence could get us what we wanted," Nina ultimately had to accept that she did not in fact know anything about killing. But she did know music. As she explained, "I sat down at my piano. An hour later I came out of my apartment with the sheet music for 'Mississippi Goddam.'"[46] The song, decrying racial injustice and mainstream entreaties for African Americans to be more patient about civil rights, tapped into and unleashed the mounting rage and frustration taking hold among African Americans and among Black people throughout the diaspora.

Nina's political evolution occurred alongside that of her fellow artist Lorraine Hansberry, whose radical intellectual contributions were indispensable to social justice movements. Lorraine, who died in 1965 at age thirty-four, was a Black Nationalist and internationalist who associated and collaborated with many Black figures of her day, including James Baldwin and Paul Robeson. After the success of her ground-breaking, award-winning play *A Raisin in the Sun*, she used her stature to challenge President Kennedy and his brother Attorney General Robert F. Kennedy to take bolder stances on civil rights while simultaneously supporting African anticolonial leaders.[47]

But in America, while protestors sang of freedom and equal rights, others had begun to groove to the mainly apolitical sounds of Motown. The independent Black record label had begun to churn out popular sounds from their Hitsville office in Detroit. Legendary artists such as Mary Wells, Diana Ross, Martha and the Vandellas, Tammi Terrell, and the Marvelettes cultivated a decidedly young and Black popular sound that was as infectious as it was largely carefree. But as the social movements continued in America, and civil rights started to give way to Black Power, and as urban uprisings ripped through cities including Watts in Los Angeles in 1965, and Newark, New Jersey, in 1968, even Motown artists such as Marvin Gaye had to ask in his record-breaking 1971 track, "What's going on?"

The short answer was that African Americans, who had been demanding an end to racial injustice and discrimination using civil disobedience, had continued to move away from purely nonviolent social protest. Gloria Richardson and the Cambridge Movement marked a pivotal shift in this regard and existed as a kind of bellwether for many Black activists. Richardson came of age on Maryland's Eastern Shore. Although she was from a middle-class background, behind the idyllic sandy beaches along the Chesapeake Bay, many of the area's Black residents languished in crippling poverty. Low wages, unemployment upwards of 30 percent, and substandard housing compounded the daily hardships spawned by racial segregation. As historian Sharon Harley explains, "Two thirds of all black families earned less than $3,000 per year." Spending that money itself sometimes proved a challenge, as segregation had placed ridiculous limitations on the most minute aspects of Black life. For example, Black people in Cambridge, Maryland, could shop in white clothing stores, but they were not allowed to use the dressing rooms. They could buy food from white restaurants, but they had to take it home rather than eat in. Black people could go to mainstream movie theaters, but they were forced to sit in segregated seats in the balcony—usually in the last row.[48] It was an area that simmered with intensifying racial tensions in the early 1960s, when Richardson, aged thirty-nine and a single mother, decided to co-chair the Cambridge Nonviolent Action Committee. Richardson and Enez Grubb led sit-ins, marches, and boycotts. They also routinely responded to violence with violence.[49]

Keenly aware of the role of poverty in maintaining racism and power structures that kept Black people down, Richardson mixed calls for civil rights with income equity, as well as exhibiting a growing affinity for self-defense. The economic evolution was in step with nonviolent civil rights stalwarts such as Martin Luther King Jr., whose own activities increasingly spotlighted poverty and the need to eradicate it in American society. At the same time, Richardson's embrace of self-defense mirrored and informed the Black Nationalist ideologies espoused by Malcolm X. It also pointed to a schism developing as calls for civil rights began to give way to something else.[50] By the late 1960s prominent SNCC activists had begun to embrace the call for Black Power, a phrase made popular in 1966 by Kwame Ture, who at the time was known as Stokely Carmichael. (Richard Wright had published a book titled *Black Power* over a decade earlier, and Black abolitionist David Walker lost his life because he essentially called for it in 1829.)[51] Growing numbers of young Black people joined and formed chapters of the Black Panther Party, which was founded by Huey Newton and Bobby Seale in 1966 in Oakland, California. Black women would, again, serve as both foot soldiers and top strategists, with many bringing to this new movement important lessons and organizational skills honed during the civil rights movement.

AURELIA BROWDER WOULD WITNESS some of these new political developments unfolding, before her death in 1971 at age fifty-two. Aurelia's funeral was a large one, filled with church members and her children and extended family. They remembered her as doing what she believed was right, without seeking fame or greater recognition. For Aurelia, "her highest aspiration was to be treated as an equal in all respects of life."[52] Aurelia's bravery, in refusing to capitulate to segregated seating and in serving as the lead plaintiff in *Browder v. Gayle*, constituted important steps toward meeting that goal for herself and everyone else.

CHAPTER TEN

SHIRLEY'S RUN, BLACK POWER, POLITICS, AND BLACK FEMINISM, 1970–2000

Doc, you'd better know what you're talking about because I am running for Congress and I am not going to have a baby.

—SHIRLEY CHISHOLM

ON A BLUSTERY DAY IN JANUARY, inside a local parochial school auditorium in the Bedford-Stuyvesant neighborhood of Brooklyn, New York, Shirley Chisholm announced that she would be seeking the Democratic presidential nomination. At the time, she entered a crowded arena—already eight men had announced their intentions to run. Though the press was skeptical, her announcement was well received by the roughly five hundred in attendance. The *New York Times* noted that Black women made up the majority of the audience. Shirley emphatically declared that in seeking the nomination she aimed to "repudiate the ridiculous notion that the American people will not vote for a qualified candidate simply because he is not white or because she is not a male."[1] Born Shirley Anita St. Hill in New York to Caribbean immigrants, Shirley credited her political ideals as being heavily influenced by her father, a voracious reader, a "union man," and a "Garveyite." But she, like many Black women of that time, had been profoundly influenced by the struggles for civil rights, Black Nationalism, Black Power, and Black feminist activism, together with African Americans' growing push into politics.[2]

Shirley, who directed a local daycare center before becoming an assemblywoman, ran for Congress in 1967, and became the first Black woman to serve in that chamber. She overcame a great deal to do so, confronting everything from moving up through local party politics as a state representative who defied the democratic machine in Albany, to contending with the discovery of a large mass in her abdomen during her campaign. When her doctor explained that she was either pregnant or suffering from a massive tumor, Shirley responded in true New York fashion: "Doc, you'd better know what you're talking about because I am running for Congress and I am not going to have a baby."[3] The tumor was benign and removed in short order. Shirley continued her run but confronted other "female problems"—namely, her Republican opposition, James Farmer. The former national chairman of CORE, had been, as Shirley wrote, "using my sex against me." Farmer's campaign assumed that depicting Shirley as "a bossy female, [and] a would-be matriarch," would resonate negatively with voters, since this critique of Black women undergirded much of Black Nationalism at the time. But in their corner of the world, the Twelfth Congressional District in Brooklyn, there were more than two female voters for every one male. As Shirley explained, "What Farmer thought was his strength was his Achilles' heel."[4] Moreover, Shirley knew how to hustle.

Armed with very little money, her own unvarnished slogan (Vote for Chisholm for Congress—Unbought and Unbossed), shopping bags printed with said slogan, and roughly twenty-five volunteers, Shirley and her team canvassed public housing and grocery stores. She also went to house parties hosted in her honor, recalling, "In the black neighborhood I ate chitlins, in the Jewish neighborhood bagels and lox, in the Puerto Rican neighborhood arroz con pollo." Meanwhile her competition had a national reputation and sound trucks manned by "young dudes with Afros, beating tom-toms: the big, black, male image." The press followed Farmer everywhere, while Shirley received little attention. When she complained, one television station staffer bluntly replied: "Who are you? A little schoolteacher who happened to go to the Assembly." That "little schoolteacher" won in November, drawing 34,885 votes to Farmer's 13,777, while a conservative candidate, Ralph J. Carrane, pulled 3,771.[5] As congresswoman, Shirley refused appointments that she did not feel were in the best interest of her constituents in the Twelfth. The other part of her political mission, as she informed one Southern white congressman, was to pave the way for a "whole lot of folks" who looked like her.[6]

Shirley's decision to run for the presidency pushed boundaries and raised awareness about the political issues impacting not just Black women and men but poor and working-class people across the racial and political spectrum. Moreover, even though she was largely a protest candidate, Shirley stilled faced significant dangers. Her campaign was inundated by racist hate mail, which included multiple death threats, and her campaign materials were routinely destroyed and vandalized. In one frightening episode, a man wielding a ten-inch blade stalked Shirley at a campaign event; fortunately, the would-be assailant was captured before he had the opportunity to stab her in the back, as he had planned.[7]

Shirley's candidacy also tested the limits of feminist allegiances and those of race. Most Black men in the Democratic Party could not get behind her campaign, and the National Organization for Women (NOW), formed in 1966 by middle-class white women like Betty Friedan but also longtime activist Pauli Murray, while supportive, also fell short of giving Shirley its full support. She did receive the endorsement of the Black Panther Party, and a number of white feminists and other liberal whites volunteered for her campaign. Shirley's political activism, in many ways, embodied the difficulties that many progressive Black women faced. She was clearly a product of the legacy of Black Nationalist thought as made popular by Malcolm X and by civil rights and Black Power activism. But though she served her communities and broke open the halls of Congress with the aim of helping more oppressed folks get through, many of those would-be beneficiaries not only failed to support her but, in extreme instances, resented her. Under the circumstances, her embrace of feminism was a necessity as much as it was a calling, because many proponents of Black Power, both male and female, believed that the 1970s marked a moment when African American women needed to stand down and let Black men lead. Shirley's historic presidential run, then, also spotlights these challenges, at the same time that it shows how Black women continued to transform barriers. Against an onslaught of damning caricatures about their womanhood, and against renewed efforts at criminalization and incarceration, African American women reclaimed and clarified feminism and continued to play central roles in domestic and international justice causes, and a few became pioneers in a new form of Black expressive culture.

EVEN AS SHIRLEY CHISHOLM blazed a new path for Black women's political engagement, she and other Black women had to face the harmful vestiges of the report by assistant secretary of labor Daniel Patrick Moynihan on the status of Black families and what supposedly ailed them. *The Negro Family: The Case for National Action*, published in 1965, rather than homing in on systematic racism, suggested that Black matriarchies, or female headed-households, had contributed to a kind of Black urban pathology. The report concluded that not only were many of these women on welfare and thus deemed a drain on the state, but it also alleged that the women had failed to raise their children, particularly their sons, to be productive members of society. This deficit was seen as contributing to a cycle of poverty and welfare dependency. Initially, prominent Black leaders and intellectuals condemned the report, but the notion that Black women were emasculating and the cause of Black dysfunction dovetailed with the current strain of Black Nationalist ideology and longstanding sexist attitudes within the Black community. In particular, it was believed that the liberation of Black people rested in the Black man being restored to his rightful place at the head of Black families and of Black social justice movements. African American women from every stratum, especially those active in civil rights and Black power, found themselves caught between wanting to support Black men and Black communities while at the same time carving out a space for their immense talents as leaders, strategists, protesters, and grassroots organizers.[8]

How Black women responded was neither simple nor uniform, though most opted to work within Black communities. Few could align themselves with white women's feminist activism of the 1960s, as it was so heavily based on middle-class white women's needs. In Black organizations, African American women forged their own versions of Black female liberation. In 1970, Dara Abubakari, a vice president of the Republic of New Africa, a group that believed in a return to African principles and separation from whites, felt that Black women needed to focus on supporting Black men:

> At one time the black woman was the only one that could say something and not get her head chopped off. You could say certain things, you could raise the banner high. But the law was strictly against the black man. So he could not do anything. Now that he speaks, we speak together. We cannot separate, and this is what I say to the Women's Lib movement. You cannot separate men from women when you're black. The black woman is not undergoing the same kind of oppression that white women have gone through in the homes. The black woman is liberated in her own mind, because she has taken on responsibility for the family and she works. Black women had to get in the labor force, because black men didn't have jobs.[9]

Though Black women's history is laden with examples of violence and incarceration, too, the idea that such dangers only jeopardized Black men remained stubbornly in place. So, too, did the sexism and misogyny that plagued most Black organizations at the time (issues that also plagued white organizations and American society generally).

However, African American female members found ways to critically shape social justice groups and to assume key leadership roles. Though Huey Newton and Bobby Seale founded the Black Panther Party (BPP) in Oakland in 1966, Black women made up the majority of its membership, by 60 percent, and some powerfully steered the organization.[10] Kathleen Cleaver served as the BPP communications secretary from 1967 to 1971; Elaine Brown became the only female chairperson to lead the party, from 1974 to 1977; and Ericka Huggins, who served on the party's Central Committee from 1977 to 1979, ran the party's Oakland Community School from 1973 to 1981. Moreover, in BPP chapters across the country, Black women created free breakfast programs for schoolchildren, which would become models for public schools nationwide. Black women also organized free medical care by working with Black doctors and nurses who volunteered time and resources to poor and working-class Black people. In addition to establishing the People's Free Medical Clinics, BPP members such as Norma Armour, who sported a halo Afro, a white clinician's coat, and badge reading "Black Panther Party Community Survival Programs," made follow-up house calls to check the results of previously administered tuberculosis tests. Black women also sponsored food and clothing drives, and they trained for the revolution, as many were as ready to wield a firearm as they were to make plates for hungry kids.[11]

Even as the BPP formed alliances with women's liberation organizations and groups fighting for gay and lesbian rights, many Black women in the party fought sexual harassment and, in a number of instances, sexual assault by party members. Such instances were usually covered up or dismissed, as few Black women wanted to send Black men to the "pigs." In her autobiography, Elaine Brown recounts numerous instances of harassment, everything from being told that "a true Sister would be happy to sleep with a revolutionary Brother" to other male party members' tolerance of another brother having savagely beaten her, because, in his mind, "don't no bitch disrespect me!" For hours he pummeled her listless body. Brown later wrote: "It was a serious, careful beating, the kind in which he was obviously expert, the kind designed to do serious damage without leaving a visible mark." As harrowing as Brown's recollections are, the sexism and exploitation that marked the experiences of some Black women in the BPP were hardly unique, though there were chapters that developed a hard line against gender discrimination.[12] Moreover, the gender skirmishes taking place in the BPP were occurring throughout a host of political organizations.

Black women like Dorothy Jamal and Brenda Haiba Karenga were among the founders and earliest organizers of the Us Organization, though Maulana (Ron) Karenga, Brenda's husband, is most associated with its origins and subsequent leadership. The group evolved from a Black studies group in Los Angeles in 1965. The women helped to create the structure, recruited female members, and participated in protests. Us aimed to liberate Black people through an embrace of its leaders' studies of African social, cultural, and political ideologies. As such, in 1967, Us male leadership, championed a construction of the ideal "African woman" as one whose primary aim was to "inspire her man, educate her children, and participate in social development." Us members also practiced polygamy and expected subservience and submission from female members.[13]

But like their sisters of yesteryear, Black women in Us used their positions as caretakers of the family to build institutions such as the Us School of Afro-American Culture. The school taught local area children using a curriculum based on Us's Kawaida theory, which at its base held "culture as the 'crucible in which black liberation takes form' and the idea that cultural autonomy is the cornerstone of Black liberation." Moreover, female members served on a number of committees with men, and by 1969 the women's group, Malaika, began to redefine the group's original articulation of African womanhood. Published in Us's newspaper, *Harambee*, "The View from the Women's Side of the Circle" used the tenets of the Nguzo Saba (a Kawaida-centered value system), particularly "Ujamaa," which references collective work and responsibility, to broaden women's roles. As historian Ashley Farmer explains, "The Malaika argued that fulfilling the principle of Ujamaa required increased political, military, and educational development of women and the breakdown of the gendered division of labor within Us organizing."[14] Similar to women in the Black Panther Party, Us female members found ways to serve and to be active in the organization despite restrictive gender ideals.

When violence between the two groups claimed the lives of BPP members Alprentice "Bunchy" Carter and John Huggins in 1969 (stemming from tensions largely instigated by the FBI's counterintelligence program), it erected an insurmountable divide between the two organizations, but that tension would serve as an unlikely catalyst for women's empowerment within the BPP. In the aftermath of her husband's murder, Ericka Huggins would find herself just a few months later imprisoned and painfully separated from her infant daughter, at the time just three months old. Facing charges for allegedly recording a violent interrogation by other BPP members in New Haven, Connecticut, Huggins languished in prison for two years before her acquittal. During that time, she wrestled with an immobilizing sadness and isolation, explaining, "I felt very alone and despondent. . . . One of the reasons I taught myself to meditate is so that I could bear seeing my daughter for an hour on a Saturday once a week. . . . Once I recognized that I could use meditation as a way to keep myself sane and balanced in prison then I could focus on my inner work."[15]

Ericka Huggins's imprisonment, as well as that of dozens of female BPP members, prompted some especially virulent misogynists in the party to reconsider their position on sisters' equality in the revolution. Even Eldridge Cleaver, who admitted in his book *Soul on Ice* that he raped Black women as "practice" for when he intended to rape white women as revenge against white men, wrote: "The incarceration and suffering of Sister Ericka should be a stinging rebuke to all manifestations of male chauvinism within our ranks. . . . A woman can be just as revolutionary as a man and . . . we cannot relegate her to an inferior position."[16] Huggins subsequently found herself in a unique position to advocate for Black women. While she did not call herself a feminist at the time, because many Black women associated the word with white women's struggle for equal pay, Huggins believed strongly in the "political, economic, and social equality of the sexes."[17] Huggins's confinement, and later that of other revolutionaries such as Angela Davis and Assata Shakur, also helped lift the veil surrounding Black women's experience on the inside.

Davis, the iconic Black Power activist, ex-political prisoner, and renowned scholar and professor, and Shakur, the Black Power revolutionary who escaped confinement and remains on the FBI's most-wanted list, would each pen weighty autobiographies detailing the pain, isolation, neglect, and abuses Black women suffered in prison. In many ways political prisoners endured some of the harshest treatment from prison guards. Yet, while Huggins's time highlighted one type of experience for Black female prisoners, the experience of Joan Little offers disturbing testimony of another.[18]

Born and raised in Beaufort County in eastern North Carolina, Joan came from a "dead-end" town punctuated by a history of racism and violent KKK activity. As a youth she had petty brushes with the law running the street at night rather than being left alone with her stepfather. Her mother convinced a Beaufort County judge to send her daughter to the Dobbs Training School for delinquent girls in 1968.[19] Joan escaped a month later and stayed with family in Newark and then Philadelphia before returning to North Carolina when she was eighteen. She eked out a living with low-paying jobs, though by the early 1970s, Joan had a racked up a number of arrests for shoplifting, with most of the charges dismissed. But she had developed a reputation among law enforcement as being of low character and rumors about her abounded—everything from Joan running a prostitution ring with her brother to being a lesbian.[20]

In 1974 Joan was arrested for a string of felonies involving breaking into Black-owned trailers. In a trial fraught with problems, she pled guilty and received two consecutive seven-to-ten-year sentences. In custody, Joan was raped by a white jailer named Clarence Alligood. During the attack, she managed to stab him eleven times with an icepick, which Alligood kept in his drawer, before escaping. Although Alligood's corpse was found "naked from the waist down . . . [a] trail of dried semen trickled down his left thigh," the grand jury wasted no time indicting her for murder, and Joan faced a death sentence in North Carolina's gas chamber. However, what looked like another open-and-shut case typical of racist railroading in the justice system would be upended entirely as Black, white, and Latinx women rallied to Joan's defense. Tamanika, of the Afrikan People's Congress, helped fund-raise for Joan's defense, explaining that what happened to Joan highlighted widespread abuses against Black female prisoners. Tamanika went on to point out, "The sentence for rape in North Carolina is the death sentence. Miss Little was raped and she is facing the death sentence." Joan was acquitted in 1975. Her experiences offer an ugly accounting of what the justice system looked like for everyday Black women—those who might not have been fortunate enough to have a "Free Joan Little" campaign behind them. But the outcome also showed the ongoing evolution and utility of Black women's activism and of Black feminism.[21]

Black feminism, in many ways, had been in the making for centuries, but some of its most deliberate iterations were produced during the Black Power era. Longtime activists such as Frances M. Beal, who had organized in SNCC and also embraced aspects of Black Power principles, became a vocal critic of the sexism and misogyny. Beal, who helped found the Third World Women's Alliance, penned a powerful essay that critiqued sexism and patriarchy in Black social movements. In her essay "Double Jeopardy: To Be Black and Female," Beal addressed the issue head-on:

> Unfortunately, there seems to be some confusion in the movement today as to who has been oppressing whom. Since the advent of black power, the black male has exerted a more prominent leadership role in our struggle for justice in the country. He sees the system for what it really is for the most part, but where he rejects its values

and mores on many issues, when it comes to women, he seems to take his guidelines from the pages of the *Ladies' Home Journal.* Certain black men are maintaining that they have been castrated by society but that black women somehow escaped this persecution and even contributed to this emasculation.[22]

Beal was also among the contributors to Toni Cade Bambara's pathbreaking anthology *The Black Woman*, published in 1970. The collection of essays, poems, and stories marked a pivotal moment in Black women's thought, as the civil rights and Black Power movements laid the groundwork for a coalescing Black feminist doctrine. Writers explored important issues facing Black women, and Bambara herself took on changing attitudes toward birth control, explaining that Black women's ability to free herself from poverty, welfare, and social and political exclusion was directly tied to "seizing control of their bodies through contraception and legalized abortion."[23] Moreover, these essays, including unique voices like that of radical Black feminist Florynce "Flo" Kennedy, chart Black women's contribution to Black Power and its impact on Black feminist ideals. Flo, a Columbia Law School graduate and known for being foul-mouthed and unorthodox, expressed herself with no filter, writing, "I think we should all be kicking ass fairly regularly, and one of my favorite targets is the media." Encouraging women to move to alternative media sources, Flo stressed the need for women to read feminist writing. Simultaneously picking up the mantle of Black female writers in the centuries and decades before them, Black women cultivated and amplified their own voices, ones reflective of their connection to the Black community but also distinctly their own.[24]

It was not a moment too soon.

Damning depictions, whether from the Moynihan report or from Black psychiatrists such as William H. Grier and Price M. Cobbs, plagued Black womanhood. In their book *Black Rage*, Grier and Cobbs suggested that oppression stunted healthy emotional growth in Black girls and that as women they neglected themselves, becoming obese and asexual (as if these two automatically went hand-in-hand). The pair went further, noting that Black women controlled their families and contributed to diminishing Black manhood by raising subservient boys. Their characterizations aligned with those promoted by Moynihan, and the notions harmed Black women in many ways, though it never stopped them from standing up for themselves and their families. African American women like Johnnie Tillmon, who helped lead the National Welfare Rights Organization during the late 1960s, knew how women like her were regarded. As Johnnie put it, "I'm a woman, I'm a black woman. I'm a poor woman. I'm a fat woman. I'm a middle-aged woman. And I'm on welfare. In this country, if you're any one of those things—poor, black, fat, female, middle-aged, on welfare—you count less as a human being. If you're all those things, you don't count at all." Tillmon, who had spent her childhood and early adulthood in a rural Black community in Arkansas, had a deep respect for hard work and had labored most of her life, from picking cotton to domestic service. She had worked as a laundress until health problems rendered her unable to continue at that job.[25]

Bucking the stigma and the threat of retaliation from welfare agencies, Johnnie and thousands of poor women begin to organize. They fought stereotypes and lobbied against dehumanizing practices such as social workers raiding recipients' homes at night hoping to catch boyfriends or rifling through women's belongings as new items might indicate additional financial support—support that would render the women ineligible for benefits. Similarly, poor women across the country began to mobilize to demand better conditions in public housing.[26]

It wasn't just urban areas that suffered crippling poverty. Throughout the rural South, Black people lived in substandard housing and had limited access to healthcare, and many Black children suffered from malnutrition. Activists like Unita Blackwell fought for state funding to repair Black neighborhoods, while Fannie Lou Hamer organized local farms to create food co-ops. But in her battles against poverty and low wages, Hamer called attention to internal class battles, commenting, "A few years ago throughout the country the middle-class black woman—I used to say not really black women, but the middle-class colored woman, c-u-l-l-u-d, didn't even respect the kind of work that I was doing. But you see now, baby, whether you have a Ph.D., D.D., or no D, we're in this bag together."[27] Indeed. Black women everywhere in America were suffering. In public housing in Baltimore, for instance, poor and working-class Black women also established food co-ops. Though many programs would be short lived, historian Rhonda Williams noted, "Tenant leaders clearly viewed the [food buying club] as financially and socially valuable to residents. In Murphy Homes, black female tenants ran a food store well into the 1990s."[28]

Black women in every part of the country and in every social stratum engaged in forms of social protest. Dorothy Bolden, a Black domestic, organized in the Household Technicians of America, founded in 1969, to advocate for domestic workers' rights and improve the conditions under which they labored. Black domestics, who had begun organizing for better pay since the 1950s when they won access to Social Security benefits, had obtained two hard-won victories in 1974 and 1976. First, domestic workers successfully fought for inclusion into minimum wage laws and then obtained access to unemployment insurance.[29]

The 1970s also found Black women such as Marsha P. Johnson breaking ground on a new frontier. Born Malcolm Michaels Jr. in Elizabeth, New Jersey, on August 24, 1945, Marsha P. (for "Pay it no mind") Johnson ended up on the streets of New York in her teens because her family could not accept her. Making her way as a sex worker and drag performer, Marsha found and created a community for herself and toured with an avant-garde drag troupe called the Hot Peaches. Her travels found her in the company of famed artists such as Andy Warhol, who photographed and painted her as a part of his transgender portrait series, "Ladies and Gentleman." Although Marsha P. had a reputation for being carefree and an icon around Christopher Street in Greenwich Village, friends noted that in dressing and adorning herself she always stashed a razor in her dress. Black women like Marsha P. endured untold bias attacks daily; to live meant essentially existing as the flesh-and-blood, breathing embodiment of a moving target.[30] That persecution, however, would fuel her commitment to advocating for her rights.

Marsha witnessed firsthand the 1969 uprising at the Stonewall Inn. Although stories about her role in the events that day vary, it is likely that she was among the first to resist. Lasting six days, the uprising against police brutality and harassment of queer communities helped propel grassroots organizing for gay rights. Moreover, Marsha and her longtime friend Sylvia Rivera formed the Street Transvestite Action Revolutionaries (STAR) and established STAR House, a communal space for homeless transgender women. The house and organization suffered from a lack of funding, however, and Marsha continued to live on and off the street. As poverty and discrimination dogged Marsha P. in life, it also contributed to her death. Her body was recovered from the Hudson River in New York City on July 2, 1992. Authorities listed the cause of death as suicide, but most who knew her believed it was more likely an accident or the result of a transphobic attack.[31] Marsha P. punctuates the revolutionary spirit of the era and sketches the arc of sexualities and political ideologies emerging for Black women.

By the late 1970s, Black women politicians, activists, students, and scholars continued to define and embrace Black feminism with and against Black Power ideologies. Writers and artists in the Black Arts Movement (BAM), such as Gwendolyn Brooks and Sonia Sanchez, also wrestled with notions of Black feminism. In Sanchez's play *The Bronx Is Next* (1968), the lead character, a Black woman who has been abused by Black men in her past, plans to teach her sons to love Black women. However, the defiant Black woman is castigated and the white cop who pays her for sex dies in a fire "set by Black militants." Layered and jarring, the texts and subtexts of Black female artists' themes reveal the complexities of Black womanhood and of Black artists' own political sensibilities.

Nina Simone, the revolutionary Black poet Nikki Giovanni, the artist-sculptor Elizabeth Catlett, and the poet-playwright Ntozake Shange enhanced Black culture and Black power, and they critically challenged chauvinism and racism. These women were entering when, where, and how they wanted. As Faith Ringgold, a BAM visual artist, explained in 1971, "No other creative field is as closed to those who are not white and male as is the visual arts. After I decided to be an artist, the first thing that I had to believe was that I, a black woman, could penetrate the art scene, and that, further, I could do so without sacrificing one iota of my blackness or my femaleness or my humanity."[32]

Black women artists, activists, and intellectuals captured and reflected the mood of African American women across political, social, and class strata, and many worked to create an organization that could move in this new direction. However, the struggles of the National Black Feminist Organization (NBFO) detailed the active fault lines among Black women. Founded in 1973, the NBFO, in its mission statement, quickly distinguished itself from white feminism, but it also took the larger society to task, noting, "Black women have suffered cruelly in this society from living the phenomenon of being *both* black and female, in a country that is both racist and sexist. . . . Because we live in a patriarchy, we have allowed a premium to be put on male suffering." The statement goes on to note, "We, not white men or black men, must define our self-image." Stressing the need for Black women and men to work together to challenge racism as well as sexism, it was a bold declaration that echoed Anna Julia Cooper's imperative nearly a century earlier, at the same time that it crackled with the energy of the era.[33]

The fervor fueling the NBFO ended up pulling its members in many different directions, and it struggled to "balance power between lesbians and non-lesbians."[34] Whereas the NBFO sought to be an umbrella organization, its inner workings surfaced fractures around sexuality as well as class, as its leadership was not always attuned to the concerns of poor and working-class Black women. As the NBFO membership and activities dwindled, former members of a New England chapter formed the Combahee River Collective, in 1974. The Combahee mission statement distinguished Black feminism from white feminism by rooting it in the Black community and in a commitment to the interrelated struggle for race, gender, and class equality. Founders Barbara Smith, Beverly Smith, and Demita Frazier also incorporated attacking homophobia and the destructive forces of capitalism into the message. Though the organization was mainly active up until the 1980s, its statement has been foundational for framing principles of contemporary Black feminism and Black feminist theory.[35]

Some African American women, however, did not identify with the term "feminist." Alice Walker advanced the term "womanism," which she defined as Black feminists or feminists of color who love women (sexually and nonsexually) and who were "committed to the survival and wholeness of entire people, male and female." According to Walker, "Womanist is to feminist as purple is to lavender."[36]

Black lesbian and feminist luminary Audre Lorde created a body of work, poems and essays, that eloquently mapped the importance of Black women's voices and activism on a range of issues, from sexism and homophobia to Black women's access to safe, effective healthcare. Lorde, ever the visionary, tapped into a critical issue plaguing Black women. Black feminists, particularly in the 1980s, played critical roles in advancing Black women's health projects and advocating for reproductive rights, especially by fighting to keep unsafe forms of birth control such as Depo-Provera from being thrust onto women of "low economic status," which included those who were "uneducated" and on welfare.[37]

Black feminism also powerfully shaped Black women's political activism, including their demand for political power. Shirley Chisholm's election to the US House of Representatives in 1968 was history making, but she would not be the only Black woman in Congress for long. In 1972 Barbara Jordan became the first Black woman elected to the House from the Deep South. The Texan broke barriers to become the first Black woman elected to the Texas State Legislature, in 1966. In moving past the stringent racism of her white colleagues, Barbara managed to earn their respect. More importantly, she also helped pass that state's first minimum wage law and was instrumental in erecting the Texas Fair Employment Commission. However, she garnered national acclaim for her moral fortitude during the years of Richard Nixon's administration. Barbara, the daughter of a Baptist minister, took to the floor of Congress and delivered a stirring address to demand that the country's elected officials do what was right and impeach the president.[38] Barbara balanced being a state and national legislator at the same time that she kept her longtime life partner, Nancy Earl, out of the public eye. Multiple sclerosis eventually ended Jordan's career as a public servant in 1979, though she would remain passionate about educational access and eventually served as a professor at the University of Texas at Austin, where today a statue dedicated to her service stands in her honor.

Carol Moseley Braun would continue the legacies of Chisholm and Jordan in 1992, when she became the first Black woman elected to the US Senate. Braun's achievement is especially significant because it occurred amidst a pronounced conservative backlash that deeply impacted Black women in 1980s and 1990s. The previous decades had witnessed the end of racial segregation, a new phase of voting rights, and a seismic shift in women's rights, including access to birth control and legal abortion. A significant drug culture also developed during that period, and illegal narcotics ravaged Black and Latinx inner cities. Conservative politicians ran on a series of law-and-order platforms that appealed to white Americans, many of whom had grown tired of social protests, so much so that lofty aims such as the War on Poverty would eventually give way to the War on Drugs. Legislation such as the 1968 Omnibus Crime Control and Safe Streets Act sharply altered criminal justice, particularly after the passage of stringent anti-narcotics laws known as the Rockefeller Drug Laws. These statutes mandated lengthy prison sentences for drug crimes and included stark sentencing disparities with racial implications that devastated Black and Latinx communities. The impact of the policies under Lyndon B. Johnson and Richard Nixon were amplified during the Reagan era. The sentences for possession of crack cocaine versus those for powdered cocaine showed the close relationship between race, class, and legal bias. Defendants with five grams of crack cocaine received the same ten-year sentence as those with five hundred grams of powered cocaine. Crack, which cost as little as five to ten dollars per vial, was prevalent in African American and Latinx communities, while powdered cocaine, which was more expensive, was more commonly used by middle- and upper-class whites.[39]

The culmination of these policies gave rise to the mass incarceration of citizens nationwide, but African Americans were disproportionately represented, and Black women especially saw their numbers in prison grow nearly 800 percent by the 1990s, due to drug crimes. In this climate, African American women who lacked prior criminal records found themselves facing years and years of confinement once they had been arrested and found guilty. In New York City in 1983, Elaine Bartlett, a Black woman, was sentenced to twenty years to life for a first offense. The mother of four lived in public housing, received welfare, and worked off the books at a beauty salon and local bar to help make ends meet. But when the Christmas holidays approached, she decided to transport four ounces of cocaine. Arrested by undercover officers, Elaine would become like thousands of African American women who were netted by harsh drug laws and overrepresented in prison. In 1984 in New York, 23 percent of the women prisoners were Latinx, 26 percent were white, and an astounding 51 percent were African American, though Black women only accounted for 14 percent of the state's population.[40]

This criminalization of Black women was part of a multipronged attack that also invoked damning images of Black women in the news to advance repressive political agendas. For example, local newspapers first used the phrase "welfare queen" to describe Linda Taylor, a Black Chicagoan who was arrested in 1974 for using a number of aliases and false addresses to collect food stamps, welfare, and veterans' benefits. During political campaigns of the 1980s, Ronald Reagan and other conservatives in the Republican Party used Taylor's history and the term "welfare queen" as a racist dog-whistle to imply that poor Black women were lazy, dishonest, and immoral and lived off government benefits at taxpayers' expense. The stereotype eclipsed the fact that white women were the majority of welfare recipients, and it promoted false notions about exactly how much money women getting benefits actually received.[41]

The hysteria whipped up around false depictions of Black women did not stop African American women activists from focusing their attention on issues that mattered to them and their communities, both in domestic and international arenas. Mary Frances Berry, the renowned legal scholar, historian, distinguished professor, civil rights activist, and former chair of the US Commission on Civil Rights, cofounded the Free South Africa Movement in 1984. On November 21 of that year, Mary and two of her colleagues, Randall Robinson of Trans-Africa and US Representative Walter Fauntroy of Washington, DC, entered the South African Embassy to demand an end to apartheid. They refused to leave the building and were arrested by uniformed US Secret Service officers. Undaunted, upon her release Mary set about building a movement, mobilizing the Congressional Black Caucus and participating in antiapartheid action on the ground. A groundswell of pressure from African Americans aimed sharp criticism at the Reagan administration's policy of "constructive engagement" with the South African government.[42]

Advising citizens to organize and join campaigns, form media watch groups, boycott entertainers who performed in South Africa, protest the sale of Krugerrands (South African currency), host teach-ins, and make support for antiapartheid a voting issue, the Free South Africa Movement rallied Americans and supported South African freedom fighters such as Winnie Madikizela-Mandela and Archbishop Desmond Tutu. Masses of college students joined the movement and also spearheaded their own organizations, including Black women such as Tanaquil Jones, who in the 1980s in New York was a member of the Coalition for a Free South Africa. The group mobilized and networked with other student organizations to spur protests, hunger strikes, and campus blockades to eventually compel Columbia University to divest from South Africa.[43] Considering the perils Black women confronted daily in the United States, one might wonder, why organize on behalf of Black people in South Africa? For Mary Frances Berry the answer was obvious: "The predicament of black folks in the U.S. has always seemed connected to colonialism and continued underdevelopment on the African continent. Participating in Pan African meetings and finding a way to visit South Africa and seeing how segregation there was . . . made it obvious that their cause should be supported. It hasn't turned out to benefit the poor as I had hoped but attacking apartheid has never diminished my actions against white supremacy in the U.S."[44]

Black women's activism would again confront acts against their womanhood, as Anita Hill captured the attention of the nation when she testified about her experience of on-the-job sexual harassment. However, Sandra Bundy, a Black woman, had laid the legal precedent for recognizing sexual harassment on the job roughly a decade earlier. In 1977 Bundy sued the Washington, DC, Department of Corrections after having been repeatedly sexually propositioned by her superiors. Bundy had sought a government position for financial stability and, as a working single mother, needed her job. Her federal suit seemed like a longshot at best, yet the judgment in her favor recognized that sexual harassment itself was in fact sex discrimination.[45] By 1991, on-the-job sexual harassment and responses to it would be the subject of discussions among families, legislators, policymakers, and places of business countrywide.

In 1991, after Thurgood Marshall, the first African American appointed to the Supreme Court, announced his plans to retire, President George H. W. Bush nominated a conservative Black judge named Clarence Thomas to replace Marshall. During Thomas's confirmation hearing, Anita, an African American attorney who had worked with Thomas when he headed the Equal Employment Opportunity Commission (EEOC), came forward with stunning allegations. Hill, educated, attractive, and soft-spoken, in her appearance before Congress, caused communities nationwide to grapple with the implications of workplace harassment. She detailed how Thomas had spoken to her about pornography and made crass sexual jokes that made her uncomfortable. Although the nominee had up until that point largely dismissed the existence of racial discrimination, Thomas claimed that he was the victim of a "high-tech lynching."[46] Sukari Hardnett, another Black woman, who also worked as a special assistant to Clarence Thomas at the EEOC from 1985 to 1986, wanted to testify to corroborate Anita Hill's testimony. She had presented herself to the Senate Judiciary Committee and wound up submitting a sworn affidavit, because, as she said, "what was happening to Anita Hill, it was unconscionable to see the way that she was being treated by the committee. And I knew that what she was saying was true because I'd observed some of those very same situations myself." Sukari added that when she worked for Thomas, she tried to avoid him: "I would run down to a friend of mine's office and hide just to avoid being in the situation with Clarence where I would have uncomfortable conversations."[47] Sukari would not testify, however, because then Democratic senator Joseph Biden ended the hearings, apparently worried that the committee looked racist. Clarence Thomas was confirmed and remains on the bench.[48]

The willingness of Sandra, Anita, and other Black women like Sukari Hardnett to come forward shows the reach of Black feminist ideals, as well as Black women's incredible bravery. Anita initiated a national discourse on workplace sexual harassment. Moreover, not only did thousands more women come forward about their experiences, but substantial legislative and employment policies changed to protect women and vulnerable employees. At the time, however, many in the Black community felt that Anita had betrayed the race by testifying against a Black man publicly, let alone before Congress. For feminists everywhere, though, Anita was a hero for bringing this issue to light. In 1991, 1,600 Black women paid for and signed a full-page ad in the *New York Times* professing their support for Anita Hill. The ad also contained a powerful statement under the heading "African American Women in Defense of Themselves," which expressed outrage at the racist and sexist treatment Anita had been subjected to, and it warned, "The malicious defamation of Professor Hill insulted all women of African descent and sent a dangerous message to any woman who might contemplate a sexual harassment complaint."[49] The Black women signatories insisted that they would not be silenced.

Anita's actions were significant but also timely, especially as more Black women entered professions that had been previously dominated by men. Though their ability to access jobs in the private sector remained limited, Black women had begun to make headway in public service, not only as teachers but also as civil servants in government, and greater numbers of Black women were pursuing college and advanced degrees.

But the patriarchal stigma surrounding Black women's advancement endured. Black feminist luminary Michelle Wallace summarized the sentiment this way: "The black woman had gotten out of hand. She was too strong, too hard, too evil, too castrating. She got all the jobs, everything. The black man never had a chance. No wonder he wanted a white woman. He needed a rest. The black woman should be more submissive and, above all, keep her big, black mouth shut."[50] Wallace's book *Black Macho and the Myth of the Superwoman* (1978) was controversial at the time of its publication, though history would largely affirm her assessment of the situation, in the late 1970s and sadly well beyond. In 1995, when Louis Farrakhan and the Nation of Islam summoned one million Black men to Washington, DC, for the Million Man March, organizers asked Black women to stay home and take care of the children.

Black feminists objected, but polling at the time suggests that Black women's support for the march being single-sex actually outstripped that of Black men, with only 18 percent of Black men expressing support, as opposed to 50 percent of Black women. Historian Deborah Gray White notes that Black women's support for the march was rooted in a desire to "reverse a particularly harsh postmodern condition faced by African American women." Black women who had been doing double-duty as both caretakers of children and, at times, the elderly and as breadwinners found the transition from the 1970s to the 1980s painful. In the 1970s they had earned almost the same amount as their white female counterparts and held solid union manufacturing jobs, but deindustrialization erased many of those jobs and the financial stability that had come along with it. These women wanted Black men to finally stand up, and they hoped the march would change what they perceived as Black men's diminishing presence in the Black community.[51]

Two years later, in Philadelphia, Black women held the Million Woman March, spearheaded by Phile Chionesu, a South Philadelphia businesswoman, and Asia Coney, a fellow Philadelphia entrepreneur.

Its ambitions were decidedly smaller, but the march was well-attended, with estimates ranging between four hundred thousand and eight hundred thousand women.[52] Speakers included US Representative Maxine Waters of California and Winnie Madikizela-Mandela. The march's twelve-point platform called for the establishment of independent Black schools, for the government to halt CIA drug operations in Black communities, and for support for women who are ex-prisoners, substance abusers, and homeless. With prayers and entertainers, the march also featured Leona Smith, president of the National Union of the Homeless and a local grassroots activist, who reminded the crowd: "This will all be in vain if you return back to your communities and do not get involved, if you do not put petty jealousies aside, if you do not continue to organize and mobilize. This day will mean nothing."[53] Yet for Qamar Mateen, who chaired the local organizing branch in Chicago, the march was for healing, for families, and for their communities. Another Black attendee, Queen Makeda, also stressed, "We're not bashing our men. We love our men. We can't live without our men, and we're just glad to know that they are learning that they can't live without us."[54]

The Million Woman March was not without its critics. Some Black feminists believed it would prove as meaningless as the Million Man March, which largely failed to produce substantive change. Because the women's march heavily advertised vendors and items for sale, some dubbed it the "Million Shopping Mall March."[55] And still others objected to the heterosexual emphasis of the march and its overarching agenda. Yet the Million Woman March is arguably an important symbol of the twentieth century for Black women. It acknowledged a desire to celebrate and empower Black women while at the same time seeking not to threaten or rival the efforts of Black men. Moreover, the hallmark strengths of Black womanhood were easily visible, since its organizers, most with little to no experience managing a national event, created a platform about protecting Black communities and particularly Black children, and successfully drew thousands of Black women for a program about them.

LOLITA SHANTÉ GOODEN, known as Roxanne Shanté, at fourteen years old, recorded the first answer record in 1984, a track in response to the popular single "Roxanne, Roxanne," by the U.T.F.O. Crew. Black women and Black girls had been steadily crafting their artistic voices, and beginning in the 1980s, used their talents as rap emcees to reach wide audiences and create a new musical genre in hip-hop. "Roxanne's Revenge" was wildly popular and sold over 250,000 copies in New York City alone.[56] Gooden was followed by a bevy of female rappers such as Sweet Tea, Nikki D, and the duo Salt N Pepa. More Afrocentric or conscious rappers emerged in the 1990s with Queen Latifah, MC Lyte, Sista Souljah, and Ling Q of X-Clan, which took its name from Black Power godfather Malcolm X. However, African American women's forays into the industry were not without controversy or struggle. Dee Barnes, who hosted a popular hip-hop talk show, was beaten by gangster rapper Dr. Dre after he took offense at an interview she conducted with another rapper who Dre felt had disrespected him. Though she sued Dr. Dre for $22.7 million and settled for an undisclosed amount out of court, Barnes's physical health and career never fully rebounded. In 2019 Barnes was reportedly homeless.[57]

Black women rappers follow in the footsteps of other Black women in history because not only were they at the start of a new industry, but they were also record-breaking pioneers in it. In 1999 New Jersey–born rapper Lauryn Hill made history by winning five Grammy awards for her debut solo album *The Miseducation of Lauryn Hill*, a riff on the title of historian Carter G. Woodson's classic text *The Mis-Education of the Negro*. Lauryn's lyrics blended pro–Black Nationalist sentiments, with liberatory Black feminist undertones and an innovative, eclectic musical style, which encompassed traditional hip-hop beats to doo-wop vibes to soul and rhythm and blues to reggae dancehall. Lauryn's music, like her stage persona, reflected decades of music, politics, and culture that had come before—with natural hair and pride in her dark skin, she was respected for her music and prowess as a Black female emcee with street credibility and mass appeal. She effectively laid to rest any confusion over Black women's status in the game.[58]

ALTHOUGH ANY CONNECTION BETWEEN rappers and Congresswoman Shirley Chisholm might seem like a stretch, Shirley's politics and presidential run inspired broad cross-sections of Black people, including hip-hop youth. As rap pioneer Biz Markie rhymed in his 1988 anthem "Nobody Beats the Biz": "cooperate with the rhythm, that is what I give em, Reagan is the Pres but I voted for Shirley Chisholm."[59] The Brooklyn politician, unbought and unbossed, embodied the kind of Black Nationalist ideals and urban fight that early rappers admired and grew up watching. After she retired from Congress, in 1983, Shirley taught at Mount Holyoke College before relocating to Florida. She died in 2005. In the documentary *Chisholm '72*, Shirley said, "When I die, I want to be remembered as a woman who lived in the twentieth century and who dared to be a catalyst of change. I don't want to be remembered as the first black woman who went to Congress. And I don't even want to be remembered as the first woman who happened to be black to make a bid for the presidency. I want to be remembered as a woman who fought for change in the twentieth century. That's what I want."[60]

Shirley was indeed a catalyst in the twentieth century, but her role in Black women's history encompasses the activism and struggle of Black women who came centuries before and touches the lives of Black women and girls who have come in the decades since she powerfully changed an era.

PATRICIA'S CLIMB AND THE SISTERS HOLDING DOWN LIBERTY

*Hold them in contempt, fine them, and throw
the shackles on them (the same electronic monitor the
U.S. Department of Justice had me wearing).*

—THERESE PATRICIA OKOUMOU

ON JULY 4, 2018, media outlets across the country blazed images of a Black woman clad in dark shorts and a gray T-shirt with bright-white lettering that read "TRUMPCARE MAKES US SICK." The unknown woman had somehow scaled the base of the Statue of the Liberty on Liberty Island and planted herself at its feet to protest the treatment of migrant children, primarily from Central America, separated from their families and placed in cages when they approached the US border seeking asylum. The detainments (under the zero-tolerance policy of the Trump administration) had been widely denounced, especially after a number of children died in custody and thousands more showed signs of physical, sexual, and mental abuse. In 95-degree heat, forty-four-year-old Therese Patricia Okoumou, refused to come down and was not dislodged until two officers forcibly removed her after a three-hour standoff. She was arrested, along with seven other members of Rise and Resist, a direct-action group dedicated to advocating for immigrants' rights.

Patricia, as she prefers to be called, immigrated to the United States in 1994 from the Republic of Congo. Her desire to come to the United States was motivated by what she described as an idealized notion of the country; she thought it actually would be the land of freedom, complete with brave citizens. However, this changed as she realized, "I had a false notion of diversity and inclusiveness." Arriving on a temporary visa, Patricia worked as an undocumented personal trainer after the visa expired. She managed to obtain her green card in 2010 and became a naturalized citizen in 2016. Patricia is adamant that her own immigration story is not what motivated her activism; rather, she felt compelled to resist on principle, because "it's immoral to put children in cages."[1]

Patricia's climb, on the Fourth, and at the Statue of Liberty, embodies Black women's history in the United States. Her arrival in the country harkens back to the exploration of African-descended women such as Isabel de Olvera, who arrived as part of a Spanish expedition in the sixteenth century. Although her feet touched firmament as a free woman, Isabel did so against the backdrop of violent colonization and imperialism spurred by European desires for greater wealth—through land grabs and, eventually, by trading in human chattel. Isabel's early demand to maintain her freedom from both "marriage or slavery" summons the aims of many Black women across time and space. It also stands, much like Patricia's climb, as a genuine pursuit of liberty.

Even as the Statue of Liberty was the brainchild of French abolitionist Édouard de Laboulaye and French designer Frédéric-Auguste Bartholdi, Black women's imprint on the figure and their role in marshalling freedom and democracy are fundamental. The early plans for building Lady Liberty, which were likely based on Bartholdi's earlier designs of Black Egyptian women, initially depicted a "broken shackle and chain in the statue's left hand."[2] Though the chains and shackles were replaced by a tablet commemorating Independence, "references to the Civil War and abolition occur repeatedly from its first introduction to the United States in 1871 up to and including the dedication celebrations in 1886." The chains now lay at the statue's feet. Indeed, the notion that it is a monument to American immigrants is largely a twentieth-century construction, though one that manages to buttress a principled Black woman's demand for justice against tyrannical policies harming vulnerable children in the twenty-first century.

That Patricia went to jail on behalf of migrant children's rights exists as an extension of Black women's radical organizing, because in just about every battle that Black women have undertaken in the United States, every barrier that they have shattered, and every first accomplishment they have secured, their actions have paved the way not just for other Black women but for all marginalized peoples. Even against their will, Black women's bodies, knowledge, labor, and off-spring have helped develop the country and contributed to its wealth, which laid the foundation for the colonies' move toward independence. The ideologies and activism of colonial Black people also lauded and called for freedom, tying the destiny of enslaved Africans to the burgeoning cause for a democratic revolution in the eighteenth century. They knew whites did not have Black people in mind, but that did not stop Black women from grasping onto the liberatory concepts.

Ellen Craft, Harriet Tubman, and other Black women of the early nineteenth century found ways to take their own liberty by freeing themselves as well as other enslaved Black people, as they embraced fugitivity. And those Black women who were already freed, such as Maria Stewart, used their status to champion the cause for freedom from enslavement but also for Black women's larger political rights. Black women such as Mary Ann Shadd Cary fiercely lobbied for suffrage. When civil war ravaged the land, Black women took flight, worked for, and resisted abuse in contraband camps, and some, like Mary Bowser, spied on the Confederacy, to help usher in abolition for all. Later, as citizens under the Fourteenth Amendment, African American women created whole industries for themselves and founded the nation's first Black-owned bank. As early as 1898, Callie House spearheaded a national movement for reparations.

Early gender rebels Edmonia Lewis and Gladys Bentley challenged traditional ideas about Black womanhood and Black sexuality, both by cross-dressing and by living openly with female lovers. Black women would continually defy restrictive gender codes, whether by becoming award-winning athletes, at times when Black women and girls were expected to remain on the sidelines, or by joining the Women's Army Corps. African American women have gone to war with and against America, but their combat ultimately was in the service of making the country a real democracy for all—something that would make America great in earnest. Patricia Okoumou drew her inspiration from another pathbreaking Black woman: "Michelle Obama, our beloved First Lady, that I care so much about, said 'When they go low, we go high,' and I went as high as I could." The poignant words, a combination from the two, look backward and forward, as our history shows that our nation's inaugural African American First Lady, and the first African American president, owe a debt to Black women such as Shirley Chisholm, who had the audacity to run for the presidency in the 1970s.

We know every battle has not been successful, and we know that going high does not always work, but even Black women's losses served generations to come. For example, despite tireless work for antilynching laws, none was ever passed. Yet, Ida B. Wells-Barnett's relentless pursuit of justice ultimately drafted the political resistance playbook for Black people for decades. Recall that Ida employed the legal system in her drive for civil rights, and she created her own newspaper and used the press generally to call attention to injustices against Black people. Ida urged and supported Black boycotts, and she recommended Black self-defense, advising African Americans to hang rifles over their hearths. Ida also went abroad, bringing international attention to racial violence against Africa Americans, and she canvassed the South, counting and documenting lynchings. Ida also networked with other African Americans as well as whites, and she collectively organized through one of the earliest African American civil rights organizations in the country, the National Association of Colored Women. And Ida was hardly alone. We know that African American women and girls put their bodies on the line during social justice movements, even though their voices were stifled and national memory often elides their sacrifice, whether by oversimplifying the work of lifelong, well-known activists such as Rosa Parks or all but erasing critical decisions made by everyday Black women who stood up when their moment came: Mamie Till-Mobley made the world see her tragedy, and Aurelia Browder gave her name to the lawsuit that was the final blow in breaking the yoke of segregated busing in Montgomery, Alabama.

African American women have remained underprotected and overpoliced, beginning with colonial laws that treated them as things rather than human beings, to more recent disparities that rendered them as largely ignored victims of the War on Drugs and mass incarceration. Yet as Black women served lengthy prison sentences, they made demands on the state for justice. Joann Walker spotlighted Black women battling HIV/AIDS, which reached epidemic levels between 1990 and 2000 and remains a pressing health issue. Diagnosed in the late 1980s, Joann showed how women prisoners with HIV/AIDS were neglected on the inside, including helping to win the compassionate release of a prisoner who was dying due to AIDS-related complications while imprisoned at the Central California Women's Facility at Chowchilla (CCWF). Joann managed this while serving four years for stealing a $200 coat in 1992. Outspoken and defiant, she wanted other prisoners to know: "I raise pure hell around here, because there is no other way to get things done. . . . I often run into trouble all the time because I will speak up and out. I have no problem fighting the system. I want to put a call out around the world: *HELP THE HIV/ AIDS INCARCERATED WOMEN AT CCWF!*"[3] Joann's advocacy led to the formation of the Coalition to Support Women Prisoners with HIV/AIDS, an organization outside CCWF. After weeks of complaining about headaches and coughing up blood, Joann was sent to an outside hospital, where she was diagnosed with having fungal meningitis, which had spread throughout her body. She died two months after her own compassionate release in 1994, but her legacy has generated attention and assistance for female prisoners battling HIV/AIDS long after.[4]

AFRICAN AMERICAN WOMEN writers and performers have given voice to Black women's history in ways that have served as a balm as well as a source of education for African American women, in addition to substantially contributing to American culture and the ongoing cause of freedom. Contemporary African American women writers such as Alice Walker celebrate and lament the complex spaces they have occupied throughout our history. Walker's Pulitzer Prize– and National Book Award–winning work *The Color Purple* (1982) highlighted intraracial legacies of domestic violence, incest, and rape, as well as white racial and sexual violence and Black women's incarceration. Yet the story is also about love—sibling love, adoptive love, lesbian love—and faith, as the story's protagonist writes directly to God. Going from rural Georgia to the African continent, the story weaves together critical themes from Black women's history.

Performers from Sissieretta and Gertrude "Ma" Rainey to Ethel Waters and Nina Simone prefigured and anticipated singers such as Kathleen Battle, Diana Ross, and Beyoncé, and actresses from Cicely Tyson to Halle Berry, and even the Black women behind critical

TV and film productions, such as Julie Dash, Ava DuVernay, Shonda Rhimes, and Shola Lynch, or network bosses like Oprah Winfrey. All of these women exist along a historical continuum, at the same time that they have expanded upon the reimagined boundaries of Black womanhood artistically.

African American womanhood is steeped in the central organizing themes of travel and migration, violence, activism and resistance, labor and entrepreneurship, criminalization, art and creativity in the broadest sense, and in human beings laying claim to their womanhood and sexuality in spite of social, structural, and political limitations. Yet all of this is intimately tied to the ferocity with which Black women have cleaved and clarified notions of liberty—Black women's history in its truest sense serves as a historical road map of the failures of mainstream approaches to democracy and an incisive tutorial on how to correct it. Among the most oppressed and marginalized, Black women in the United States have nonetheless routinely defied otherwise near all-encompassingly negative messages denying their right to be, to push back and demand more—from the nation, from their communities, from their partners, and from themselves.

The twenty-first century is rife with unabashed anti-Blackness in government, but Black women have emerged as some of its most formidable opponents. From Representative Maxine Waters famously reclaiming her time and Bree Newsome scaling a flagpole to tear down the Confederate flag from the South Carolina statehouse grounds to the bravery of everyday Black women such as Angela Whitehead. On May 5, 2019, Angela threw two white police officers out of her Wisconsin home after they entered illegally. Letting the police know that they "got the wrong Black girl on the right day," Whitehead yelled: "This is *my* house. *I pay* these bills. Are you crazy? . . . Now tell me that I'm fuckin' wrong; you can't. . . . You *do not* come in my home without permission. Period."[5] Angela was not in denial about the potential deadly consequences of asserting her rights as a Black woman. She was frightened, but she stood up to protect her family. She screamed at the officers: "If I hadn't just came in the house from smoking a cigarette, this door would have been closed and your ass would have had to knock. You do not come up in my fucking house without my permission, with your white ass, and I'm black and I'm scared of you . . . this is my home, where my kids live, how I know you wasn't coming up in here with a fuckin' gun? Cop, black people killer. I don't know that, I don't. So, guess what? I'm aggressive." Angela and Patricia and so many other Black women, from one corner of the country to the next, typify the courage, intelligence, iron core, and backbone of Black women throughout history. Black women like them also currently make up one of the most dedicated voting blocs combatting the dangerous surge of white supremacy in the United States. But as Angela's and Patricia's actions reveal, Black women are also actively embodying resistance.

After her protest at the Statue of Liberty, Patricia Okoumou was convicted of trespassing, disorderly conduct, and "interference with agency functions." Appearing at her sentencing hearing with tape across her face to protest the limitations placed upon her freedom of speech, she went before the criminal justice system unbowed. She answered the prosecution's sentencing recommendation, that she serve thirty days behind bars and three years of probation, by telling the court: "I do not need probation and I do not belong in prison. I am not a criminal." Based on the charges, Patricia could have been sent to prison for over a year. However, in the early part of 2019, she was sentenced instead to five years of probation and two hundred hours of community service. As with all Black women clapping back against power, as well as organizing against its corrupt and bigoted applications, Patricia spoke truth to it. As she wrote on April 26, 2019, "Hold them in contempt, fine them, and throw the shackles on them (the same electronic monitor the U.S. Department of Justice had me wearing)." Further, she has already done the community and the country a service. She reminded us again of how the country is far short of living up to its professed democratic ideals, and she stayed in formation by demanding justice and liberty for all. Patricia's climb also speaks to us in an extraordinary combination of harsh, insistent, and exuberant tones. That rhythm is in keeping with the historical vein of Black women's efforts to remake the country in their own image, toward a pure rendering of freedom.[6]

AFTERWORD

Writing *A Black Women's History of the United States* has been thrilling, challenging, and exhausting. The process has become a part of our individual and collective histories in profound ways. When we began this work, in 2014, Daina's father was still alive and so was Kali's mother. Dr. Melvin "Mel" Ramey passed away in June 2017 at the age of seventy-eight, and Mrs. June Maria Gross passed away in December 2017, just shy of her seventy-seventh birthday. On January 9, 2019, Londa Ann Lovell, Kali's first cousin, with whom she was raised as a sister, suffered a fatal heart attack at age fifty-one. These deaths changed how we approach history. It deepened our understanding of the weight of the sacrifice, pain, and loss in so many of the stories we told. It also complicated our mission, because we struggled to bridge putting forward the raw, unadulterated truth of African American women's experiences in this country with the desire to produce a book that would feed and inspire today's Black women. So, we followed routes trodden by our foremothers and sisters, and decided we needed to commune and process with other Black women on the matter.

We planned to convene an amazing constellation of sister-scholars in the field for an all-day manuscript workshop on March 1, 2019, at Rutgers University in New Brunswick, New Jersey. The night before, however, found a broad swath of the Mid-Atlantic covered in snow. In response to the storm, flights were cancelled and many schools were closed, while others expected to open on a two-hour delay. For Kali, a single mother by choice, the delayed start of school for her third-grader, coupled with icy road conditions, meant that she might not be able to attend. For Daina and her mother, Dr. Felicenne Ramey, who also planned to attend, there were concerns about whether trains would be running; they had been in New York a day earlier and intended to use mass transit to get to New Jersey. We agonized over what to do, especially since we had already lost one participant—Dr. Rhonda Williams's flight from Nashville, Tennessee, was canceled, and she was unable to get another. Mercifully, save starting a little behind schedule, nine of the ten invited scholars were present. Drs. Brittney Cooper, Erica Armstrong Dunbar, Tiffany Gill, Sharon Harley, Cheryl Hicks, Stephanie E. Jones-Rogers, Talitha LeFlouria, Donna Murch, and Deborah Gray White graciously read outlines and rough chapters in advance of the meeting. Rhonda scanned and emailed her handwritten notes.

Words fail when attempting to describe what happened at the workshop, yet for us the day was a critical nexus of the historical themes and work we were writing about. We sat around a set of tables arranged in a hollow square and for hours discussed, debated, argued, laughed, and damn near cried, as we set ourselves to the task at hand. Each sister understood the importance of the goals as well as the difficulties in trying to write a sweeping historical study about Black women that was educational, engaging, and designed to reach a multigenerational audience from different socioeconomic backgrounds. We will never forget their vital contributions, generosity, and kindness. Most writers know that obtaining critical feedback is essential and truly invaluable, but it also means being incredibly vulnerable—ideas (deep flaws and hilarious fails) are laid bare. We were so fortunate to have been blessed with a brilliant group of dynamic scholars who worked beautifully together. Moreover, the meeting, in addition to transforming the book, was itself historic, as Black women make up less than 2 percent of the professoriate in the United States.

We realize, and have experienced ourselves, that some of the stories here are viscerally painful and psychologically difficult, but if this book has taught us—and, we hope, all who read it—anything, it's that CeCe McDonald and Laverne Cox exist along a continuum with Frances Thompson. There would be no Cardi B without Roxanne Shanté or Lauryn Hill or Lil' Kim for that matter. Athletes have reached new heights because Black women like Alice Coachman made Olympic history before they were born. Likewise, there would be no Naomi Osaka or Cori "Coco" Gauff or Sloane Stephens without Venus Williams and Serena Williams. At the same time, the racist double standards that plague Black women like Serena, whether we examine her disproportionate number of drug tests for steroids or the racist media depictions of her dominance in tennis or her near-death experience giving birth, show that despite her achievements and wealth, as a Black woman she remains vulnerable to the lethal structural racism in the medical profession and beyond.

Serena's incredible talent is too often clouded by racist white tennis officials' misogynistic policing of her body, attacks enacted under the guise of sports and fashion regulations. For example, after rocking a black catsuit that hugged her muscular curves on the court, an outfit that Serena felt empowered in, the president of the French Tennis Federation announced in 2018 that the French Open would implement a dress code, because players had gone too far. Targeting Serena, in particular, he stated, "One must respect the game and the place."

Serena, well accustomed to taking to the court as both a player and a freedom fighter in her own right, attended the 2019 French Open in a custom-designed zebra-striped ensemble emblazoned with the words "Mother, Champion, Queen, Goddess." The words were written in French to make certain the crowd could understand the legend before them (as if anyone could forget). When a reporter still tried it, telling her that the words were a lot to carry, she eloquently responded, "It is a lot to carry, but so is being Serena Williams." She also won the day's match. Her retort, like her game, was perfect, a response that evinced decades of having to quickly shut down someone trying to diminish her greatness. The win attested to her ability to triumph in hostile terrain. The twenty-three-time Grand Slam champion, in that moment, could easily have spoken for any one of us, though, because being a Black woman, like being a Black girl, in the United States is a lot to carry. Fortunately, we, like Serena, have a rich, extensive history to draw upon for strength and guidance.

The book release in January 2020 was quite successful, and we were humbled by the outpouring of support. We gave individual and joint book talks in Texas, New Jersey, and Pennsylvania, and planned a robust speaking tour that would take us well into the summer. However, the world literally shut down because of the coronavirus pandemic, with Black and Brown communities disproportionately impacted. Like most, we hunkered down with family and did all we could to stay safe. Eventually, we moved to virtual presentations and began speaking to book clubs, and we gave a virtual keynote address at an annual conference hosted by the University of Missouri's Carter Center for K-12 Black History Education—this year's subject was "Teaching Black Herstories." We also appeared on several syndicated radio shows and podcasts. We were happy that people wanted to learn this history and that they engaged our work during such trying times.

While we continued to speak to wide audiences, Beacon Press approached us about creating a young adult (YA) version of the book. This incredible opportunity has been an important outgrowth that we did not initially anticipate. After several conversations, the press hired the award-winning Tonya Bolden as the adapter, and she started right away on the new book. We also decided that we wanted to speak to young readers prior to publication and created a junior editorial board with youth from all over the United States. The names of potential advisors came pouring in, and we look forward to these conversations. In the spring of 2021, we expect to host virtual focus groups in order to receive direct feedback from school-age students.

Even as this reception to the book has been heartening, and with the YA version on the horizon, Black women's history has marched on, and with it, so too have a number of the themes we highlighted, particularly those related to violence and criminal justice. Little did we know we were heading for more challenges in an area that was all too familiar to us as scholars of Black women's history.

On March 13, 2020, white police officers in Louisville, Kentucky, shot and killed an unarmed, twenty-six-year-old Black woman in her home. Breonna Taylor was an innocent, vibrant, beautiful young woman who worked as an emergency room technician. Between 12 and 1 a.m. officers burst into the apartment she shared with her boyfriend, Kenneth Walker, using a no-knock warrant based on outdated information. Alarmed by loud noises and then having their front door breached with a battering ram, Walker fired using his legally purchased and registered firearm. One officer was hit and two officers returned fire. In the hail of thirty-two bullets, Breonna Taylor was hit five times and died at the scene. She lay on the floor of her apartment for hours while her distraught mother, Tamika Palmer, had been sent to a hospital waiting room.

Initially, Breonna Taylor's case did not receive widespread attention until it was paired with two other high-profile cases, that of Ahmaud Arbery, twenty-five, who was murdered by a father-son duo of white men while out for a run in the Satilla Shores neighborhood near Brunswick, Georgia, on February 23, 2020, and George Floyd, forty-six, who died after police officers pinned him facedown, with one kneeling on his neck for eight minutes and forty-six seconds in Minneapolis, Minnesota, on May 25, 2020. Video footage of Floyd's death ignited national and international protests against racism and police brutality. His death also helped buoy Tamika Palmer's quest for justice for Breonna. But while the men involved in the Arbery shooting have since been arrested and indicted on murder charges and officers in the Floyd case, too, face murder and manslaughter charges, the grand jury failed to indict anyone in Breonna Taylor's case based on the limited options presented by the Kentucky attorney general, Daniel Cameron. Breonna's family continues to fight, even after one officer was fired and after winning a multimillion-dollar settlement and the city's passage of Breonna's Law, which bans the use of no-knock warrants. Breonna Taylor's image, which made history gracing *Vanity Fair* and *O Magazine*, has become a rallying cry for Black Lives Matter, as well as for calls to defund the police and demands for substantive criminal justice reform. Athletes like Naomi Osaka wore a mask honoring Breonna Taylor at the US Open while the WNBA dedicated their season to Breonna Taylor, following a long tradition of Black women's sports activism. Breonna Taylor did not have a choice, but like so many Black women before her, her sacrifice has resulted in changes that benefit everyone, not just her family or Black women or Black people.

Black women also mobilized around another common cause: political change. In record numbers, they did not just vote, but they also played major roles in shaping the direction of the Democratic presidential campaign. From Symone Sanders being among the leadership of President-elect Joseph R. Biden's campaign, to a record six Black women being considered as possible Democratic presidential running mates, to Stacey Abrams, transforming a stolen race for the governorship of Georgia in 2018 into a statewide rebuke of voter suppression and helping to turn the state blue for the first time in twenty-eight-years, Black women effectively wielded their many powers and were embraced for it. Four days after the nation voted, on November 3, 2020, when the race was finally called, Vice President–elect Kamala Harris made history as the first woman, the first

Black woman, and the first woman of South Asian descent to win that office. We know that Harris's victory follows the advances made by a long line of trailblazers, like Charlotta Bass, who made history in 1952, when she ran as the vice presidential nominee for the Progressive Party, and Charlene Mitchell, who ran for president as the Communist Party USA nominee in 1968.

We hope that the future is bright for Black women and girls. We hope that Black women and aspiring young girls will continue to hold political office like Representative Cori Bush of Missouri and the twenty-five other Black women elected or reelected to serve in Congress in the 2020 election cycle. After all, Black women arrived in the country advocating for their rights, and we should continue to be vigilant so that Isabel de Olvera's words "I DEMAND JUSTICE" are not in vain.

We owe a debt to the Black women who came before us, those who persevered and those who did not, because the totality of their history is what informs our present and readies us to continue to fight for justice, for ourselves and, by extension, for all.

ACKNOWLEDGMENTS

We have labored feverishly on this book. We've always focused on Black women's history and were honored when Beacon provided an extraordinary opportunity to expand on that work. We hope that the stories shared in this volume introduce readers to Black women's dynamism. We wrote this book under great stress and have several people to thank for helping us push through the literal and figurative loss of family and friends. Daina wishes to give all power and glory to God. She also wishes to thank her mother, a strong Black woman who has been with the project all the way, including reading drafts, attending the manuscript workshop, and encouraging us through the writing process. She did so while grieving the loss of her husband of more than fifty years of marriage. This volume is dedicated to him. Daina is forever grateful to her family, including her husband and son for enduring another book so soon after the last one was published.

Kali wishes to thank God for helping her survive losing her mother, who passed away before seeing the book's final publication. Mrs. June Maria Gross believed in her daughter's intellect and potential when no one else did. She struggled to put her through school and set her on this path years ago. Kali loved her very much, misses her every day, and has dedicated this book to her. This book is also dedicated to Londa Ann Lovell, not only a cousin and sister, but she was also Kali's cherished friend. Kali would also like to thank her family and friends, especially the Abraham, Bowleg, Cohen, Gross, Irons, Johnson, Kirby, Lafayette, Lovell, and Ramos clans. She especially would like to thank her daughter, who put up with her mother working late and being away from home while researching and writing. Kali loves her very much and wrote much of this history with her in mind.

Daina would like to thank her graduate and undergraduate student researchers for their support, the "UT Cartel": Nakia Parker, Lauren Henley, Signe P. Fourmy, Maria Esther Hammack, Ron W. Davis, Zaria El-Fil, and Ashton Sauseda. Kali would like to thank Dean Michelle Stephens; all of her Rutgers History colleagues, especially Carolyn Brown, Kim Butler, Erica Armstrong Dunbar, Marisa Fuentes, Donna Murch, and Deborah Gray White; and the following graduate students: Pamela Walker, Brooke A. Thomas, Beatrice J. Adams, Shaun Armstead, Tracey Johnson, Joseph Williams, Jerrad Pacatte, and Leo Valdes. She would also like to thank Steven Fullwood for his important critical interventions and research assistance. I must also thank Jackie Carroll for taking care of my daughter—you have been in the trenches on weekends and late nights, and I am very grateful.

We also wish to thank Mary Frances Berry, Brittany Cooper, Pero G. Dagbovie, Erica Armstrong Dunbar, Ashley D. Farmer, Paula Giddings, Tiffany Gill, Sharon Harley, LaShawn Harris, Leslie M. Harris, Cheryl Hicks, Jacqueline Jones, Stephanie E. Jones-Rogers, Talitha LeFlouria, Donna Murch, and Deborah Gray White. We owe a special debt to Rhonda Williams, who read and critiqued multiple drafts of the book. We are also grateful to Janette Beckman for graciously allowing us to use her iconic photograph of rap music's female pioneers. Finally, we are grateful to work with Beacon Press, especially Gayatri Patnaik, Susan Lumenello, Maya Fernandez, and Marcy Barnes, as well as our editors Cecelia Cancellaro and Cynthia Yaudes, who have helped make this a better book.

IMAGE CREDITS

1. (McKoy sisters): WikiCommons.

2. (Edmonson sisters): Library of Congress, Prints and Photographs Division, Washington, DC.

3. (Susie King Taylor): Library of Congress, Prints and Photographs Division, Washington, DC.

4. (Edmonia Lewis): Harvard Art Museums/Fogg Museum, transfer from Special Collections, Fine Arts Library, Harvard College Library, bequest of Evert Jansen Wendell.

5. (woman outside slave pen): Library of Congress, Prints and Photographs Division, Washington, DC.

6. (Frances Thompson): *Days' Doings* (NY), August 12, 1876.

7. (Nannie Burroughs): Photographs and Prints Division, Schomburg Center for Research in Black Culture, New York Public Library.

8. (Augusta Savage and friends): Photographs and Prints Division, Schomburg Center for Research in Black Culture, New York Public Library.

9. (women farmworkers): Photographs and Prints Division, Schomburg Center for Research in Black Culture, New York Public Library.

10. (domestic workers): Photographs and Prints Division, Schomburg Center for Research in Black Culture, New York Public Library.

11. (Mary Petty): Photographs and Prints Division, Schomburg Center for Research in Black Culture, New York Public Library.

12. (WACs): Photographs and Prints Division, Schomburg Center for Research in Black Culture, New York Public Library.

13. (Shirley Chisholm): US House of Representatives; Photographs and Prints Division, Schomburg Center for Research in Black Culture, New York Public Library.

14. (Gladys Bentley): Collection of the Smithsonian National Museum of African American History and Culture.

15. (Rappers, "Class of '88"): Collection of the Smithsonian National Museum of African American History and Culture. Courtesy of Janette Beckman.

NOTES

AUTHORS' NOTE

1. Maria Stewart, "Why Sit Ye Here and Die?," printed in Marilyn Richardson, *Maria W. Stewart: America's First Black Woman Political Writer: Essays and Speeches* (Bloomington: Indiana University Press, 1987), 45–49.

2. Scholars too numerous to name here have published important work in Black women's history. This short list of scholarship reflects the comprehensive studies and anthologies published before the millennium. See Paula Giddings, *When and Where I Enter: The Impact of Black Women on Race and Sex in America* (New York: Morrow, 1984); Darlene Clark Hine and Kathleen Thompson, *A Shining Thread of Hope: The History of Black Women in America* (New York: Broadway, 1998); Sharon Harley and Rosalyn Terborg-Penn, eds., *The Afro-American Woman: Struggles and Images* (Port Washington, NY: Kennikat, 1978); Darlene Clark Hine, Wilma King, and Linda Reed, eds., *"We Specialize in the Wholly Impossible": A Reader in Black Women's History* (Brooklyn, NY: Carlson, 1995); and Darlene Clark Hine, Elsa Barkley Brown, and Rosalyn Terborg-Penn, eds., *Black Women in America: An Historical Encyclopedia, Vol. 1 (A–L) and Vol. 2 (M–Z)* (Bloomington: Indiana University Press, 1993). Deborah Gray White published the first comprehensive study of enslaved women, *"Ar'n't I a Woman?: Female Slaves in the Plantation South* (New York: W. W. Norton, 1985), while Gerda Lerner and Dorothy Sterling created the first set of primary document readers in the field. See Lerner, ed., *Black Women in White America: A Documentary History* (New York: Vintage, 1972), and Sterling, ed., *We Are Your Sisters: Black Women in the Nineteenth Century* (New York: W. W. Norton, 1984). Jacqueline Jones, who explored labor from enslavement to the twentieth century, rounds out this early list of scholarship. See Jones, *Labor of Love, Labor of Sorrow: Black Women, Work, and the Family, from Slavery to the Present* (New York: Vintage, 1985).

INTRODUCTION: NANNIE'S LEGACY AND THE HISTORIES OF BLACK WOMEN

1. The school's earlier motto, "Work, Support Thyself, to Thine Own Powers Appeal," was supplanted by the later motto, "We Specialize in the Wholly Impossible." See Darlene Clark Hine, Elsa Barkley Brown, and Rosalyn Terborg-Penn, eds., *Black Women in America: An Historical Encyclopedia, Vol. 1 (A–L)* (Bloomington: Indiana University Press, 1993), 204.

2. Sharon Harley, "Nannie Helen Burroughs: 'The Black Goddess of Liberty,'" *Journal of Negro History* 81, nos. 1–4, Vindicating the Race: Contributions to African-American Intellectual History (Winter–Autumn 1996): 63; Hine, Brown, and Terborg-Penn, eds., *Black Women in America*, 201–5.

3. Quoted in Harley, "Nannie Helen Burroughs," 66–67, 65; "With All They Getting," *Southern Workman* 56, no. 7 (July 1917): 299–301, in Lerner, *Black Women in White America*, ed. Gerder Lerner (New York: Vintage Books, 1992); Nannie Helen Burroughs, "The Negro Woman and Suffrage," 1923, box 46, Nannie Helen Burroughs Papers, Library of Congress (hereafter LOC), Washington, DC; "From a Woman's Point of View, Vote for Justice and Jobs," 1936, Nannie Helen Burroughs Papers; *Black Women in America*, 204.

4. Jennifer L. Morgan, *Laboring Women: Reproduction and Gender in New World Slavery* (Philadelphia: University of Pennsylvania Press, 2004), 50. For more on the middle passage, see Sowandé Mustakeem, *Slavery at Sea: Terror, Sex, and Sickness in the Middle Passage* (Urbana: University of Illinois, 2016); and Stephanie E. Smallwood, *Saltwater Slavery: A Middle Passage from Africa to American Diaspora* (Cambridge, MA: Harvard University Press, 2007).

5. "Misogynoir," a term coined by Moya Bailey and Trudy aka @thetrudz, describes the anti-black misogyny that Black women experience. For more on the term and how its framers have experienced it, see Moya Bailey and Trudy, "On Misogynoir: Citation, Erasure, and Plagiarism," *Feminist Media Studies* 18, no. 4 (2018): 762–68.

6. Rikki Byrd, "The American Flag Was Sewn in Part by a Teenage Black Girl," *Teen Vogue*, July 4, 2018; Sally Johnston and Pat Billing, *Mary Young Pickersgill Flag Maker of the Star Spangled Banner* (Bloomington, IN: Author House, 2014), 17–20; Seth Rockman, *Scraping By: Wage Labor, Slavery, and Survival in Early Baltimore* (Baltimore: Johns Hopkins University Press, 2009), 260–62; Michelle Wilkinson, ed., *For Whom It Stands: The Flag and the American People* (Reginald F. Lewis Museum of Maryland African American History & Culture, 2016).

7. Tiffany M. Gill, *Beauty Shop Politics: African American Women's Activism in the Beauty Industry* (Urbana: University of Illinois Press, 2010), 7–15.

CHAPTER ONE: ISABEL'S EXPEDITION AND FREEDOM BEFORE 1619

1. George Hammond, ed., *Don Juan Oñate: Colonizer of New Mexico, 1595–1628*, vol. 5 (Santa Fe: University of New Mexico Press, 1953), 560; and Dedra S. McDonald, "To Be Black and Female in the Spanish Southwest: Toward a History of African Women on New Spain's Far Northern Frontier," in *African American Women Confront the West, 1600–2000*, ed. Quintard Taylor and Shirley Ann Wilson Moore (Norman: University of Oklahoma Press, 2008), 31–52, quote on 31–32.

2. McDonald, "To Be Black and Female in the Spanish Southwest," 37.

3. The term "mulatto" was not offensive at that time, and it meant one who was of African and Indian descent, according to scholar Jack D. Forbes, *Black Africans and Native Americans: Color, Race, and Caste in the Evolution of Red-Black Peoples* (New York: Basil Blackwell, 1988). Racial mixing was common in this time period, as indigenous peoples, Europeans, Mexicans,

Africans, Spaniards, and other groups shared offspring. We do not know if these relationships were consensual or not, but there is great evidence of multiracial people. See Herman L. Bennett, *African Kings and Black Slaves: Sovereignty and Dispossession in the Early Modern Atlantic* (Philadelphia: University of Pennsylvania Press, 2018); Gary B. Nash, "The Hidden History of Mestizo America," *Journal of American History* 82, no. 3 (December 1995): 941–64; and Gwendolyn Midlo Hall, *Slavery and African Ethnicities in the Americas: Restoring the Links* (Chapel Hill: University of North Carolina Press, 2007).

4. Bruce Glasrud, ed., *African American History in New Mexico: Portraits from Five Hundred Years* (Albuquerque: University of New Mexico Press, 2013), 32–33.

5. Herbert Aptheker, *American Negro Slave Revolts* (1943) (New York: Columbia University Press, 1983); Paul E. Hoffman, *A New Andalucía and a Way to the Orient: The American Southeast During the Sixteenth Century* (Baton Rouge: Louisiana State University Press, 2015); William Loren Katz, *The Black West: A Documentary and Pictorial History of the African American Role in the Westward Expansion of the United States* (New York: Random House, 2005); and Woodbury Lowery, *The Spanish Settlements: Within the Present Limits of the United States: Florida, 1562–1574* (New York: Knickerbocker Press, 1905).

6. Rafel Valdez Aguilar, *Sinaloa Negritud y Olvido* (1993) (Culiacán, Sinaloa: El Diario de Sinaloa, 2004), 45.

7. F. W. Hodge, *History of New Mexico by Gaspar Pérez de Villagrá, 1610* (Los Angeles: Quivira Society, 1933), 76.

8. Hammond, *Don Juan Oñate*, 560.

9. Hammond, *Don Juan Oñate*, 310.

10. Hodge, *History of New Mexico*, quoted on 73 fn1, and in *The Handbook of Texas Online*, W. H. Timmons, "Oñate Expedition," http://www.tshaonline.org/handbook/online/articles/upo02, accessed August 8, 2018.

11. Figures calculated by the author and Ashton Sauseda based on the "Inspection Made by Juan De Frías Salazar of the Expedition," published in Hammond, *Don Juan Oñate*, 199–308.

12. Hammond, *Don Juan Oñate*, 557–60.

13. Hammond, *Don Juan Oñate*. For quoted material, see Martha Menchaca, *Recovering the History, Constructing Race: The Indian, Black, and White Roots of Mexican Americans* (Austin: University of Texas Press, 2001), 85.

14. Frederick W. Hodge, ed., "The Narrative of Alvar Nunez Cabeza de Vaca," in *Spanish Explorers in the Southern United States, 1528–1542* (New York: Charles Scribner's Sons, 1907), 107.

15. Hodge, "The Narrative of Alvar Nunez Cabeza de Vaca," 107.

16. R. R. Wright, "Negro Companions of the Spanish Explorers," *American Anthropologist* (1904): 217–28.

17. References for the history of Maria come from Jennifer L. Morgan, "Partus Sequitur Ventrem: Law, Race, and Reproduction in Colonial Slavery," *Small Axe* 55, no. 1 (March 2018): 1–17, esp. 6–8.

18. Morgan, "Partus Sequitur Ventrem," 7.

19. Morgan, "Partus Sequitur Ventrem," 6–7.

20. Hodge, *History of New Mexico*, 110–11.

21. Hodge, *History of New Mexico*, 100–101.

22. Hodge, *History of New Mexico*.

23. "The Story of Africa: Slavery Timeline," BBC World Service, http://www
.bbc.co.uk/worldservice/africa/features/storyofafrica/9generic3.shtml, accessed
July 29, 2019.

CHAPTER TWO: ANGELA'S EXODUS OUT OF AFRICA

1. Engel Sluiter, "New Light on the '20. and Odd Negroes' Arriving in
Virginia, August 1619," *William and Mary Quarterly* 54, no. 2 (April 1997):
395–98, quote on 397.

2. "The First Africans," Jamestown Rediscovery, Historic Jamestowne website, https://historicjamestowne.org/history/the-first-africans, accessed May 4,
2019.

3. International Slavery Museum, "Extracts from John Newton's Journal,"
National Museums Liverpool, http://www.liverpoolmuseums.org.uk/ism/slavery
/middle_passage/john_newton.aspx, accessed April 7, 2019.

4. This is a rare account of the capture experience of a Mandingo woman
who later settled in Bluefields, Nicaragua. See Charles Napier Bell, *Tangweera:
Life and Adventures Among Gentle Savages* (London: Edward Arnold, 1899),
21–30, quotes on 24–25.

5. *Boston Gazette*, April 26–May 3, 1731.

6. Gwendolyn Midlo Hall, *Africans in Colonial Louisiana: The Development of Afro-Creole Culture in the Eighteenth Century* (Baton Rouge: Louisiana
State University Press, 1992), 69.

7. Hall, *Africans in Colonial Louisiana*, 69–70.

8. Jane Landers, *Black Society in Spanish Florida* (Urbana: University of Illinois Press, 1999), 18.

9. Landers, *Black Society in Spanish Florida*, 19.

10. Madaline W. Nichols, "Las Siete Partidas," *California Law Review* 20,
no. 3 (1932): 260.

11. Leslie M. Harris, *In the Shadow of Slavery: African Americans in New
York City, 1626–1863* (Chicago: University of Chicago Press, 2003), 14.

12. Christopher Moore, "A World of Possibilities: Slavery and Freedom in
Dutch New Amsterdam," in *Slavery in New York*, ed. Ira Berlin and Leslie M.
Harris (New York: New Press, 2005), 31–56, quoted material on 37–38.

13. Harris, *In the Shadow of Slavery*, 14–15.

14. Moore, "A World of Possibilities," 38.

15. Moore, "A World of Possibilities," 45–46.

16. Nearly one hundred years later, Susanna Jones filed a freedom suit in
1754 (Lancaster County, VA). Such suits appeared in this court record until the
end of slavery in 1865.

17. Virginia, Brown, W. Morle, Cochran, G., Gray, W. Waller, Desilver, T.,
Hening, W. Waller, J. & G. Cochran, Franklin Press (Richmond: V., R. &
W. & G. Bartow), *The statutes at large;: being a collection of all the laws of
Virginia, from the first session of the legislature, in the year 1619. Published
pursuant to an act of the General Assembly of Virginia, passed on the fifth day of*

February one thousand eight hundred and eight. : Volume I [–XIII] (New York: Printed for the editor, by R. & W. & G. Bartow, 1823, 1819, 1823), Vol. II, 270.

18. Kelly Buchanan, "Slavery in the French Colonies: Le Code Noir (the Black Code) of 1685," *Library of Congress Blog*, January 13, 2011, https://blogs.loc.gov/law/2011/01/slavery-in-the-french-colonies.

19. Full text of the 1724 Louisiana Code Noir, found on the Black Past website, July 28, 2007, https://www.blackpast.org/african-american-history /louisianas-code-noir-1724.

20. Susan Stessin-Cohn and Ashley Hurlburt-Biagini, *In Defiance: Runaways from Slavery in New York's Hudson River Valley, 1735–1831* (Delmar, NY: Black Dome Press, 2016), 27.

21. *American Weekly Mercury* (Philadelphia), October 31– November 7, 1723.

22. *American Weekly Mercury*, January 4–January 11, 1732.

23. *Weekly News-Letter* (Boston), December 12–December 19, 1728.

24. *New-England Weekly Journal* (Boston), October 4, 1731.

25. *New-England Weekly Journal*, December 25, 1732.

26. *Boston Gazette*, from May 21 to May 29, 1733.

27. Richard Price, ed., *Maroon Societies: Rebel Slave Communities in the Americas* (1979) (Baltimore: Johns Hopkins University Press, 1996), 1.

28. Sylviane A. Diouf, *Slavery's Exiles: The Story of American Maroons* (New York: New York University Press, 2014), 18.

29. Diouf, *Slavery's Exiles*, 27.

30. Timothy James Lockley, ed., *Maroon Communities in South Carolina: A Documentary Record* (Columbia: University of South Carolina Press, 2009), 3.

31. Diouf, *Slavery's Exiles*, 27–28.

CHAPTER THREE: BELINDA'S PETITION FOR INDEPENDENCE

1. Frederick County (VA) Coroners' Inquisitions, 1779–1927, local government records collection, Frederick County Court Records, Library of Virginia, Richmond.

2. "Belinda Sutton and Her Petitions," Royall House & Slave Quarters, http://www.royallhouse.org/slavery/belinda-sutton-and-her-petitions, accessed February 14, 2018.

3. Goochland County (VA) Judgments (Freedom Suits), 1763, Local Government Records Collection, Goochland County Court Records, Library of Virginia, Richmond.

4. Taunya Lovell Banks, "Elizabeth Freeman," in *Black Women in America: An Historical Encyclopedia*, 2nd ed., Vol. 1, ed. Darlene Clark Hine et al. (New York: Oxford University Press, 2005), 499–500.

5. *Virginia Gazette* (Williamsburg), April 25, 1766. It appears that Heriter captured her but she ran away again in 1768.

6. See *Virginia Gazette*, September 17, 1767, and September 8, 1768.

7. *Virginia Gazette*, June 1, 1769.

8. *Virginia Gazette*, October 26, 1769.

9. *Virginia Gazette*, June 27, 1770.

10. *Virginia Gazette*, August 3, 1769.

11. Benjamin Quarles, *The Negro in the American Revolution* (New York: W. W. Norton, 1961), vii and 27fn28.

12. Quarles, *The Negro in the American Revolution*, 27–28.

13. James Burton, Provision Return, 1 May 1777, accession 44302, personal papers collection, Library of Virginia, Richmond.

14. "American Revolutionary War, 1775–1783," http://revolutionarywar.us /continental-army/virginia, accessed May 6, 2019.

15. Quarles, *The Negro in the American Revolution*, 94.

16. Quarles, *The Negro in the American Revolution*, 99.

17. Jacqueline Jones, *A Dreadful Deceit: The Myth of Race from the Colonial Era to Obama's America* (New York: Basic Books, 2013), 91.

18. Book of Negroes, Book 1, "Black Loyalists: Our History, Our People," Canada's Digital Collections, ape.lac-bac.gc.ca/100/200/301/can_digital _collections/backloyalists/documents/official/black_loyalist_directory.htm, accessed May 9, 2019.

19. Book of Negroes, Book 1.

20. Book of Negroes, Book 1.

21. Commissioner of Public Records, Nova Scotia Archives, RG 1, vol. 170, p. 333 (microfilm no. 15282), available at http://novascotia.ca/archives/Africans /archives.asp?ID=20, accessed May 9, 2019.

22. Commissioner of Public Records, Nova Scotia Archives, 338.

23. William Waller Hening, ed., *The Statutes at Large; Being a Collection of All the Laws of Virginia from the First Session of the Legislature, in the Year 1619* (Philadelphia: R. & W. & G. Bartow, 1823), 447–48, 450–51, and 453–54 (emphasis added).

24. Hening, *The Statutes at Large*, 459, 460–62 (emphasis added).

25. Race and Slavery Petitions Project, "Compensation Claims," PAR 11381402 and 11380109, April 15, 2014.

26. Richard Peters, ed., *The Public Statutes at Large of the United States of America, from the Organization of the Government in 1789, to March 3, 1845* (Boston: Charles C. Little and James Brown, 1845), 1:302–5.

27. Richard Demone Pulley, "The Role of the Virginia Slave in Iron and Tobacco Manufacturing," master's thesis, University of Richmond, 1962.

28. Charles Dew, "David Ross and the Oxford Iron Works: A Study of Industrial Slavery in the Nineteenth-Century South," *William and Mary Quarterly* 31, no. 2 (April 1974): 189–224, quotes on 193, 194, and 196.

29. Dew, "David Ross and the Oxford Iron Works," 198–99.

30. Dew, "David Ross and the Oxford Iron Works," 211–12.

31. Daina Ramey Berry, *Swing the Sickle for the Harvest Is Ripe: Gender and Slavery in Antebellum Georgia* (Urbana: University of Illinois Press, 2007).

32. Maurie D. McInnis and Kirt von Daacke, eds., *Educated in Tyranny: Slavery at Thomas Jefferson's University* (Charlottesville: University of Virginia Press, 2019).

33. Leslie M. Harris, James Campbell, and Alfred Trophy, eds., *Slavery and the University: Histories and Legacies* (Athens: University of Georgia Press, 2018); Marisa Fuentes, Deborah Gray White, and Beatrice J. Adams, *Scarlett and Black: Slavery and Dispossession in Rutgers History* (New Brunswick, NJ:

Rutgers University Press, 2016); and Craig Wilder, *Ebony & Ivy: Race, Slavery, and the Troubled History of America's Universities* (New York: Bloomsbury Publishing, 2014).

34. *New York Gazette and Weekly Mercury*, January 16, 1775.

35. *New York Gazette and Weekly Mercury*, January 19, 1775.

36. *New York Gazette and Weekly Mercury*, January 23, 1775.

37. Daina Ramey Berry, *The Price for Their Pound of Flesh: The Value of the Enslaved, from Womb to Grave, in the Building of a Nation* (Boston: Beacon Press, 2017), chapters 1–3.

38. Erica Armstrong Dunbar, *Never Caught: The Washingtons' Relentless Pursuit of Their Runaway Slave, Ona Judge* (New York: 37 Ink, 2017); Elizabeth Dowling Taylor, ed., *A Slave in the White House: Paul Jennings and the Madisons* (New York: St. Martin's Griffin, 2012); and "James Madison's Slavery Interpretation Manual," unpublished manuscript, 2017.

39. Ira Berlin, *Slaves Without Masters: The Freedom Negro in the Antebellum South* (New York: New Press, 1974), 47.

40. Lillian Ashcraft-Eason, "'She Voluntarily Hath Come': A Gambian Woman Trader in Colonial Georgia in the Eighteenth Century," in *Identity in the Shadow of Slavery*, ed. Paul E. Lovejoy (New York: Bloomsbury, 2000), 202–21, quoted material on 202, 204, and 207.

41. Ashcraft-Eason, "'She Voluntarily Hath Come,'" 213.

42. Excerpted document in *Escrituras*, reel 172, bundle 378, 17–A–B, 18–A–B, of the East Florida Papers, LOC (microfilm copy at P. K. Yonge Library of Florida History, University of Florida). Document is in Spanish; this version was translated by Caleb Finnegan and may be found online at http://www.nps .gov/timu/learn/education/upload/ak_lesson.pdf, accessed May 27, 2019.

43. *Escrituras*, 6. Two of their daughters stayed in the United States with their white husbands.

44. Virginia (Colony), Colonial Papers, Order of the Court of Oyer and Terminer of Brunswick County, 1773 Jan. 11, Accession 36138, state government records collection, Library of Virginia, Richmond.

45. Frederick County (VA) Coroners' Inquisitions, 1779–1972, local government records collection, Frederick County Court Records, Library of Virginia, Richmond.

46. Lunenburg County (VA) Coroners' Inquisitions, 1752–1924, local government records collection, Lunenburg County Court Records, Library of Virginia, Richmond.

47. Virginia (Colony), Colonial Papers, Order of the Court of Oyer and Terminer of Brunswick County, 1772 June 3, accession 36138, state government records collection, Library of Virginia, Richmond.

48. Frederick County (VA) Coroners' Inquisitions, 1779–1972, local government records collection, Frederick County Court Records, Library of Virginia, Richmond.

49. Diouf, *Slavery's Exiles*, 217.

50. Frederick Douglass, *The Heroic Slave*, in *Autographs for Freedom*, ed. Julia Griffiths (Cleveland: John P. Jewett and Company, 1853), 192.

51. Richard Grant, "Deep in the Swamps, Archaeologists Are Finding How Fugitive Slaves Kept Their Freedom," Smithsonian.com, September 2016, http://www.smithsonianmag.com/history/deep-swamps-archaeologists-fugitive-slaves-kept-freedom-180960122.

52. Historic Hudson Valley, "What Is Pinkster?," http://hudsonvalley.org/article/what-is-pinkster, accessed May 27, 2019.

53. "Edict of Good Government, July 2, 1784, Digest of the Acts and Deliberations of the Cabildo Laws," vol. 1, book 3, pp. 105–12.

CHAPTER FOUR: MILLIE AND CHRISTINE'S PERFORMANCE AND THE EXPANSION OF SLAVERY

1. Richardson, *Maria W. Stewart*, 56.

2. *Biological Sketch of Millie Christine, the Carolina Twin: Surnamed the Two-Headed Nightengale* [sic] *and the Eighth Wonder of the World* (1882) (Cincinnati: Hennegan & Co., 1902–12); *The History of the Carolina Twins: Told in "Their Own Peculiar Way" by "One of Them"* (Buffalo: Buffalo Courier Printing House, 1869); and Ellen Samuels, "Examining Millie and Christine McCoy: Where Enslavement and Enfreakment Meet," *Signs* 37, no. 1 (September 2011): 53–81. Their mother's name is often spelled Monemia and sometimes Menemia in different publications. We chose to use the former.

3. Deirdre Cooper Owens, *Medical Bondage: Race, Gender, and the Origins of American Gynecology* (Athens: University of Georgia Press, 2017); and Rana A. Hogarth, *Medicalizing Blackness: Making Racial Difference in the Atlantic World, 1780–1840* (Chapel Hill: University of North Carolina Press, 2017).

4. Chapter I, article I, Vermont Constitution, found in *The Federal and State Constitutions Colonial Charters, and Other Organic Laws of the States, Territories, and Colonies Now or Heretofore Forming the United States of America, Compiled and Edited Under the Act of Congress of June 30, 1906 by Francis Newton Thorpe* (Washington, DC: Government Printing Office, 1909); Patrick Rael, *Eighty-Eight Years: The Long Death of Slavery in the United States, 1777–1865* (Athens: University of Georgia Press, 2015), 64–66.

5. Act for the Gradual Abolition of Slavery, 1780, Avalon Project: Documents in Law, History & Diplomacy, http://avalon.law.yale.edu/18th_century/pennst01.asp; Edward Raymond Turner, "The Abolition of Slavery in Pennsylvania," *Pennsylvania Magazine of History and Biography* 36, no. 2 (1912): 137; Erica Armstrong Dunbar, *A Fragile Freedom: African American Women and Emancipation in the Antebellum City* (New Haven, CT: Yale University Press, 2008), 3; Negley K. Teeters, *The Cradle of the Penitentiary: The Walnut Street Jail at Philadelphia, 1777–1845* (Philadelphia: The Pennsylvania Prison Society, 1955); Leslie Patrick-Stamp, "Numbers that Are Not New: African Americans in the Country's First Prison, 1790–1835" in the *Pennsylvania Magazine of History & Biography*, Vol. CXIX, Nos. 1/2, (January/April 1995), 96, 98–100.

6. Joanne Pope Melish, *Disowning Slavery: Gradual Emancipation and "Race" in New England, 1780–1860* (Ithaca, NY: Cornell University Press, 1998), 66–69.

7. James J. Gigantino II, *The Ragged Road to Abolition: Slavery and Freedom in New Jersey, 1776–1865* (Philadelphia: University of Pennsylvania Press, 2015), 95–97.

8. Du Bois, *The Philadelphia Negro*, 32–39; Charles L. Blockson, *Philadelphia: 1639–2000* (Charleston, SC: Acadia Press, 2000), 28; Charles L. Blockson, *African Americans in Pennsylvania: A History and Guide* (Baltimore: Black Classic Press, 1994), 50.

9. Elizabeth Keckley, *Behind the Scenes: Thirty Years a Slave, and Four Years in the White House*, ed. Frances Smith Foster (Urbana: University of Illinois Press, 1998), 13–14.

10. *Alexandria (VA) Expositor*, May 24, 1804.

11. *Telegraph and Texas Register* (Houston), September 23, 1837.

12. *Northern Standard* (Clarksville, TX), July 28, 1849.

13. "Sarah Ashley," *Federal Writers' Project: Slave Narrative Project, Vol. 16, Texas, Part 1*, 34, https://hdl.loc.gov/loc.mss/mesn.161, accessed May 30, 2019.

14. Steven Deyle, *Carry Me Back: The Domestic Slave Trade in American Life* (New York: Oxford University Press, 2005), 17.

15. J. W. C. Pennington, *A Narrative of Events of the Life of J. H. Banks, an Escaped Slave, from the Cotton State, Alabama, in America* (Liverpool: M. Rourke, Printer, 1861), 46–47.

16. Pennington, *A Narrative of Events of the Life of J. H. Banks*.

17. Harriet Jacobs, "Letter from a Fugitive Slave," *New York Daily Tribune*, June 21, 1853, 6.

18. "Jordon Smith," *Federal Writers' Project: Slave Narrative Project, Vol. 16, Texas, Part 4*, 38, https://www.loc.gov/resources, accessed July 6, 2019.

19. "Millie Simkins," *Federal Writers' Project: Slave Narrative Project, Vol. 15* (Tennessee: Batson-Young, 1936), 66, manuscript/mixed material, https://www.loc.gov/item/mesn150. Several other bondpeople testified about being naked on the auction block. See "Campbell Armstrong," *Federal Writers' Project: Slave Narrative Project, Vol. 2, Arkansas, Part 1, Abbott-Byrd* (November–December 1936), manuscript/mixed material, https://www.loc.gov/item/mesn021/; and "Andrew Boone," *Federal Writers' Project: Slave Narrative Project, Vol. 11, North Carolina, Part 1, Adams-Hunter* (1936), manuscript/mixed material, https://www.loc.gov/item/mesn111.

20. C. Abner to E. Kingsland, Esq., November 18, 1859, MSS# 2Ab7221, Virginia Historical Society.

21. For the latter, see Daina Ramey Berry, "The Ubiquitous Nature of Slave Capital," in *After Piketty: The Agenda for Economics and Inequality*, ed. Heather Boushey, J. Bradford Delong, and Marshall Steinbaum (Cambridge, MA: Harvard University Press, 2017), 126–49.

22. Deirdre Cooper Owens, *Medical Bondage: Race, Gender, and the Origins of American Gynecology* (Athens: University of Georgia Press, 2017); and Nicole Ivy, "Materia Medica: Black Women, White Doctors and Spectacular Gynecology in the 19th Century U.S.," PhD diss., Yale University, 2013.

23. Samuels, "Examining Millie and Christine," 54.

24. "Biographical Sketch of Millie Christine," 21–22.

25. "Biographical Sketch of Millie Christine," 7–10.

26. Here we are referring to the Moynihan Report. See US Department of Labor, Office of Policy Planning and Research, *The Negro Family: The Case for National Action* (Washington, DC: US Government Printing Office, 1965).

27. As quoted in "James Madison's Slavery Interpretation Manual," 31.

28. Berry, *Swing the Sickle for the Harvest Is Ripe* , 56–61, quote on 57.

29. Tera W. Hunter, *Bound in Wedlock: Slave and Free Black Marriage in the Nineteenth Century* (Cambridge, MA: Belknap Press of Harvard University Press, 2017), 21.

30. H. W. Flourunoy, *Calendar of Virginia State Papers and Other Manuscripts from January 1, 1836 to April 15, 1869 Col. XI* (Richmond, 1893), 310–11. For more on Harriet's husband, Dangerfield Newby, see Berry, *The Price for Their Pound of Flesh*.

31. "James Madison's Slavery Interpretation Manual," 36–37.

32. "Rose Williams," in *Federal Writers' Project, Slave Narrative Project, Vol. 16, Texas, Part 4, 1936*, www.loc.gov/item/mens164. For a detailed analysis of the exchange between Rose and Rufus, see Tom Foster, *Rethinking Rufus: Sexual Violations of Enslaved Men* (Athens: University of Georgia Press, 2019).

33. Amrita Chakrabarti Myers, *Forging Freedom: Black Women and the Pursuit of Liberty in Antebellum Charleston* (Chapel Hill: University of North Carolina Press, 2011).

34. Larry Koger, *Black Slaveowners: Free Black Slave Masters in South Carolina, 1790–1860* (Columbia: University of South Carolina Press, 1985), 25.

35. Wilma King, *The Essence of Liberty: Free Black Women During the Slave Era* (Columbia: University of Missouri Press, 2006), 77–80, quoted material on 77–8.

36. William Still, *Underground Railroad Records* (Philadelphia: Williams Still Publisher, 1888), 282–84.

37. Rosetta Douglass Sprague, "My Mother as I Recall Her," *Journal of Negro History* 8, no. 1 (January 1923): 93–101, quote p. 93.

38. Talitha L. LeFlouria, *Frederick Douglass: A Watchtower of Human Freedom* (Washington, DC: Eastern National, 2008), 10.

39. Darlene Clark Hine, Elsa Barkley Brown, and Rosalyn Terborg-Penn, eds., *Black Women in America, Vol. 2* (New York: Oxford University Press, 2005), 367.

40. Sprague, "My Mother," 95.

41. Sprague, "My Mother," 100.

42. William Craft, *Running a Thousand Miles for Freedom; or, the Escape of William and Ellen Craft from Slavery* (London: William Tweedie, 1860).

43. See "Harriet Robinson Scott," *Historic Missourians: The State Historical Society of Missouri*, https://shsmo.org/historicmissourians/name/s/scotth, accessed May 30, 2019; Lea VanderVelde, *Mrs. Dred Scott: A Life on Slavery's Frontier* (New York: Oxford University Press, 2009); and Martha S. Jones, *Birthright Citizens: A History of Race and Rights in Antebellum America* (Cambridge, UK: Cambridge University Press, 2018), 128–46; and Tera Hunter, *Bound in Wedlock: Slave and Free Black Marriage in the Nineteenth Century* (Cambridge, MA: Belknap Press of Harvard University Press, 2017).

44. "James Madison's Slavery Interpretation Manual," 43–45.

45. "James Madison's Slavery Interpretation Manual," 43–45.

46. William Pierson argues that slaves "committed suicide under a depressed mental state brought on by a sense of loss and separation exacerbated by the hopelessness of what seemed an increasingly harsh regime of bondage." See

Pierson, "White Cannibals, Black Martyrs: Fear, Depression, and Religious Faith as Causes of Suicide Among New Slaves," *Journal of Negro History* 62, no. 2 (April 1977): 147–59, quote on 150.

47. Deposition of Francis S. Key to John Randolph, 22 April 1816, "Trafficking in Slaves," Congressional Records HR 14A–17.4 NARA, Washington, DC.

48. Jesse Torrey, *American Slave Trade* (London: C. Clement, 1822), 72.

49. Torrey, *American Slave Trade*.

50. E. A. Andrews, *Slavery and the Domestic Slave-Trade in the United States* (Boston: Light & Stearns, 1836), 112–13.

51. John Hawkins Simpson, *Horrors of the Virginian Slave Trade and of the Slave-Rearing Plantations. The True Story of Dinah, an Escaped Virginian Slave, Now in London, on Whose Body are Eleven Scars Left by Tortures which were Inflicted by her Master, Her Own Father. Together with Extracts from the Laws of Virginia, Showing That Against these Barbarities the Law Gives not the Smallest Protection to the Slave, but the Reverse* (London: A. W. Bennett, 1863), 34.

52. Ruthie Winegarten, *Black Texas Women: 150 Years of Trial and Triumph* (Austin: University of Texas Press, 1995), 31.

53. Stephanie Jones-Rogers, *They Were Her Property: White Women as Slave Owners in the American South* (New Haven, CT: Yale University Press, 2019); and Thavolia Glymph, *Out of the House of Bondage: The Transformation of the Plantation Household* (New York: Cambridge University Press, 2008).

54. Douglas O. Linder, "Famous Trials: Celia, a Slave, Trial (1855): An Account," https://www.famous-trials.com/celia/180-home, accessed May 30, 2019.

55. Susan Eva O'Donovan, "Universities of Social and Political Change: Slaves in Jail in Antebellum America," in *Buried Lives: Incarcerated in Early America*, ed. Michele Lise Tarter and Richard Bell (Athens: University of Georgia Press, 2012), 124–41, quote on 125.

56. Leslie M. Harris and Daina Ramey Berry, eds., *Slavery and Freedom in Savannah* (Athens: University of Georgia Press, 2014), xviii, 98–99.

57. Norfolk County (VA) Coroner's Inquisitions, 1766–1909, Library of Virginia. Phoebe belonged to the estate of Henry Prince of Sussex County, NJ, and was hanged July 20, 1833.

58. George Rawick, *The American Slave*, vol. 13, p. 163, quote in Daina Ramey Berry, "'We Sho Was Dressed Up': Slave Women, Material Culture, and Decorative Arts in Wilkes County, Georgia," in *The Savannah River Valley up to 1865: Fine Arts, Architecture, and Decorative Arts*, ed. Ashley Callahan (Athens: Georgia Museum of Art, 2003), 73–83.

59. Berry, "'We Sho Was Dressed Up,'" 73.

60. Bert James Lowenberg and Ruth Bogin, eds., *Black Women in Nineteenth-Century American Life: Their Words, Their Thoughts, Their Feelings* (University Park: Pennsylvania State University Press, 1976), 134–41.

61. Bettye Collier-Thomas, *Daughters of Thunder: Black Women Preachers and Their Sermons, 1850–1979* (San Francisco: Jossey-Bass Publishers, 1998), 12–14, quote on 14.

62. Rosalyn Terborg-Penn, *African American Women in the Struggle for the Vote, 1850–1920* (Bloomington: Indiana University Press, 1998), 13, 16, 18.

CHAPTER FIVE: MARY'S APRON AND THE DEMISE OF SLAVERY

1. Mary Colbert, *Federal Writers' Project: Slave Narrative Project, Vol. 4, Georgia, Part 1,* 1936, https://www.loc.gov/item/mesn041.

2. Aunt Rhody Holswell, *Federal Writers' Project: Slave Narrative Project, Vol. 10, Missouri,* 1936. https://www.loc.gov/item/mesn100/.

3. Confederate States of America, "Declaration of the Immediate Causes Which Induce and Justify the Secession of South Carolina from the Federal Union, December 24, 1860," available online at Avalon Project, Yale University Law School, https:avalon.law.yale.edu/19th_century/csa_scarsec.asp, accessed June 1, 2019.

4. Thavolia Glymph, "I'm a Radical Black Girl: Black Women Unionists and the Politics of Civil War History," *Journal of the Civil War Era* 8, no. 3 (September 2018): 359–87, quote on 364.

5. "Pauline Grice," *Federal Writers' Project: Slave Narrative Project, Vol. 16, Texas, Part 2,* 1936, 98–101, quoted material on 100, https://www.loc.gov/item/mesn162.

6. "Millie Forward," *Federal Writers' Project: Slave Narrative Project, Vol. 16, Texas, Part 2,* 1936, 48. https://www.loc.gov/item/mesn162.

7. "Harriett Barrett," *Federal Writers' Project: Slave Narrative Project, Vol. 16, Texas, Part 1,* 1936, 49. https://www.loc.gov/item/mesn161/.

8. Mrs. Francena Martin Sutton, "Civil War Experience of Some Arkansas Women," unpublished manuscript, Dolph Briscoe Center, University of Texas at Austin, 4.

9. Susie King Taylor, *A Black Woman's Civil War Memoirs: Reminiscences of My Life in Camp with the 33rd U.S. Colored Troops, Late 1st South Carolina Volunteers* (1902), ed. Patricia W. Romero and Willie Lee Rose (Princeton, NJ: Markus Wiener Publishers, 1995), 29–30 and 33.

10. Taylor, *A Black Woman's Civil War Memoirs,* 38, 45.

11. Taylor, *A Black Woman's Civil War Memoirs,* 52.

12. Taylor, *A Black Woman's Civil War Memoirs,* 22–23.

13. Jane E. Schultz, *Women at the Front: Hospital Workers in Civil War America* (Chapel Hill: University of North Carolina Press, 2004), 17.

14. Frank Moore, *The Civil War in Song and Story, 1861–1865* (New York: Peter Fenelon Collier, Publisher, 1882), 264.

15. Schultz, *Women at the Front,* 21–24.

16. Berry, "'We Sho Was Dressed Up,'" 76.

17. Deborah M. Liles and Angela Boswell, eds., *Women in Civil War Texas: Diversity and Dissidence in the Trans-Mississippi* (Denton: University of North Texas Press, 2016), 104; and Angela Boswell, "Introduction," in Liles and Boswell, *Women in Civil War Texas.*

18. Thad Morgan, "How a Black Spy Infiltrated the Confederate White House," History.com, https://www.history.com/news/female-spies-civil-war-mary-bowser-elizabeth-van-lew, accessed June 9, 2019.

19. Sterling, *We Are Your Sisters,* 245–305.

20. Catherine Clinton, *Harriet Tubman: The Road to Freedom* (New York: Little, Brown, 2004), 164–170, quoted material on 166 and 168. For other accounts of Tubman's role in this raid, see Sarah H. Bradford, *Scenes in the Life of Harriet Tubman* (Auburn, NY: Dennis Brothers & Company, 1869), 87; and

Jean M. Humez, *Harriet Tubman: The Life and Life Stories* (Madison: University of Wisconsin Press, 2003), 52–62.

21. J. Brent Morris, "Life in the Swamp," *New York Times*, October 19, 2013.

22. Robert Arnold, *The Dismal Swamp and Lake Drummond: Early Recollections, Vivid Portrayal of Amusing Scenes* (Norfolk, VA: Green, Burke & Gregory Printers, 1888), 9–10.

23. Janice Sumler-Edmond, "Charlotte L. Forten Grimké," s.v. in Hine et al., *Black Women in America*. Vol. 2, 550–53, quote on 552. See also Brenda E. Stevenson, ed., *The Journals of Charlotte Forten Grimké* (New York: Oxford University Press, 1989).

24. Charlotte Forten, "Life on the Sea Islands: A Young Black Woman Describes Her Experience Teaching Freed Slaves During the Civil War," *Atlantic Monthly* 13 (May 1864): 587–96.

25. See chapter 2.

26. Forten, "Life on the Sea Islands."

27. Bettye Collier-Thomas, *Jesus, Jobs, and Justice: African American Women and Religion* (New York: Knopf, 2010), xv–xvii.

28. Harry Henderson and Albert Henderson, *The Indomitable Spirit of Edmonia Lewis: A Narrative Biography* (Milford, CT: Esquiline Hill Press, 2012).

29. Smithsonian American Art Museum, "Edmonia Lewis: Artist Biography," https://americanart.si.edu/artist/edmonia-lewis-2914, accessed May 26, 2019; Bonnie Zimmerman, ed., *Lesbian Histories and Cultures: An Encyclopedia* (New York: Routledge, 2000), 466–67; Martha Ward Plowden, *Famous Firsts of Black Women*, 2nd ed. (Gretna, LA: Pelican Publishing, 2002), 83–84.

30. "Harriett Barrett," *Federal Writers' Project: Slave Narrative Project, Vol. 16, Texas, Part 1*, 1936, 49, https://www.loc.gov/item/mesn161.

31. "Millie Forward," *Federal Writers' Project: Slave Narrative Project, Vol. 16, Texas, Part 2*, 1936, 48, https://www.loc.gov/item/mesn162.

32. "Sarah Ford," *Federal Writers' Project: Slave Narrative Project, Vol. 16, Texas, Part 2*, 1936, 45–46, https://www.loc.gov/item/mesn162.

33. "Molly Harrell," *Federal Writers' Project: Slave Narrative Project, Vol. 16, Texas, Part 2*, 1936, 115–17, https://www.loc.gov/item/mesn162.

34. "Betty Farrow," *Federal Writers' Project: Slave Narrative Project, Vol. 16, Texas, Part 2*, 1936, 34, https://www.loc.gov/item/mesn162.

35. Central Texas Juneteenth Website, http://www.juneteenthcentraltexas.com.

36. "Sarah Ashley," *Federal Writers' Project: Slave Narrative Project, Vol. 16, Texas, Part 1*, 1936, 34, https://www.loc.gov/item/mesn161.

37. "Mary Edwards," *Federal Writers' Project: Slave Narrative Project, Vol. 16, Texas, Part 2*, 1936, https://www.loc.gov/item/mesn162.

38. *Austin Daily Record*, June 25, 1869.

39. Thirteenth Amendment of the US Constitution.

40. Mrs. Francena Martin Sutton, "Civil War Experience of Some Arkansas Women." The eight thousand figure is derived from Michael Doran, "Negro Slaves of the Five Civilized Tribes," *Annals of the Association of American Geographers* 68, no. 3 (September 1978): 335–50. The Thirteenth Amendment did not apply to Indian territory until 1866 because Indian territory was not part of the United States and this land was not occupied by the Union or the Confederacy.

Five Indian nations sided with the Confederacy and had to sign separate treaties each. Also, some Cherokee freed their slaves in 1863, so the Thirteenth Amendment did not apply to them. Indian soldiers fought on both sides of the war, and the last Confederate general to surrender was the native general Stan Watie.

41. David W. Blight and James Downs, eds., *Beyond Freedom: Disrupting the History of Emancipation* (Athens: University of Georgia Press, 2017); and Jim Downs, *Sick from Freedom: African-American Illness and Suffering During the Civil War and Reconstruction* (Oxford, UK: Oxford University Press, 2012).

42. Nakia Delynn Parker, "Trails of Tears and Freedom: Black Life in Indian Slave Country, 1830–1866," PhD diss., University of Texas at Austin, 2019.

43. Quoted in Terborg-Penn, *African American Women in the Struggle for the Vote*, 33, 31; for Truth, see Nell Irvin Painter, *Sojourner Truth: A Life, a Symbol* (New York: W. W. Norton, 1997), 254–55.

44. Colbert, *Federal Writers' Project.*

CHAPTER SIX: FRANCES'S SEX AND THE DAWNING OF THE BLACK WOMAN'S ERA

1. *Memphis Daily Appeal*, July 13, 1876; "Frances Thompson (Colored) Sworn and Examined," in Lerner, *Black Women in White America*, 174; Hannah Rosen, "'Not That Sort of Woman': Race, Gender, and Sexual Violence During the Memphis Riot of 1866," in *Love, Race, Sex: Crossing Boundaries in North American History*, ed. Martha Hodes (New York: New York University Press, 1999), 267–72, 281–83; Hannah Rosen, *Terror in the Heart of Freedom: Citizenship, Sexual Violence, the Meaning of Race in the Postemancipation South* (Chapel Hill: University of North Carolina Press, 2009), 39–58.

2. For vice allegations and doubt about her testimony, see *Memphis Public Ledger*, July 11, 1876 (hereafter *MPL*). This article charges that Frances was from South Carolina, but she testified as having been raised in Maryland. For accusations of making "hoodoo bags" and fortune telling, see *MPL*, July 15, 1876. Accounts intimated that Lucy Smith's nickname was "Stumpy" and that she had been in and out of the penitentiary. See *MPL*, July 13, 1876.

3. *MPL*, July 13, 1876. A report of Lucy Smith's death appears in *MPL*, November 11, 1876. For laundry and auction, see *MPL*, July 19, 1876. Rosen, "Not That Sort of Woman," 283–84; "Francis alias Frances Thompson," *Days' Doings* (New York), August 12, 1876.

4. Deborah Gray White, *Too Heavy a Load: Black Women in Defense of the Themselves, 1894–1994* (New York: W. W. Norton, 1999), 36–37.

5. Ida B. Wells, *Crusade for Justice: The Autobiography of Ida B. Wells*, ed. Alfreda Duster (Chicago: University of Chicago Press, 1970), xvi, esp. 18; Carol Anderson, *One Person, No Vote: How Voter Suppression Is Destroying Our Democracy* (New York: Bloomsbury, 2018), 2–5.

6. "Grand Jury Will Probe Lynching," *Daily Oklahoman*, May 31, 1911. On Laura Nelson, see Crystal N. Feimster, *Southern Horrors: Women and the Politics of Rape and Lynching* (Cambridge, MA: Harvard University Press, 2009), 66. *Crisis*, July 1911, in Lerner, *Black Women in White America*, 162. For the numbers of black women lynched, see Feimster, *Southern Horrors*, 165, 171. A recent report says that 4,084 African Americans were lynched by whites

in Alabama, Arkansas, Florida, Georgia, Kentucky, Louisiana, Mississippi, North Carolina, South Carolina, Tennessee, Texas, and Virginia between 1877 and 1950. See Equal Justice Institute, *Lynching in America: Confronting the Legacy of Racial Terror*, 3rd ed. (2017), https://lynchinginamerica.eji.org/report.

7. Feimster, *Southern Horrors*, 121–22.

8. Wells, *Crusade for Justice*, 65; Giddings, *When and Where I Enter*, 29.

9. *Minutes of the Second Convention of the National Association of Colored Women: Held at Quinn Chapel, 24th Street and Wabash Avenue, Chicago, Ill., August 14th, 15th, and 16th, 1899* (LOC), 4; *Ninth Annual Convention, Grand Chapter, Delta Sigma Theta Sorority, Howard University, Washington, D.C., 1919–1927*, subject file 1884–1962, Mary Church Terrell Papers, LOC; Giddings, *When and Where I Enter*, 95.

10. Giddings, *When and Where I Enter*, 129–30.

11. White, *Too Heavy a Load*, 59; "The National Colored Women's Congress," in *The Woman's Era* 2, no. 9 (January 1896): 2–3.

12. Evelyn Brooks Higginbotham, *Righteous Discontent: The Women's Movement in the Black Baptist Church, 1880–1920* (Cambridge, MA: Harvard University Press, 1994), 195–99. "Jook joints" were essentially underground/informal night spots that often featured musical performances, allowed dancing, and served alcohol.

13. On the layered aims of black clubwomen, see Brittney Cooper, *Beyond Respectability: The Intellectual Thought of Race Women* (Urbana: University of Illinois Press, 2017), 20–23; Fannie Barrier Williams, "A Northern Negro's Autobiography," *Independent* 57, no. 2902 (July 14, 1904): 96, in Lerner, *Black Women in White America*, 165; Wanda A. Hendricks, *Fannie Barrier Williams: Crossing the Borders of Region and Race* (Chicago: University of Illinois, 2014), 1–3, 151–52.

14. Mary Church Terrell, Fifth Biennial of the National Association of Colored Women, microfilm, reel 21, box 29, Mary Church Terrell Papers: Speeches and Writings, 1866–1953 (LOC).

15. Anna Julia Cooper, *A Voice from the South* (Xenia, Ohio: Aldine Printing House, 1892), 31.

16. Jones, *Labor of Love, Labor of Sorrow*, 86–90; Nina Banks, "Uplifting the Race Through Domesticity: Capitalism, African-American Migration, and the Household Economy in the Great Migration, 1916–1930," *Feminist Economies* 12, no. 4 (2006): 603.

17. Jones, *Labor of Love, Labor of Sorrow*, 86–90.

18. Tera W. Hunter, *To 'Joy My Freedom: Southern Black Women's Lives and Labors After the Civil War* (Cambridge, MA: Harvard University Press, 1998), 85–94.

19. A Negro Nurse, "More Slavery at the South," *Independent* 72, no. 3295 (January 25, 1912): 196–200, in Lerner, *Black Women in White America*, 227–29.

20. For the moral, see Mary Church Terrell, "An If or Two," 1898, reel 20, box 28, Mary Church Terrell Papers. On labor, see Mary Church Terrell, "What It Means to Be Colored in the Capital of the United States," *Independent* 62, no. 3034 (January 24, 1907): 181–86, in Lerner, *Black Women in White America*,

380. See also Mary Church Terrell, *A Colored Woman in a White World* (Washington, DC: Ransdell, 1940).

21. Booker T. Washington's National Business League, quoted in Giddings, *When and Where I Enter*, 75. Also see Elsa Barkley Brown, "Womanist Consciousness: Maggie Lena Walker and the Independent Order of Saint Luke," *Signs* 14, no. 3 (April 1989): 610–33; Shennette Garrett-Scott, *Banking on Freedom: Black Women in U.S. Finance Before the New Deal* (New York: Columbia University Press, 2019), 7–11.

22. Sharon Harley, "For the Good of the Family and Race: Gender, Work, and Domestic Roles in the Black Community, 1880–1930," *Signs* 15, no. 2 (Winter 1990): 346.

23. Collier-Thomas, *Jesus, Jobs, and Justice*, 59.

24. Tiffany Gill, "'The First Thing Every Negro Girl Does': Black Beauty Culture, Racial Politics, and the Construction of Modern Black Womanhood, 1905–1925," in *Cultures of Commerce: Representation and American Business Culture, 1877–1960*, ed. Elspeth H. Brown, Catherine Gudis, and Marina Moskowitz (New York: Palgrave, 2006), 146–47, 149–51.

25. Quoted in Gill, *Beauty Shop Politics*, 25. Also see Harley, "For the Good of the Family and Race," 7–32.

26. Quoted in Harley, "Nannie Helen Burroughs," 67. See also Speeches and Writings, box 46–47, Nannie Helen Burroughs Papers, 1900–1963, LOC.

27. William Hannibal Thomas, *The American Negro: What He Was, What He Is, and What He May Become* (orig. 1901, Macmillan Company; repr. New York: Negro Universities Press, 1969) 195, quoted in White, *Too Heavy a Load*, 61.

28. W. E. B. Du Bois, *The Philadelphia Negro: A Social Study* (1897) (Philadelphia: University of Pennsylvania Press, 1996), 55–56, 65.

29. *Annual Report of the National League for the Protection of Colored Women, 1910*, p. 3, Urban Archives, Temple University, Philadelphia; on S.W. Layten, see *Notable Black Women in America, Book II*, ed. Jessie Carney Smith (Michigan: Gale Research, 1996), 403.

30. *A Report on Existing Conditions with Recommendations to the Honorable Rudolph Blankenburg, Mayor of Philadelphia* (Philadelphia: Philadelphia Vice Commission, 1913); Kali N. Gross, *Colored Amazons: Crime, Violence, and the City of Brotherly Love, 1880–1910* (Durham, NC: Duke University Press, 2006), 58–64; Cynthia Blair, *I've Got to Make My Livin': Black Women's Sex Work in Turn-of-the-Century Chicago* (Chicago: University of Illinois Press, 2010), 45–47; Talitha LeFlouria, *Chained in Silence: Black Women and Convict Labor in the New South* (Chapel Hill: University of North Carolina Press, 2015), 62–67.

31. For the Sanders quote, see Talitha LeFlouria, "'Under the Sting of the Lash': Gendered Violence, Terror, and Resistance in the South's Convict Camps," *Journal of African American History* 100, no. 3 (Summer 2015): 366. For a description of the work farms, see LeFlouria, "'Under the Sting of the Lash,'" 368.

32. Nicole Hahn Rafter, *Partial Justice: Women, Prisons, and Social Control* (New York: Routledge, 1990), 144; Kali Nicole Gross, "African American Women, Mass Incarceration, and the Politics of Protection," *Journal of American History* 102, no. 1 (June 2015): 28–31.

33. Quoted in Hunter, *To 'Joy My Freedom*, 133; for a discussion of "pan totting," see Hunter, *To 'Joy My Freedom*, 60–68; Gross, *Colored Amazons*, 54–60.

34. A Southern Colored Woman, "The Race Problem—An Autobiography," *Independent* 56, no. 2885 (March 17, 1904): 587–89, in Lerner, *Black Women in White America*.

35. Maureen D. Lee, *Sissieretta Jones: The Greatest Singer of Her Race, 1868–1933* (Columbia: University of South Carolina Press, 2013), 4–5, 14–29, 80–95, 31; "The Black Patti," *Philadelphia Inquirer*, November 1892.

36. "The Black Patti"; Lee, *Sissieretta Jones*, chaps. 8 and 9, 240.

37. Mary Frances Berry, *My Face Is Black Is True: Callie House and the Struggle for Ex-Slave Reparations* (New York: Vintage Books, 2006), 5, 261, 206, 215.

38. Berry, *My Face Is Black Is True*, 206, 215; "Ex-Slaves In Mass Meeting," *New York Times*, February 14, 1903.

39. Berry, *My Face Is Black Is True*.

40. Jacqueline Jones, *Goddess of Anarchy: The Life and Times of Lucy Parsons, American Radical* (New York: Basic Books, 2017), 37, 138.

41. Jones, *Goddess of Anarchy*, 75–76, and chap. 6.

42. Jones, *Goddess of Anarchy*, chaps. 6 and 7, esp. 248, 342; "Lucy Parsons Harangues an Audience," *New York Times*, August 21, 1893.

CHAPTER SEVEN: AUGUSTA'S CLAY, MIGRATION, AND THE DEPRESSION

1. Folder 2, box 1, Augusta Savage Papers, 1926–1987, Schomburg Center for Research in Black Culture, New York Public Library; Jill Lepore, *Joe Gould's Teeth* (New York: Vintage Books, 2016), 60; Sharif Bey, "Augusta Savage: Sacrifice, Social Responsibility, and Early African American Art Education," *Studies in Art Education: A Journal of Issues and Research* 58, no 2 (2017): 127.

2. Quoted in Bey, "Augusta Savage," 129, 128–30. "Persons and Achievements to be Remembered in March," *Negro History Bulletin* 2, no. 6 (March 1939): 51. Also see "Color Line Drawn by Americans," *New York Amsterdam News*, April 25, 1923.

3. Lepore, *Joe Gould's Teeth*, 60, 62; T. Denean Sharpley-Whiting, *Bricktop's Paris: African American in Paris Between Two World Wars* (New York: SUNY Press, 2015), 134. For images of Savage's work, see Schomburg Center for Research in Black Culture, Photographs and Prints Division, New York Public Library: "Bust of Unidentified Youth by Augusta Savage," http://digital collections.nypl.org/items/f97273e0-77da-0136-fa16-294a5a9c3aa4; "Laughing Boy," http://digitalcollections.nypl.org/items/13ad6870-10eb-0136-d4d7 -0d185348eda3; "James Weldon Johnson," http://digitalcollections.nypl.org /items/6ead8a20-10eb-0136-8453-67929ad3c29d, "Statuette by Augusta Savage Entitled 'Pumbaa,'" http://digitalcollections.nypl.org/items/65bf05a0-71af-0136 -58b9-007a4eeoc219; "Reclining Nude," http://digitalcollections.nypl.org/items /c6e522do-10eb-0136-328e-0523e682ec40, all accessed February 6, 2019. For her Harlem Renaissance contemporaries, see Lepore, *Joe Gould's Teeth*, 67. Jacob Lawrence quoted in Bey, "Augusta Savage," 130.

4. Bey, "Augusta Savage," 133; box 2, Savage Papers; "Women Sculptors at World's Fair," *Washington (DC) Evening Star* (*Sunday Star* ed.), January 1, 1939.

5. Year: 1940; Census Place: New York, New York; Roll: m-t0627-02665; Page: 61A; Enumeration District: 31–1733; Lepore, *Joe Gould's Teeth*, 66–68, 72–76, 117; Bey, "Augusta Savage," 137; "Gala Opening Friday May 10th at 1PM! City State Officials at Opening!: Negro World's Fair, Seventy-Five Years, Negro Progress Exposition," *Detroit Tribune*, May 4, 1940.

6. For FBI sources, see Lepore, *Joe Gould's Teeth*, 209–10n40. We would caution readers about the flawed, racist, and divisive ways the FBI surveilled Black people. For more recent examples about the complexities of FBI records as it pertains to African American history, see Donna Murch, "A Historian's Claims About Martin Luther King Are Shocking—and Irresponsible," *Guardian*, June 8, 2019, https://www.theguardian.com/commentisfree/2019/jun/08/martin-luther-king-david-garrow-essay-claims.

7. Deirdre Bloome, James Feigenbaum, and Christopher Muller, "Tenancy, Marriage, and the Boll Weevil Infestation, 1892–1930," *Demography* 9, no. 2 (2017): 1030.

8. Quoted in Elizabeth Clark-Lewis, *Living In, Living Out: African American Domestics and the Great Migration* (New York: Kodansha International, 1996), 20–21; Jones, *Labor of Love, Labor of Sorrow*, 81; Banks, "Uplifting the Race Through Domesticity," 603.

9. Jones, *Labor of Love, Labor of Sorrow*, 80.

10. Banks, "Uplifting the Race Through Domesticity," 605; Jones, *Labor of Love, Labor of Sorrow*, 132–34.

11. Quoted in Clark-Lewis, *Living In, Living Out*, 48–49.

12. Quoted in Clark-Lewis, *Living In, Living Out*, 70.

13. Banks, "Uplifting the Race Through Domesticity," 606; Giddings, *When and Where I Enter*, chap. 8.

14. Quoted in Addie W. Hunton and Kathryn M. Johnson, *Two Colored Women with the American Expeditionary Forces* (Brooklyn, NY: Brooklyn Eagle Press, 1920), 15, 19–20. See also Nikki L. Brown, *Private Politics and Public Voices: Black Women's Activism from WWI to the New Deal* (Bloomington: Indiana University Press, 2006), 89–92.

15. For lyrics to "Black Eye Blues," see Angela Y. Davis, *Blues Legacies and Black Feminism: Gertrude "Ma" Rainey, Bessie Smith, and Billie Holiday* (New York: Vintage Books, 1998), 204. On Ma Rainey, see Davis, *Blues Legacies and Black Feminism*, 40. Hazel Carby, "Policing the Black Woman's Body in an Urban Context," *Critical Inquiry* 18, no. 4 (Summer 1992): 738–55.

16. Langston Hughes, *The Big Sea: An Autobiography* (1940) (New York: Hill and Wang, 1993), 226.

17. Eric Garber, "Gladys Bentley: The Bulldagger Who Sang the Blues," *Outlook* 1 (Spring 1988): 52–61.

18. Quoted in Cookie Woolner, "'Woman Slain in Queer Love Brawl': African American Women, Same-Sex Desire, and Violence in the Urban North, 1920–1929," *Journal of African American History* 100, no. 3 (Summer 2015): 406.

19. Cheryl Hicks, *Talk with You Like a Woman: African American Women, Justice, and Reform in New York, 1890–1935* (Chapel Hill: University of North Carolina Press, 2010), 221.

20. Quoted in Clark-Lewis, *Living In, Living Out*, 83–85; LaShawn Harris, "Dream Books, Crystal Balls, and 'Lucky Numbers': African American Female Mediums in Harlem, 1900–1930s," *Afro-Americans in New York Life and History* 35, no. 1 (January 2011): 83–85.

21. Hicks, *Talk with You Like a Woman*, 132–33; Gross, "African American Women, Mass Incarceration, and the Politics of Protection," 25–33.

22. Hicks, "'She Would Be Better Off in the South,'" in Hicks, *Talk with You Like a Woman*.

23. On Terrell, see Treva B. Lindsey, *Colored No More: Reinventing Black Womanhood in Washington, D.C.* (Urbana: University of Illinois Press, 2017), 97–99. For examples of Terrell's speeches, see "Remarks Made at the Memorial Services Held in Honor of Susan B. Anthony in New York City," 1906, Mary Church Terrell Papers: Speeches and Writings, 1866–1953; "The Woman Suffrage Movement and Frederick Douglass," 1908, Mary Church Terrell Papers; and "Black People and Arguments Made by Democrats in Favor of League of Nations," 1920, Mary Church Terrell Papers.

24. Terborg-Penn, *African American Women*, 148–49; "Woman Makes Fight for Senate Seat," *Chicago Defender*, August 31, 1918.

25. Terborg-Penn, *African American Women*, 154; "Tinkham Has New Bill for Reapportionment," *New York Times*, May 15, 1922.

26. Suzanne O'Dea, *From Suffrage to the Senate: An Encyclopedia of Leaders, Causes & Issues* (Armenia, NY: Grey House Publishing, 2013), 510; Evelyn Brooks Higginbotham, "Religion, Politics, and Gender: The Leadership of Nannie Helen Burroughs," in *This Far by Faith: Readings in African-American Women's Religious Biography*, ed. Judith Weisenfield and Richard Newman (New York: Routledge, 1996), 152–53.

27. Gill, "The First Thing Every Negro Girl Does," 144.

28. Ula Y. Taylor, *The Veiled Garvey: The Life and Times of Amy Jacques Garvey* (Chapel Hill: University of North Carolina Press, 2002), 25–34; Natanya Duncan, "The 'Efficient Womanhood' of the Universal Negro Improvement Association: 1919–1930," PhD diss., University of Florida, 2008, 40–46; also see Tony Martin, *Amy Ashwood Garvey: Pan-Africanist, Feminist, and Wife No. 1; or a Tale of Two Amies* (Dover, MA: Majority Press, 2007).

29. Keisha Blain, *Set the World on Fire: Black Nationalist Women and the Global Struggle for Freedom* (Philadelphia: University of Pennsylvania Press, 2018), 23.

30. Amy Jacques-Garvey, "Women as Leaders," in *Words of Fire: An Anthology of African American Feminist Thought*, ed. Beverly Guy-Sheftall (New York: New Press, 1995), 94.

31. Erik S. McDuffie, "The Diasporic Journeys of Louise Little: Garveyism, the Midwest, and Community Feminism," in *Women, Gender, and Families of Color* 4, no. 2 (Fall 2016): 146–47; Blain, *Set the World on Fire*, 22.

32. Joe William Trotter, Jr., *From Raw a Deal to a New Deal? African Americans, 1929–1945* (New York: Oxford University Press, 1996), 21; Hine and Thompson, *A Shining Thread of Hope*, 242–43.

33. Hine and Thompson, *A Shining Thread of Hope*, 244; "Negro Actors Guild Stage Big Memorial," *Chicago Defender*, April 23, 1938.

34. Hine and Thompson, *A Shining Thread of Hope*, 243. Ella Baker and Marvel Cooke, "The Bronx Slave Market," *Crisis* 42, no. 11 (November 1, 1935): 330; for the quote, see Louise Mitchell, "Slave Markets Typify Exploitation of Domestics," *Daily Worker*, May 5, 1940. Also see LaShawn Harris, "Marvel Cooke: Investigative Journalist, Communist, and Black Radical Subject," *Journal for the Study of Radicalism* 6, no. 2 (2012): 91–92.

35. Baker and Cooke, "The Bronx Slave Market"; Giddings, *When and Where I Enter*, 233; "'Slave Market' in City Protested," *New York Times*, May 19, 1938.

36. "Detroit Housewives League Celebrates," *Chicago Defender*, June 27, 1931; "Bank Head Talks to Housewives," *Chicago Defender*, March 8, 1930; Hine and Thompson, *A Shining Thread of Hope*, 245–46.

37. Giddings, *When and Where I Enter*, 217.

38. Trotter, *From a Raw Deal*, 60; Cheryl Lynn Greenberg, *To Ask for an Equal Chance: African Americans in the Great Depression* (New York: Rowman and Littlefield, 2009), 50–51.

39. Greenberg, *To Ask for an Equal Chance*, 46, 47–48.

40. Giddings, *When and Where I Enter*. Also see National Council of Negro Women, Records, NABHW 001, Mary McLeod Bethune Council House National Historic Park Site, Washington, DC.

41. Giddings, *When and Where I Enter*, 220–21.

42. Harris, "Marvel Cooke," 103–5; LaShawn Harris, "Running with the Reds: African American Women and the Communist Party During the Great Depression," *Journal of African American History* 94, no. 1 (Winter 2009): 23.

43. Harris, "Running with the Reds," 26; Erik S. McDuffie, "'[She] devoted twenty minutes condemning all other forms of government but the Soviet': Black Women Radicals in the Garvey Movement and in the Left during the 1920s," in *Diasporic Africa: A Reader*, ed. Michael A. Gomez (New York: New York University Press, 2006), 219–50.

44. On Jones, see Rhonda Y. Williams, *Concrete Demands: The Search for Black Power in the 20th Century* (New York: Routledge, 2015), 54–55; Carole Boyce Davies, *Left of Karl Marx: The Political Life of Black Communist Claudia Jones* (Durham, NC: Duke University Press, 2007), 3, 138; Denise Lynn, "Socialist Feminism and Triple Oppression: Claudia Jones and African American Women in American Communism," *Journal for the Study of Radicalism* 8, no. 2 (Fall 2014): 8–10; Claudia Jones, *Jim-Crow in Uniform* (New York: New Age Publishers, 1940), 23, object no. 2010.55.1, Smithsonian National Museum of African American History and Culture, Washington, DC.

45. Zora Neale Hurston, *Poker!*, 1931, Deposit Drama Collection, manuscript/mixed material, LOC.

CHAPTER EIGHT: ALICE'S MEDALS AND BLACK WOMEN'S WAR AT HOME

1. Alice Coachman quoted in "Good Things Happening for One Who Decided to Wait," *New York Times*, April 27, 1995. "It was a really rough time," quoted in Jennifer H. Lansbury, *A Spectacular Leap: Black Women Athletes in Twentieth-Century America* (Fayetteville: University of Arkansas Press, 2014), 43, 41–42.

2. Lansbury, *A Spectacular Leap*, 44, 53. Historically Black colleges and universities tended to be divided on the role of Black women in sports. Tuskegee tended to encourage strong athleticism on the part of women and men and had a number of competitive teams. However, at Bennett College, in Greensboro, North Carolina, notions of gender and class plagued the basketball team, as Black female players faced strong criticism and regulation during their involvement in the sport. See Rita M. Liberti, "We Were Ladies, We Just Played Like Basketball Boys: African-American Women and Competitive Basketball at Bennett College, 1929–1942," *Journal of Sports History* 26, no. 3 (October 1999): 567–84.

3. Lansbury, *A Spectacular Leap*, 58–59.

4. "Georgia to Honor Alice Coachman Olympic Star," *Chicago Defender*, August 21, 1948.

5. "Alice Coachman Gives Up Track," *Chicago Defender*, November 12, 1949; "Georgia to Honor Alice Coachman Olympic Star," *Chicago Defender*, August 21, 1948; "Good Things Happening for One Who Decided to Wait," *New York Times*, April 27, 1995.

6. See "Mable Gilvert, 1225 Poydres St., New Orleans, La.," in Lerner, *Black Women in White America*, 403.

7. "Mt. Pleasant, Texas, 4/25–41," in Lerner, *Black Women in White America*, 404.

8. Giddings, *When and Where I Enter*, 232; white, *Too Heavy a Load*, 148–49.

9. Giddings, *When and Where I Enter*, 405; white, *Too Heavy a Load*, 143.

10. Giddings, *When and Where I Enter*, 236, 236–37; Jones, *Labor of Love, Labor of Sorrow*, 197.

11. Sharon Harley, Francille Wilson, and Shirley Wilson Logan, "Introduction: Historical Overview of Black Women and Work," in *Sister Circle: Black Women and Work*, ed. Sharon Harley and the Black Women and Work Collective (New Brunswick, NJ: Rutgers University Press, 2002), 7–8.

12. Giddings, *When and Where I Enter*, 236–37.

13. Sandra M. Bolzenius, *Glory in the Spirit: How Four Black Women Took On the Army During World War II* (Chicago: University of Illinois Press, 2018), 46–47, 41.

14. Bolzenius, *Glory in the Spirit*, 75–76, 79, 107; "Negro WACS in Protest," *New York Times*, March 12, 1945; "Army Court Convicts 4 Negro WACS of Disobeying Superior," *Washington Post*, March 21, 1945.

15. Bolzenius, *Glory in the Spirit*, 122, 128, 140; "Ask WAC Convictions Inquiry," *New York Times*, March 23, 1945; "Negro WACs Back on Duty: Conviction of Court-Martial Is Reversed," *New York Times*, April 4, 1945.

16. Charity Adams Earley, *One Woman's Army: A Black Officer Remembers the WAC* (College Station: Texas A&M University Press, 1989). British

newspaper quoted in Richard Goldstein, "Charity Adams Earley, Black Pioneer in Wacs, Dies at 83," *New York Times*, January 22, 2002; Hine and Thompson, *A Shining Thread of Hope*, 263.

17. Hine and Thompson, *A Shining Thread of Hope*, 263; "Negro Nurses Would Serve" *New York Times*, December 19, 1944; "Negro Nurses Ban By Services Cited," *New York Times*, January 14, 1945; "Army Nurse to Get a Medal," *New York Times*, June 8, 1945.

18. "Program of Rights Issued By Negroes: Representatives of 25 Groups Call on Conventions of Major Parties to Recognize It," *New York Times*, June 20, 1944; Harley, Wilson, and Logan, "Introduction," 8.

19. Hine and Thompson, *A Shining Thread of Hope*, 264.

20. File No. 85113, Commonwealth of Pennsylvania, Department of Health, Bureau of Vital Statistics, Philadelphia; "Corrine Sykes Pays with Life for Knife Slaying," *Chicago Defender*, October 26, 1945.

21. Census Data on Corrine Sykes see Year: 1940; Census Place: Philadelphia, Philadelphia, Pennsylvania; Roll: m-t0627-03719; Page: 11B; Enumeration District: 51-1006; Ron Avery, *City of Brotherly Mayhem: Philadelphia Crimes and Criminals* (Philadelphia: Otis Books, 1997), 75–79; John H. Maurer, *No. 1020, In the Supreme Court of the United States: Corrine Sykes alias Heloise T. Parker (Petitioner) v. The Commonwealth of Pennsylvania, October Term, 1945* (Washington, DC: US Supreme Court Records, 2011), 9–10 (hereafter *Sykes v. Commonwealth*).

22. "2d Man Hunted in Theft, Slaying," *Philadelphia Inquirer*, December 21, 1944; *Sykes v. Commonwealth*, 3.

23. *Sykes vs. Commonwealth*, 3–5.

24. For more on Sadie T. M. Alexander, see the Alexander Family Papers, 1817–2005, University Archives, University of Pennsylvania, Philadelphia.

25. *Sykes v. Commonwealth*, 6–7; Commonwealth v. Sykes, Supreme Court of Pennsylvania, 353 Pa. 392 45 A.2d 43 (Jan. 7, 1946). Appeal No. 162, January term, 1945, from judgment and sentence of Court of Oyer and Terminer, Philadelphia County, December term, 1944, No. 407; "Corrine Sykes Dies in Chair," *Philadelphia Inquirer*, October 13, 1945; "Police Data Asked on House Maids," *Philadelphia Inquirer*, March 21, 1945; Avery, *City of Brotherly Mayhem*, 79; *Severed Souls*, dir. Tina Morton, Vimeo, 2014, https://vimeo.com/110002983.

26. Year: 1940; Census Place: Montgomery, Montgomery, Alabama; Roll: m-t0627-00068; Page: 61A; Enumeration District: 51–37B; Jeanne Theoharis, *The Rebellious Life of Mrs. Rosa Parks* (Boston: Beacon Press, 2013), 48, 108.

27. Pauli Murray, *Song in a Weary Throat: Memoir of an American Pilgrimage* (1987) (New York: W. W. Norton, 2018), 46.

28. Patricia Bell-Scott, *The Firebrand and the First Lady: Portrait of Friendship; Pauli Murray, Eleanor Roosevelt, and the Struggle for Social Justice* (New York: Vintage Books, 2017), 8–9.

29. Bell-Scott, *The Firebrand and the First Lady*, 32–34.

30. Bell-Scott, *The Firebrand and the First Lady*, 56–57; Rosalind Rosenberg, *Jane Crow: The Life of Pauli Murray* (New York: Oxford University Press, 2017), 39–42.

31. Bell-Scott, *The Firebrand and the First Lady*, 61–65; Rosenberg, *Jane Crow*, 79. We thought Pauli and Adelene might have been lovers, but "school friend" is how Murray described her in an oral interview with Genna Rae Mc-Neil. See "Interview with Pauli Murray," February 13, 1976, interview G-0044, Southern Oral History Program Collection, Chapel Hill, North Carolina. See also Murray, *Song in a Weary Throat*, 178.

32. Bell-Scott, *The Firebrand and the First Lady*, 61–65.

33. Charlene Regester, *African American Actresses: The Struggle for Visibility, 1900–1960* (Bloomington: Indiana University Press, 2010), 244. On black women in early pornographic films, see Mireille Miller-Young, *A Taste for Brown Sugar: Black Women in Pornography* (Durham, NC: Duke University Press, 2014), chapter 1.

34. Regester, *African American Actresses*, 244–47. The dancing was co-choreographed by Katherine Dunham and George Balanchine. For an image of Dunham in the Broadway production in 1940, see Special Collections Research Center, Morris Library, Southern Illinois University, Carbondale.

35. Regester, *African American Actresses*, 254, 245.

36. Ann Petry, *The Street: A Novel* (Boston: Houghton Mifflin, 1946), 3; Farah Jasmine Griffin, *Harlem Nocturne: Women, Artists and Progressive Politics during World War II* (New York: Basic Civitas, 2013), 96–98.

37. Quoted in Dorothy Roberts, *Killing the Black Body: Race, Reproduction, and the Meaning of Liberty* (New York: Vintage Books, 1997), 99.

38. Davies, *Left of Karl Marx*, 134, 150, xxiv–xxvii, 134, 150.

39. Ula Yvette Taylor, *The Promise of Patriarchy: Women and the Nation of Islam* (Chapel Hill: University of North Carolina Press, 2017), 60–63, 65–67.

40. Taylor, *The Promise of Patriarchy*, 68.

41. "Gov. Sparks To Probe Taylor Rape Case," *Chicago Defender*, December 16, 1944; *The Rape of Recy Taylor*, dir. Nancy Buirski, Augusta Films, 2017.

42. "Charge Two Cops in Rape," *Chicago Defender*, April 16, 1949; "Refuse to Nab Cops for Rape," *Chicago Defender*, May 7, 1949; Danielle L. Mc-Guire, *At the Dark End of the Street: Black Women, Rape, and Resistance—A New History of the Civil Rights Movement from Rosa Parks to the Rise of Black Power* (New York: Vintage Books, 2011), 63–66; Theoharis, *Rebellious Life of Mrs. Rosa Parks*, 28.

43. Danielle L. McGuire, "'It Was Like All of Us Had Been Raped': Sexual Violence, Community Mobilization, and the African American Freedom Struggle," *Journal of African American History* 91, no. 3 (December 2004): 910–11; "Charge Two Cops in Rape," *Chicago Defender*, April 16, 1949; "Refuse to Nab Cops for Rape," *Chicago Defender*, May 7, 1949.

44. Giddings, *When and Where I Enter*, 264.

45. "Alice Coachman, 90, Dies; First Black Woman to Win Olympic Gold," *New York Times*, July 14, 2014.

CHAPTER NINE: AURELIA'S LAWSUIT AGAINST JIM CROW

1. Year: 1930; Census Place: Walkers, Montgomery, Alabama; Page: 24B; Enumeration District: 0057; FHL microfilm: 2339779; Alabama, County Marriage Records, 1805–1967, available at Ancestry.com; Aurelia S. Browder v.

W. A. Gayle, District Court of the United States, Middle District of Alabama, Northern Division, Civil Action No. 1147, N, May 11, 1956, Series: Civil Cases 9/1938–11/26/1968, RG 21 (Washington, DC: National Archives), 3–7; Blair L. M. Kelly, *Right to Ride: Streetcar Boycotts and African American Citizenship in the Era of Plessy v. Ferguson* (Chapel Hill: University of North Carolina Press, 2010); phone conversation with Butler Browder, Aurelia Browder's son, May 24, 2019, 9:18 a.m.

2. Giddings, *When and Where I Enter*, 263.

3. *Browder v. Gayle*, 3–22. For Smith's fines, see *Browder v. Gayle*, 11; Paul Hendrickson, "The Ladies Before Rosa," *Washington Post*, April 12, 1998.

4. Browder v. Gayle, 352 US 903 (1956), 4–5; Joyce A. Hanson, *Rosa Parks: A Biography* (Santa Barbara, CA: Greenwood Biographies, 2011), 89–90.

5. Pauli Murray, *States' Laws on Race and Color* (Athens, GA: Women's Division of Christian Service, Board of Missions of the Methodist Church, 1950); Genna Rae McNeil, *Groundwork: Charles Hamilton Houston and the Struggle for Civil Rights* (Philadelphia: University of Pennsylvania Press, 1984); Bernice McNair Barnett, "Invisible Southern Black Women Leaders in the Civil Rights Movement: The Triple Constraints of Gender, Race, and Class," *Gender and Society* 7, no. 2 (June 1993): 168–69.

6. Mamie Till Bradley, "Mamie Till Bradley: October 29, 1955, Bethel AME Church, Baltimore, Maryland," in *Women and the Civil Rights Movement, 1954–1965*, ed. Davis W. Houck and David E. Dixon (Jackson: University Press of Mississippi, 2009), 17–18; *The Untold Story of Emmett Louis Till*, dir. Keith Beauchamp, Velocity, 2005: 1:45–2:30, 5:25–5:30.

7. Bradley, "Mamie Till Bradley," 19.

8. Bradley, "Mamie Till Bradley," 22.

9. *The Untold Story of Emmett Louis Till*: 26:49–28:52.

10. Bradley, "Mamie Till Bradley," 24; examples of these reactions may be seen in *The Untold Story of Emmett Louis Till*: 31:26–34:00.

11. Bradley, "Mamie Till Bradley," 20.

12. "'I Wanted the Whole World to See': Race, Gender, and Construction of Motherhood in the Death of Emmett Till," in *Motherhood in Black and White: Race and Sex in American Liberalism, 1930–1965*, ed. Ruth Feldstein (Ithaca, NY: Cornell University Press, 2000); Richard Pérez-Peña, "Woman Linked to 1955 Emmett Till Murder Tells Historian Her Claims Were False," *New York Times*, January 27, 2017.

13. Hine and Thompson, *A Shining Thread of Hope*, 275; "Another Woman Has Been Arrested—Don't Ride the Bus," December 5, 1955, Montgomery County District Attorney's Files (Montgomery County Court House, Montgomery, AL); Martin Luther King Jr. Papers Project, Stanford University, Stanford, CA. See also Jo Ann Robinson interview by Willie Mae Lee, February 7, 1956, Preston Valien Collection, Amistad Research Center, Tulane University, New Orleans.

14. Giddings, *When and Where I Enter*, 265; Jo Ann Robinson, *The Montgomery Bus Boycott and the Women Who Started It: The Memoir of Jo Ann Gibson Robinson* (Knoxville: University of Tennessee Press, 1987).

15. "Montgomery Bars Bus Runs At Night," *New York Times*, December 30, 1956; Theoharis, *Rebellious Life of Mrs. Rosa Parks*.

16. Cooper, *Beyond Respectability*, introduction, chap. 3; quoted in Giddings, *When and Where I Enter*, 274; Barbara Ransby, *Ella Baker and the Black Freedom Movement: A Radical Democratic Vision* (Chapel Hill: University of North Carolina Press, 2005).

17. Unita Blackwell, *Barefootin': Life Lesson from the Road to Freedom* (New York: Crown, 2006).

18. "Interview of Diane Nash," *American Experience*, season 23, episode 12, WGBH Educational Foundation, 2017, at 09:25.

19. Benjamin Houston, *Nashville Way: Racial Etiquette and the Struggle for Social Justice in a Southern City* (Athens: University of Georgia Press, 2012), 80–81; Giddings, *When and Where I Enter*, 272–75.

20. Jennifer Stollman, "Diane Nash: 'Courage Displaces Fear, Love Transforms Hate': Civil Rights Activism and the Commitment to Nonviolence," in *The Human Tradition in the Civil Rights Movement*, ed. Susan M. Glisson (New York: Rowman and Littlefield, 2006).

21. Gwendolyn Zoharah Simmons, interview by Joseph Mosnier, September 14, 2011, Gainesville, Florida, AFC 2010/039, LOC.

22. Vicki Crawford, "African American Women in the Mississippi Freedom Democratic Party," in *Sisters in the Struggle: African American Women in the Civil Rights–Black Power Movement*, ed. Bettye Collier-Thomas and V. P. Franklin (New York: New York University Press, 2001), 121–22.

23. Chana Kai Lee, "Anger, Memory, and Personal Power," in Collier-Thomas and Franklin, *Sisters in the Struggle*, 144, 145, 146.

24. Crawford, "African American Women in the Mississippi Freedom Democratic Party," 126; Lee, "Anger, Memory, and Personal Power," 151.

25. Lee, "Anger, Memory, and Personal Power," 9, 161; Julius Paul, "The Return of Punitive Sterilization Proposals: Current Attacks on Illegitimacy and the AFDC Program," *Law and Society Review* 3, no. 1 (1968): 88–92.

26. Quoted in Lee, *For Freedom's Sake*, 100.

27. Melba Pattillo Beals, *Warriors Don't Cry: A Searing Memoir of the Battle to Integrate Little Rock's Central High* (New York: Simon and Schuster, 1995), 75–76, 112.

28. Quoted in Rachel Devlin, *A Girl Stands at the Door: The Generation of Young Women Who Desegregated America's Schools* (New York: Basic Books, 2018), 238, also see 235–38; Charlayne Hunter-Gault, *In My Place* (New York: Vintage Books, 1992), 1–3, 201–2; Giddings, *When and Where I Enter*, 274.

29. Rhonda Y. Williams, *The Politics of Public Housing: Black Women's Struggles Against Urban Inequality* (New York: Oxford University Press, 2005), 112, 120.

30. McGuire, "'It Was Like All of Us Had Been Raped,'" 906–7.

31. McGuire, "'It Was Like All of Us Had Been Raped,'" 914–17; McGuire, *At the Dark Ennd of the Street*, 167; "FAMU Students Vow to Press for Fight for Justice," *Daily Defender*, May 2, 1959; "Tension Up over Rape of Coed, FAMU Students Stage Protest," *Daily Defender*, May 4, 1959.

32. McGuire, "'It Was Like All of Us Had Been Raped,'" 920.

33. McGuire, "'It Was Like All of Us Had Been Raped,'" 922–31; "Nation Eyes FAMU Coed Attack Trial," *Daily Defender*, June 9, 1959.

34. McGuire, "'It Was Like All of Us Had Been Raped,'" 927; McGuire, *At the Dark End of the Street*, 323n52; "Florida Rape Sentence Due in 2 Weeks," *Washington Post*, June 15, 1959.

35. Shaun L. Gabbidon, Helen Taylor Greene, and Vernetta D. Young, eds., *African American Classics in Criminology and Criminal Justice* (New York: Sage, 2002), 144; U.S. Supreme Court, *Hamilton v. Alabama*, No. 793, 376 US 650 (1964).

36. Donna M. Owens, "Stolen Girls," *Essence* 37, no. 2 (June 2006): 162–66, 168.

37. Owens, "Stolen Girls."

38. Bayard Rustin, *I Must Resist: Bayard Rustin's Life in Letters* (San Francisco: City Lights Books, 2012); John D'Emilio, *Lost Prophet: The Life and Times of Bayard Rustin* (Chicago: University of Chicago Press, 2004).

39. "March on Washington for Jobs and Freedom," Part 6, Open Vault, WGBH, http://openvault.wgbh.org/catalog/A_CB387942466C46F6BAE6528BAFD53055.

40. *4 Little Girls*, dir. Spike Lee, 40 Acres and a Mule Filmworks, 2007, at 1:07:27–1:09.

41. *4 Little Girls*, at 1:03:37, 1:05:25.

42. Bradley, "Mamie Till Bradley," 26.

43. For Maxine McNair and Alpha Robertson, see *4 Little Girls*, at 1:35:18–1:36:25.

44. The phrase "shouting troubles over" is a riff off of a verse in Clara Ward's gospel song "How I Got Over" (1951), which Mahalia Jackson recorded in 1961 and performed at the March on Washington in 1963. See Willa Ward-Royster, *How I Got Over: Clara Ward and the World-Famous Ward Sisters* (Philadelphia: Temple University Press, 1997), 104.

45. For the description of Simone, see Langston Hughes, "Week By Week: Spotlight on Nina Simone," *Chicago Defender*, November 12, 1960. See also Nina Simone, *I Put A Spell On You: The Autobiography of Nina Simone* (1992) (Boston: Da Capo Press, 2003), 89.

46. Simone, *I Put a Spell on You*, 90.

47. Imani Perry, *Looking for Lorraine: The Radiant and Radical Life of Lorraine Hansberry* (Boston: Beacon Press, 2018).

48. Sharon Harley, "'Chronicle of a Death Foretold': Gloria Richardson, the Cambridge Movement, and the Radical Black Activist Tradition," in Collier-Thomas and Franklin, *Sisters in the Struggle*, 178–80.

49. Harley, "'Chronicle of a Death Foretold.'"

50. Harley, "'Chronicle of a Death Foretold,'" 190.

51. Williams, *Concrete Demands*, 7, 51; Richard Wright, *Black Power: A Record of Reactions in a Land of Pathos* (New York: Harper Collins, 1954); David Walker, *David Walker's Appeal in Four Articles; Together with a Preamble, to the Coloured Citizens of the World, but in Particular, and Very Expressly, to Those of the United States of America* (Boston, 1829).

52. *Washington Post*, April 4, 1998.

CHAPTER TEN: SHIRLEY'S RUN, BLACK POWER,
POLITICS, AND BLACK FEMINISM

1. Frank Lynn, "New Hat in Ring: Mrs. Chisholm's," *New York Times*, January 26, 1972.

2. *Chisholm '72: Unbought and Unbossed*, dir. Shola Lynch, PBS, 2005; Bayard Rustin, "From Protest to Politics: The Future of the Civil Rights Movement," in *Commentary* 39, no. 2 (February 1965), Box 1, Folder 122, American Left Ephemera Collection, 1894–2008, AIS.2007.11, Archives Service Center, University of Pittsburgh.

3. Shirley Chisholm, *Unbought and Unbossed* (1970) (Washington, DC: Take Root Media, 2010), 88.

4. Chisholm, *Unbought and Unbossed*, 91.

5. Chisholm, *Unbought and Unbossed*, 86–88, 94.

6. *Chisholm '72*, at 0:14:31–0:14:37

7. *Chisholm '72*.

8. US Department of Labor, *The Negro Family*.

9. Gerda Lerner interview of Dara Abubakari (Virginia E. Y. Collins), October 11, 1970, New Orleans, in Lerner, *Black Women in White America*, 585–86.

10. Christina Greene, "Women in the Civil Rights and Black Power Movements," in *Oxford Research Encyclopedia of American History* (November 2016), 9, available at Oxfordre.com, doi: 10.1093/acrefore/9780199329175.013.212.

11. For dates when women held key positions, see Hine et al., *Black Women in America, Vol. 1*, 135–36; Alondra Nelson, *Body and Soul: The Black Panther Party and the Fight Against Medical Discrimination* (Minneapolis: University of Minnesota Press, 2011), 96–97, 77–82. For Norma Armour, see Nelson, *Body and Soul*, 85; Robyn Spencer, *The Revolution Has Come: Black Power, Gender, and the Black Panther Party in Oakland* (Durham, NC: Duke University Press, 2016), 45–46, 173–76; Ashley Farmer, *Remaking Black Power: How Women Transformed an Era* (Chapel Hill: University of North Carolina Press, 2017), 10–12. The Afro was rooted in a longer history at the same time that it became emblematic of broader style consciousness being modeled by radical black women and appropriated domestically and internationally. See Tanisha Ford, *Liberated Threads: Black Women, Style, and the Global Politics of Soul* (Chapel Hill: University of North Carolina, 2015), 1–2, 91–99.

12. For an examination of how Huey Newton and the Black Panther Party came up with the idea of calling police "pigs," see Donna Jean Murch, *Living for the City: Migration, Education, and the Rise of the Black Panther Party in Oakland, California* (Chapel Hill: University of North Carolina Press, 2010), 135–36. For examples of sexism and misogyny, see Elaine Brown, *A Taste of Power: A Black Woman's Story* (New York: Doubleday, 1992), 115, 306–10, 313. Historian and former BPP member in the DC area Sharon Harley explained that their chapter did not countenance sexism and/or sexual harassment or sexual assault; shared with authors March 1, 2019.

13. Ashley D. Farmer, "Renegotiating the 'African Woman': Cultural Nationalist Theorizing in the Us Organization and the Congress of African People, 1965–1975," *Black Diaspora Review* 4, no. 1 (Winter 2014): 85–86; Brown, *A Taste of Power*, 108–10.

14. Farmer, "Renegotiating the 'African Woman,'" 77, 93; Farmer, *Remaking Black Power*, 100–101.

15. Mary Phillips, "The Feminist Leadership of Ericka Huggins in the Black Panther Party," *Black Diaspora Review* 4, no. 1 (Winter 2014): 191.

16. Phillips, "The Feminist Leadership of Ericka Huggins in the Black Panther Party," 197; Farmer, *Remaking Black Power*, 76.

17. Phillips, "The Feminist Leadership of Ericka Huggins in the Black Panther Party," 198.

18. Angela Davis, *Angela Davis: An Autobiography* (New York: Random House, 1974); Assata Shakur, *Assata: An Autobiography* (Westport, CT: L. Hill, 1987).

19. Christina Greene, "'She Ain't No Rosa Parks': The Joan Little Rape-Murder Case and Jim Crow Justice in the Post–Civil Rights South," *Journal of African American History* 100, no. 3 (Summer 2015): 431–32.

20. Greene, 'She Ain't No Rosa Parks,' 433–34.

21. Greene, 'She Ain't No Rosa Parks,' 428; "Area Groups Help Pay for N.C. Woman's Defense," *Pittsburgh Post-Gazette*, February 3, 1975.

22. Frances Beal, "Double Jeopardy: To Be Black and Female," in Guy-Sheftall, *Words of Fire*, 147–48.

23. Toni Cade Bambara, "The Pill: Genocide or Liberation?," in *The Black Woman: An Anthology*, ed. Toni Cade Bambara (New York: Mentor Books, 1970), 162–69.

24. Flo Kennedy, *Color Me Flo: My Hard Life and Good Times* (Englewood Cliffs, NJ: Prentice Hall, 1976), 14–15, 132; Sherie M. Randolph, *Florynce "Flo" Kennedy: The Life of a Black Feminist Radical* (Chapel Hill: University of North Carolina Press, 2015), 3–7, 99–102.

25. Quoted in *White, Too Heavy a Load*, 234; also see William H. Grier and Price M. Cobbs, *Black Rage* (Oregon: Wipf and Stock, 2000), 47, 48–51; Premilla Nadasen, "'We Do Whatever Becomes Necessary': Johnnie Tillmon, Welfare Rights, and Black Power," in *Want to Start a Revolution? Radical Black Women in the Black Freedom Struggle*, ed. Dayo Gore, Jeanne Theoharis, and Komozi Woodard (New York: New York University Press, 2009), 318–19; and Premilla Nadasen, *Welfare Warriors: The Welfare Rights Movement in the United States* (New York: Routledge, 2005), 19–20.

26. Williams, *The Politics of Public Housing*, 199.

27. Fannie Lou Hamer, "The Special Plight and the Role of Black Women," speech, NAACP Legal Defense Fund Institute, New York City, May 7, 1971.

28. Williams, *The Politics of Public Housing*, 199.

29. Premilla Nadasen, *Household Workers Unite: The Untold Story of African American Women Who Built a Movement* (Boston: Beacon Press, 2015), 19–20, 58, 60–62.

30. *Pay It No Mind: Marsha P. Johnson*, dir. Michael Kasino (1987), Redux Pictures, 2012.

31. *Pay It No Mind*; Hugh Ryan, "Power to the People: Exploring Marsha P. Johnson's Queer Liberation," *Out*, August 24, 2017.

32. Quoted in *Ms.*, January 1973, 55.

33. Jeanne-Marie A. Miller, "Black Women Playwrights from Grimke to Shange: Selected Synopses of Their Works," in *All the Women Are White, All the Blacks Are Men, but Some of Us Are Brave* (1982), ed. Gloria T. Hull, Patricia Bell-Scott, and Barbara Smith (New York: Feminist Press, 1992), 287–88.

34. Michelle Wallace, "On the National Black Feminist Organization," *Redstockings*, June 1975.

35. Kimberly Springer, *Living for the Revolution: Black Feminist Organizations, 1968–1980* (Durham, NC: Duke University Press, 2005), 166–67; *How We Get Free: Black Feminism and the Combahee River Collective*, ed. Keeanga-Yamahatta Taylor (Chicago: Haymarket Books, 2017); Luritta DuBois, PhD diss., "United in Our Diversity," University of Texas, Austin, 2019, 24–25.

36. Alice Walker, *In Search of Our Mothers' Gardens: Womanist Prose* (Orlando, FL: Harcourt Brace, 1983).

37. For examples of Lorde's work, see Audre Lorde, *Sister Outsider: Essays and Speeches* (Berkeley, CA: Crossing Press, 2007); DuBois, "United in Our Diversity," 24–25.

38. Barbara Jordan, *Barbara Jordan: A Self-Portrait* (Austin: University of Texas Press, 1979). For more on Jordan, see the Barbara Jordan Papers, 1975–2009, Box 2.325/A76c and Box 2.325/D26f, Briscoe Center for American History Manuscripts, University of Texas at Austin.

39. Heather Ann Thompson, "Why Mass Incarceration Matters: Rethinking Crisis, Decline, and Transformation in Postwar American History," *Journal of American History* 97, no. 3 (December 2010): 703–34; Heather Ann Thompson and Donna Murch, eds., "Special Section: Urban America and the Carceral State," *Journal of Urban History* 41, no. 5 (2015); Elizabeth Hinton, *From the War on Poverty to the War on Drugs: The Making of Mass Incarceration in America* (Cambridge, MA: Harvard University Press, 2016), 132–40, 158–64, 316–25; Dorothy Marie Provine, *Unequal Under Law: Race in the War on Drugs* (Chicago: University of Chicago Press, 2007), 110–25.

40. Jennifer Gonnerman, *Life on the Outside: The Prison Odyssey of Elaine Bartlett* (New York: Picador, 2004), 78.

41. "'Welfare Queen' in Court," *Chicago Defender*, February 9, 1974; "Alleged 'Welfare Queen' Is Accused of $154,000 Ripoff," *Jet*, December 19, 1974, 16; Josh Levin, "The Welfare Queen," *Slate*, December 19, 2013, http://www.slate.com/articles/news_and_politics/history/2013/12/linda_taylor_welfare_queen_ronald_reagan_made_her_a_notorious_american_villain.html.

42. Frank Dexter Brown, "Amandla! The Rallying Cry Against Apartheid," *Black Enterprise*, April 1985, 58–61; Mary Frances Berry, *History Teaches Us to Resist: How Progressive Movements Have Succeeded in Challenging Times* (Boston: Beacon Press, 2018), 87–108.

43. "Fast Ends After Sovern Meeting," *Columbia Daily Spectator* CIX, no. 100 (April 9, 1985).

44. Correspondence with Kali Gross, June 25, 2019.

45. Sandra G. Bundy, Appellant, v. Delbert Jackson, Director, D.C. Department of Corrections, 641 F.2d 934 (D.C. Cir. 1981); U.S. Court of Appeals for the District of Columbia Circuit 641 F.2d 934 (D.C. Cir. 1981); Argued March 26, 1980; Decided January 12, 1981; Luke Mullins, "#HerToo: The Story of the

DC Woman Who Helped Make Sexual Harassment Illegal," *Washingtonian*, March 4, 2018, https://www.washingtonian.com/2018/03/04/hertoo-40-year s-ago-this-woman-helped-make-sexual-harassment-illegal-sandra-bundy.

46. *New York Times*, June 28, 1991.

47. "Anita Hill Testimony: The Witness Not Called," *All Things Considered*, NPR, September 23, 2018, https://www.npr.org/2018/09/23/650956623 /anita-hill-testimony-the-witness-not-called.

48. *New York Times*, June 28, 1991.

49. Tonja Renée Stidhum, "Activists Remember a Full Page NYT Ad 1,600 Black Women Signed in Support of Anita Hill Ahead of Kavanaugh Hearings," *Blavity*, September 19, 2018, https://blavity.com/activists-remember-a-full-page -nyt-ad-1600-black-women-signed-in-support-of-anita-hill-ahead-of-kavanaugh -hearings.

50. Michelle Wallace, *Black Macho and the Myth of the Superwoman* (1978) (New York: Verso, 2015), 12.

51. Rhonda Williams quoted in Deborah Gray White, *Lost in the USA: American Identity from the Promise Keepers to the Million Mom March* (Urbana: University of Illinois Press, 2017), 72; Harley, Wilson, and Logan, "Introduction," 8–9; White, *Lost in the USA*, 84–85.

52. Michael Fletcher, DeNeen L. Brown, "'We Are Countless In Unity': Hundreds of Thousands Flock to Philadelphia for Million Women March," *Washington Post*, October 26, 1997; T. Shawn Taylor, "Million Women March: 'Getting Something Done'," *Chicago Tribune*, October 26, 1997.

53. Michael Janofsky, "At Million Woman March, Focus Is on Family," *New York Times*, October 26, 1997.

54. T. Shawn Taylor, "Million Women March: 'Getting Something Done,'" *Chicago Tribune*, October 26, 1997.

55. Told to Kali Gross, summer 1997.

56. *Icons of Hip Hop: An Encyclopedia of the Movement, Music, and Culture, Vol. 1*, ed. Mickey Hess (Westport, CT: Greenwood Press, 2007), 53.

57. Tamar Lapin, "Pioneering Hip-Hop Reporter Dee Barnes Is Homeless," *New York Post*, March 26, 2019; Dara Sharif, "Pioneering Hip-Hop Journalist Dee Barnes, Now Homeless, Gets a Hand Up from Wendy Williams," *Root*, April 18, 2019.

58. By the early part of the twenty-first century, Lauryn, now a single mother, would battle debilitating bouts of depression, as well as the reaches of the US justice system. In 2013 she served three months in a federal prison for tax evasion. See Greg Botelho, "Grammy-Winning Singer Lauryn Hill Released from Federal Prison," October 7, 2013, CNN.com.

59. Big Daddy Kane, Marley Mal, and Biz Markie, "Nobody Beats the Biz," *Goin' Off*, Cold Chillin' Records, 1988.

60. *Chisholm '72* at 1:14:53–1:15:38.

CONCLUSION

1. Chidinma Irene Nwoye, "The Congolese-American Activist Who Scaled the State of Liberty Isn't Backing Down from Taking On Trump," *Quartz Africa*, February 10, 2019.

2. Rebecca M. Joseph, "The Black Statue of Liberty Rumor: An Inquiry into the History and Meaning of Bartholdi's Liberté éclairant le Monde Final Report," Northeast Ethnography Program, Boston Support Office (Washington, DC: National Park Service, 2000).

3. Noelle Hanrahan, "To Die in Chowchilla: HIV in Prison, AIDS Has Become a Quiet Scandal in the Nation's Largest Women's Prison," *San Francisco Bay Guardian*, January 26, 1994; Joann Walker, "Medical Treatment at Chowchilla," in *Criminal Injustice: Confronting the Prison Crisis*, ed. Elihu Rosenblatt (Boston: South End Press, 1996), 125; Judy Parks, "Activists Rally at Chowchilla for Better Prisoner Healthcare," *Bay Area Reporter*, February 3, 1994, p. 11, box 5, Judy Greenspan Papers, coll. 113, Lesbian, Gay, Bisexual and Transgender Community Center, New York, NY.

4. Judy Greenspan, "Struggle for Compassion: The Fight for Quality Care for Women with AIDS at Central California Women's Facility," in *Yale Journal of Law & Feminism*. 6, no. 2, article 6 (1993): 386.

5. Aliya Semper Ewing, "You Got the Wrong Black Girl on the Right Day, Baby," *Root*, May 5, 2019.

6. Mary Ann Georgantopoulos, "The Woman Who Scaled the Statue of Liberty on the 4th of July Was Sentenced to Five Years Probation," *BuzzFeed*, March 19, 2019; US District Court, Southern District of New York, United States of America v. Therese Okoumou, July 5, 2018, case no. 118-cr-00469 UA, document 1 filed July 5, 2018, https://www.justice.gov/usao-sdny/press-release/file/1078006/download; Patricia Okoumou Facebook Page, https://www.facebook.com/officialpatriciaokoumou.

AFTERWORD

1. Joseph Fleming, "French Open Ban on Serena Williams' Catsuit Show Tennis Just Can't Get Out of Its Own Way," *USA Today*, October 18, 2019.

2. Scott Gleeson, "Serena Williams Debuts Zebra-Striped Outfit in Bold Fashion Statement at French Open," *USA Today*, May 27, 2019; Howard Fendrich, "Champion, Queen, Goddess, Mother: Serena Wins at French Open," *AP News*, May 27, 2019.

3. Richard A. Oppel Jr., Derrick Bryson Taylor, and Nicholas Bogel-Burroughs, "What to Know About Breonna Taylor's Death," *New York Times*, October 30, 2020; Dylan Lovan and Piper Hudspeth Blackburn, "Recordings Reveal Confusion Behind Breonna Taylor's Death," *AP News*, October 3, 2020.

4. Richard Fausset, "What We Know of the Shooting Death of Ahmaud Arbery," *New York Times*, November 13, 2020; "What We Know About the Death of George Floyd in Minneapolis," *New York Times*, November 5, 2020; Zak Cheney-Rice, "It Sure Looks Like Daniel Cameron Lied About Breonna Taylor's Killing," *New York Magazine: Intelligencer*, September 30, 2020; Ta-Nehisi Coates, guest editor, "Special Issue: The Great Fire," *Vanity Fair*, September 2020; "Breonna Taylor: Born June 5, 1993, Killed by Police March 13, 2020," *O: The Oprah Magazine*, September 2020; Jill Martin, "Naomi Osaka Wears Mask Honoring Breonna Taylor Before Winning US Open Match," CNN, September 1, 2020: https://www.cnn.com/2020/09/01/

us/naomi-osaka-breonna-taylor-mask-us-open-trnd/index.html, accessed November 23, 2020; Darcy Schild, "US Open Champion Naomi Osaka Wore 7 Different Masks at the Tournament to Honor Police Brutality Victims," *Insider*, September 16, 2020; Jenna West, "WNBA Dedicates Season to Breonna Taylor, Holds Moment of Silence to Honor Her," *Sports Illustrated*, July 25, 2020.

5 Mark Leibovich, "Symone Sanders Bet on Biden, and Herself," *New York Times*, August 19, 2020; Khushbu Shah, "'Textbook Voter Suppression': Georgia's Bitter Election a Battle Years in the Making," *Guardian*, November 10, 2018; David Marchese, "Why Stacey Abrams Is Still Saying She Won," *New York Times*, April 28, 2019; Pia Deshpande, "Buttigieg Says Stacey Abrams Was Robbed in Georgia Governor's Race," *Politico*, June 6, 2019; Maya King, "How Stacey Abrams and Her Band of Believers Turned Georgia Blue," *Politico*, November 8, 2020: https://www.politico.com/news/2020/11/08/stacey-abrams-believers-georgia-blue-434985, accessed November 23, 2020. For Charlene Mitchell's run for president of the Communist Party USA, see Nicholas Gagarin, "Charlene Mitchell," *Harvard Crimson*, November 5, 1968, https://www.thecrimson.com/article/1968/11/5/charlene-mitchell-pbtbhe-frederick-douglas-book, accessed November 23, 2020; and Charlene Mitchell, "First Black Woman Presidential Candidate: The Communist Party's Charlene Mitchell," *People's World*, August 19, 2020, https://www.peoplesworld.org/article/first-black-woman-presidential-candidate-the-communist-partys-charlene-mitchell, accessed November 23, 2020.

INDEX

Abbott, Cleveland, 144
Abner, C., 71
abolition: gradual abolition legislation, 56, 65–68, 74; and responses to Emancipation, 97–98; spread of in the North, 65; and the Statue of Liberty, 209–10. *See also* resistance to enslavement
abortion, legal, 194, 199. *See also* reproductive rights
"abroad" relationships, 74–75
Abubakari, Dara, 189–90
Abyssinian Baptist Church, Harlem, 137
Acoma people, resistance to Spanish explorers, 20
"An Act Concerning Servants and Slaves" (Virginia), 38, 50–51, 57. *See also* Black Codes
"An Act Respecting Fugitives from Justice, and Persons Escaping from the Service of their Masters," 52
"Act to Prevent Runaways" (South Carolina), 38
Adams, William, 78
"African American," use of term, xi
"African American Women in Defense of Themselves," 203
African Methodist Episcopal Church, Philadelphia, 84–85
Africans, Africa: accompanying Balboa, 12; arrival in North America, 9–10; enslaved, cultural diversity, 22; heritage from,

134, 190–91; holding facilities in Africa, 26; women's farming skills, 2; and work to end apartheid, 201–2. *See also* slave trade, transatlantic
Afrikan People's Conference, 193
Afro hair style, 248n11
Agnes (enslaved woman), escape, 42–43
Agricultural Adjustment Act, 139
agricultural labor: and the Black Codes, 101–2; and the boll weevil, 126; and the Cotton Gin, 68; cotton production, 54; and the Depression, 137; exclusion from Social Security program, 139; in French colonies, 34–35; pecan workers' strike, 138; during the Revolutionary Era, 54; sale of plantations, 69; sharecroppers, 95, 111, 126–27, 137, 170, 172; sugarcane production, 69; task vs. gang systems, 54; and wage-fixing activities, 111
Albany, Georgia, honoring Coachman in, 145
Albany State Teacher's College, Georgia, 144
Alexander, Raymond Pace, 152
Alexander, Sadie Tanner Mossell, 150
Alice (enslaved woman), escape, 44
Allah Temple of Islam, Chicago, 158
all-Black communities, 61–62, 94–95, 108
Allen, Richard, 84–85

rebellions by, 12; efforts to erase
identities of, 24, 26; experience
of capture and transport, 21–22,
25–26, 28–30; San Miguel de
Gualdape, 12; sea burials, 26. *See
also* resistance to enslavement
enslaved women: agricultural labor,
54; artistic creativity, 83–84;
blankets and clothing produced
for Confederate soldiers, 92;
commodification process, 22,
51; on Cortés expedition to California, 13; diversity of cultures
among, 22; erasure of the identities of, 24, 26; family relationships, 74–75; forced prostitution/
reproduction, 31; and Fugitive
Slave Acts, 52; and lynching,
107; maroons, 38; options during
the Civil War, 89–91; options
during the Revolutionary War
era, 42–44; and pregnancy,
53–55, 55; slave quarters, as
communities, 75; stereotypical
depictions, 3; transition to freedom, 95, 97–100. *See also* free
Black women; resistance to enslavement; runaways, escapees
enslavers: compensation provided to,
46, 51; industrial labor, 53; murder of, 61; reactions to resistance
by the enslaved, 82; requirements
of in Virginia slave code, 50; and
slave drivers, 54; use of term, xii,
56–57
entrepreneurship: bank, 112–13;
beauty shops, hair care, 6,
113–14; as central theme in Black
women's lives, 6, 213; divining,
fortune-telling, 7, 12, 235n2;
following passage of the Fourteenth Amendment, 210; and
gradual abolition, 67–68; and the
Great Migration, 130; hair and
body-care products, 114; Lloyd's
restaurant, 68; and survival tactics of Black women during the

Depression, 137. *See also* labor,
employment
escape efforts. *See* runaways,
escapees
Esteban the Moor, 16–17
Esther (ship), escapees on, 48
"Ethiopian Regiment," 45
Executive Order 8802, 147

factory work, 52–53
Fair Employment Practices Committee, 147
Fanny (enslaved woman), resistance
by, 53–54
Farmer, James, 186
farming. *See* agricultural labor
Farrakhan, Louis, 204
Farrell, Molly, 98–99
Fauntroy, Walter, 201
FBI, surveillance of Black people,
239n6
Federal Council on Negro Affairs
("Black Cabinet"), 140
Federal Writers Project, 75–76
femininity, concepts of, 3, 6, 144–45
feminism: Black women's relationship
to, 187–88; Black women's resis-
tance to term, 192; white dom-
inance of, 188. *See also* Black
feminism; women's suffrage
Fifteenth Amendment, 102
Fifth Virginia Regiment, Blacks serv-
ing with, 45–46
Fillifitas, Sarah, 48
Fisher, Ora, 128
Fisk University, Nashville, sit-ins, 171
Flora (enslaved woman), resistance
by, 61
Florida A&M University (FAMU),
rape of Betty Jean Owens, 176–77
food co-ops, 195–96
Ford, Sarah, 98
Fort Des Moines, Iowa, Earley's suc-
cess at, 149
Fort Devens, Massachusetts, strike by
Black WACs, 148–49
Forward, Millie, 89, 98